Heroes Masked and Mythic

Heroes Masked and Mythic

Echoes of Ancient Archetypes in Comic Book Characters

CHRISTOPHER WOOD

McFarland & Company, Inc., Publishers
Jefferson, North Carolina

ISBN (print) 978-1-4766-8315-7
ISBN (ebook) 978-1-4766-4138-6

LIBRARY OF CONGRESS AND BRITISH LIBRARY
CATALOGUING DATA ARE AVAILABLE

Library of Congress Control Number 2020054629

Front cover art by Christopher Wood

Printed in the United States of America

McFarland & Company, Inc., Publishers
Box 611, Jefferson, North Carolina 28640
www.mcfarlandpub.com

Goddess of song, teach me the story of a Hero.—Homer

A hero is someone who has given his or her life to something bigger than oneself.—Joseph Campbell

The pleasure of reading a story and wondering what will come next for the hero is a pleasure that has lasted for centuries and, I think, will always be with us.—Stan Lee

Table of Contents

Acknowledgments

If I started naming everyone who helped me write this book, it would be a book in and of itself, but there a number of particular superheroes I wish to acknowledge without whose support this volume would not have been possible. I am grateful to my wife Tracy, for her love, support, and editorial prowess, to my children who help me to see the world with new eyes, to my parents and brother and sister, and my friends for having the patience to put up with me and my book monster. Among these I wish to thank Kane Leal, Chris Aguirre, and Phil Phillips for their valuable insight. I wish to thank Todd Livingston, who suggested McFarland in the first place, and my editor Layla Milholen at the press for her tireless efforts at answering so many questions. I wish to thank the creators, writers, inkers, editors, and everyone who made comics possible for a pretentious young boy, but especially the great late Stan Lee and Jack Kirby. Many thanks to Joss Whedon for having the courage to go beyond the comics and give audiences a new vision of the Marvel Universe. To Joseph Campbell, a gentle but guiding light for so many of us. To Joseph Nagy for his guidance and support those many years ago. Finally, I wish to thank you, my reader, for choosing my book out of the millions of others out there. I hope it proves useful, and you enjoy the tales, as I have, of epic heroes old and new.

Preface

The book you now hold in your hands, *Heroes Masked and Mythic: Echoes of Ancient Archetypes in Comic Book Characters*, will elucidate the world of the epic hero and dare to suggest that it is very much alive and well entrenched in many modern storytelling traditions. A perfect example may be found in the American comic book, where artistic periods are categorized per the epic tradition. The tradition, much like Hesiod records in his *Works and Days* (109–111), begins with the *Golden Age* (1930–1950). Here we find the birth of heroes such as Superman, Batman, Wonder Woman, and Captain America. It is followed by the *Silver Age* (1956–1970) in which many comic heroes were redefined following questions of moral corruption of America's youth, the *Bronze Age* (1970–1985), and finally the *Modern Age* (1986–present). The ancient Greeks loved their superheroes, and so do we. Modern storytellers (authors, filmmakers, and the like) also know that really great stories start with really great characters, and throughout the course of this book, we will meet a few of them.

What makes their stories truly stirring, I would argue, is the modern spin we place on these heroic archetypes. Each chapter is designed to address a specific theme embracing both the worlds of ancient epic and the modern superhero, illuminating where these stories intertwine and, sometimes, where they diverge. Combined, the collected works are intended to serve as a vehicle for discussing ancient and modern storytelling archetypes, the need for the hero, how heroes interact, and what all this might reveal about ancient and modern culture. Such discussions, I believe, will help modern audiences become reacquainted with ancient storytelling traditions. The target audience ranges from students of mythology and fans of modern mythmaking in film and comics to the Homeric scholar for whom these discussions may provide avenues of further research or touchpoints for classroom discussion. The chapters are not written in any particular order or with any particular agenda in mind and are certainly not intended to serve as the definitive word on the topic.

Ultimately this book represents a somewhat eclectic amalgamation of several youthful passions, namely, comic books, films, and ancient mythology. As a boy, I cultivated a deep-wrought and lasting love for comics and ran several paper routes just to make enough money to afford next month's exciting issue of *Spider-Man*, the *Avengers*, and the *Fantastic Four*. These were stories and characters that spoke to me. They were heroic, but somehow different, marginal, but surprisingly human despite their superhuman powers. Splashes of color and stories told in frames, nevertheless echoed thousands of years of epic tradition, amplified also by the power of film. In college and graduate school, I pursued the classics and art history and began to find many striking similarities between modern and ancient epic heroes, so much so that I began to wonder if many of the patterns were being purposefully repeated, or formed some sort of nascent *habitus*, from which I found myself waking. It was a secret love affair that could not be touched while entrenched in academia.

It is surprising to me that this topic has yet to be really tackled, even by an academic market so impacted by the rush to "publish or perish" on novel or edgy ideas. Nevertheless, there are some competing titles within the academic press, though these books talk more about classics and the sword and sandals series and films such as *Gladiator*, *Troy*, and HBO's *Rome*. Monica Cyrino's *Rome, Season One: History Makes Television*, as well as her book on the second season of the series, *Rome Season Two: Trial and Triumph*, addresses the historical veracity and narrative style of the two HBO series. *Big Screen Rome* by the same author examines cinematic explorations of Hollywood films such as *Spartacus*, *Gladiator*, and *Life of Brian*, in which she typically comments upon how modern directors use ancient history and culture to make their own commentary on modern culture. As co-editor with Monica Cyrino, Antony Agoustakis in *STARZ Spartacus: Reimagining an Icon on Screen* pulls together essays related to the series, which are on topics of slavery, sexuality, spectacle, material culture, and modern reception.

As far as trade press, however, there are still other competing narratives, but none grapple with Homeric heroes and comic books but rather tend to stick to films specifically meant to reframe events and stories from the ancient world. Nevertheless, the important scholarship of those who have come before me should not be ignored but rather embraced and contemplated as companions along this road of comparative literature. This is how I conducted my own research for this book: I read, read, read. As a classicist, I was trained always to flee to the text—in this case, Homer's Greek but also the source texts of comic books and even their film representations. Yet we all stand on the shoulders of giants, and therefore I should like to take a moment here to give a brief nod to those scholars and thinkers who have strengthened my own resolve to write this, sometimes as a catalyst to change, and others with whom I couldn't agree more or have said it better myself.

The New Peplum: Essays on Sword and Sandal Films and Television by Nicholas Diak is one such book. His main focus is on the modern "sword and sandal" films, and by that he means in the past 30 years rather than including the 1960s. The author views the use of technology and narrative approaches that change the end experience of the viewer as something impossible to achieve at a time earlier than now.

Another compelling narrative approach to a specific interest area in this book is Adrienne Mayor's *The Amazons: Lives and Legends of Warrior Women Across the Ancient World*. Although Mayor is an academic, her books have been a boon to trade presses, bringing a bit of the esoteric and specialized world of classics to the general populace. This particular tome focuses on the archaeological and linguistic data as well as data gathered from relevant visual culture of the time period, all of which clarifies who the Amazons actually were, and how the stories of them were made into the stuff of myth.

In *Our Superheroes, Ourselves*, Robin Rosenberg and a host of other notable psychologists examine the relationships we have with the modern superhero as well as with the super villain and how each serves as a mirror for ourselves and our world. The final five chapters examine the humanity of the superhero as well as the idea of the not entirely human hero, Wonder Woman, Aquaman, or gifted children, Tony Stark, Bruce Wayne, and Peter Parker as examples.[1]

Marco Arnaudo's *The Myth of the Superhero* is a wide-ranging textual exploration of the influence of myth and religion on superheroes, looking at the incorporation of New Testament, and even ancient Greek ideals. His specific focus on serialization is an important observation, as he notes: "No contemporary genre exhibits the specific qualities of epic as much as the superhero comic does."[2] I could not agree more, for our modern relationship to Homer has been largely influenced by a text-based tradition, but for the ancient Greeks, the concept of serialization is embedded in the form of the oral storytelling tradition.

Andrew Bahlmann's *The Mythology of the Superhero* bears multiple readings. It is an eclectic and informed approach to looking at superheroes as modern mythology by developing a corpus of recognizable tropes rather than overgeneralizing, and why superheroes, like epic heroes, matter. In his six chapters, Bahlmann builds a formidable lexicon of superhero mythology, while examining Green Arrow and Buffy the Vampire Slayer as well as revisiting *Beowulf*. He also refers to Terrence Wandtke's work *The Meaning of Superhero Comic Books*, specifically his emphasis on oral cultures and their influence on the unfolding of the tale. As an archaeologist and art historian, I would add that while this is true, we also tend to neglect the visual stimuli that attends oral tradition—cups, vases, daggers with subtle references to Homeric heroes, all of which have an equal impact on the storytelling tradition. These objects have their own biographies, and they allow their owners to tell their own version of the myth.

In *Do the Gods Wear Capes*, Ben Saunders addresses many of the more underlying philosophical issues inherent in modern comic book heroes such as the concepts of love, justice, and whose justice, Wonder Woman as the embodiment both of female repression and liberation, and of course heroic failure. Saunders defends the genre for its ability to, like philosophy, bridge that seemingly deep gulf between experience and desire in our own lives.

The tale of the superheroine, an often neglected topic, makes for a fascinating read in Valerie Estelle Frankel's *Superheroines and the Epic Journey: Mythic Themes in Comic, Film and Television.* The book is divided into seven chapters, and its main focus is showing how superheroines are universal heroes and covers the hero birth, call to rescue, superhero tools, male influences, and finally motherhood and enlightenment, all with a feminist reading. Frankel also addresses the increasing problem of the all too familiar provocative depiction of heroines in comics and discusses Jennifer Stuller's groundbreaking book *Ink-Stained Amazons* which, like Laura Mulvey's work on the male gaze, has us wondering if we are all doing superheroines an injustice by dressing them in skimpy clothing.

Each of these works touches on the topic of the modern superhero as seen in comics and film. These are art forms that combine art and text. They are also economically and visually accessible, and thus appeal to a mass audience. For the ancient Greeks, their greatest heroes were forever immortalized in epic poetry. Epic was an equally significant part of Greek culture. Alexander the Great, for example, was said to have slept with a copy of the *Iliad* beneath his pillow and visited the tomb of Achilles, his boyhood hero.[3] Achilles, Hector, Odysseus—names that recall great deeds that defined a time and a culture—are with us still guiding our own myth-making tradition. Epic is unique in that it is cognizant of its own genre. It is a story that knows it is a story. When Odysseus visits the court of the Phaeacians, for example, and hears his own story being sung by the blind bard Demodocus, it is as though Homer himself is taking a bow.

What Is Myth?

First, we need to establish some ground rules. We need to define what we mean when we talk about myth. Seems simple enough, but it is not actually as straightforward as one might think. The word means different things to different cultures at different times. For example, the ancient Greeks, who thought of themselves more along the lines of polities rather than Greeks as a unified entity *per se* and certainly never thought they were ancient in their own time, used the term μῦθος (*mythos*), meaning *speech*, *narrative*, *fiction*, *myth*, or *plot*. Obviously, applying this term at the wrong time to the wrong person might get you stoned, and not in a good way. Suffice it to say that even in the ancient Greek there is great variability in meaning. This is great, because you could call Demosthenes' speech a myth, meaning hogwash, one day, then when he gives you the evil eye in the agora the next day you can smile and say, "Oh, by myth I really meant to say it was an 'epic' speech, thank you very much."

The term "myth," as we commonly think of it today, was borrowed by English speakers in the early 19th century to refer to a story, or series of etiological stories involving supernatural forces or beings that reinforce a religious ritual or belief.[4] Homer and Hesiod, poets of the Greek epic cycle, blamed the ills of mankind on various supernatural forces. The whole Trojan War, for example, was really the result of an *ad hoc* beauty contest among the goddesses Hera, Aphrodite, and Athena, and the poor mortal sod they made judge it made the mistake of choosing sides instead of calling in sick. A lot of the problems arise, however, from competing narratives among different city-states. Everyone wanted to claim Herakles as a hometown hero, which is why we have so many different mythic traditions. In turn, Xenophanes questioned the veracity of Homer and Hesiod, paving the way for the Socratics to clean up the mess.

Modern views of myth, of course, owe much to Carl Jung's 12 mythic archetypes. Jung suggested that certain archetypes are derived from the human subconscious and actualized in images and behavior in the waking world: the great mother, father, child, devil, god, wise man, wise old woman, trickster and hero, and the anima. Among these, however, certain figures pervaded, namely, the shadow (one's subconscious dark side), the wise old man, the child, the mother and maiden.[5] Jung's work greatly influenced anthropologists such as the late Claude Lévi-Strauss and comparative mythologists such as Joseph Campbell. Lévi-Strauss was looking at the collective nature of the unconscious, claiming that the "structure of primitive thoughts is present in our minds."[6] Obviously, ignoring the label of "primitive," we might simply recognize that the human brain from very early on is pre-wired for certain structural patterns, and it is easy to see why. Unless you live on the moon, the figure of the old mother, old man, maiden and shadow are part of the human journey and can be found in every culture's mythic archetypes.

Without a doubt, one of the most influential works on mythic archetypes is Joseph Campbell's *Hero with a Thousand Faces.* Campbell identified certain recurring actions in the mythologies of the world, which he called the monomyth: separation from society, undergoing the initiation where the hero proves his heroic nature through many trials, attaining a type of apotheosis where he is reborn a hero, and finally the return, where the hero earns recognition for his accomplishments. This is why the ancient Greek concept of *nostos*, the return of the hero, is so important to the attainment of glory. It is why Odysseus bemoans his fate. If he cannot tell his tale on his home turf, he goes unremembered by those he left behind initially. Of course, Campbell was criticized for the limited applicability of his model, but as Jung warns us in *Man and His Symbols*: "the term 'archetype' is often misunderstood as meaning certain definite mythological images or motifs, but these are nothing more than conscious representations, representations that can vary a great deal in detail without losing their basic pattern."[7] It is those differences, however, that define who we are and are thus worthy of study. For myself, Campbell's insight was not only a new way of looking at myth but also a way of drawing together various mythic traditions and making sense of them.

What Is a Hero?

What does it mean to be a hero? The answer largely depends on one's cultural context, or as Derrida has poignantly observed, one's *habitus*. Today, we may look to the skies and exalt caped crusaders such as Superman, Iron Man, or Wonder Woman as heroes, characters with superhuman powers who can leap tall buildings with a single bound, fight the good fight, and can go and do what we mere mortals can only dream of. We tend to idolize athletes who can perform incredible feats of skill and garner strength and grit against all odds, or politicians, who rise to the occasion, rallying people to a great cause, or the rock star poet who sings of a deep and common truth. Forty years ago, however, Americans eagerly clung to their televisions entranced by the tales of the gunslinger, men who settled the West and lived and died by a code. As Americans we tend to love our heroes, but heroes are also loners—Batman wages a tireless, typically one-man war against crime from the sanctity of his Batcave, Superman from his fortress of solitude, Iron Man from Avengers tower. Ironically, though we look up to them, and most want to be them, they are the quintessential Other, gods living among mortals. Heroes, multi-faceted as they generally are, serve to define our society. By being the Other, they can escape society, and so can we, by joining in their adventures. So too did the heroes of ancient Greece.

Of all the works of the ancient world, none has captured the essence of the hero more than Homer's *Iliad*. Achilles the lion-hearted, Hector breaker of horses, god-like Diomedes, and Odysseus the master strategist and weaver of tales: names that echo across time and have stirred the imagination of readers for centuries. For Homer, likewise, the ἥρως (*herōs*) was no mere mortal. Typically the offspring of a god and a mortal woman, he was expected to be fierce in battle and to adhere to a strict code of honor. Courageous and bold, he was typically endowed with some superhuman invulnerability that concealed an underlying great and tragic flaw, or *hamartia*, which served to be the source of his downfall. Hector's *hubris*, Achilles' anger, and Herakles' madness are all perfect examples. Heroes often go where others fear to tread, battling horrific monsters, braving some far flung part of the world in order to not only secure some inner wisdom but also personal glory, which ultimately demands their return home so they can recount their adventures and live on in the oral traditions of the respective cultures.

Often such warriors find themselves under the aegis of the gods. By providing some form of divine intervention, such gods often aid the hero on their quest: Hermes, for example, whispering in the ear of Odysseus how to defeat Circe. Well, can you blame them? It is, after all, rather tedious being omnipotent and ruling the universe all day, day after day, year after year, millennium after millennium. In the end, the journey of the hero is the journey of life. It is transformative. No hero who begins his quest is ever truly the same upon his return. Through the process of the quest, therefore, they undergo a death and rebirth. Just as a butterfly emerging from the chrysalis, they surrender an often young and impetuous ego in exchange for enlightenment and wisdom. Nevertheless, what a hero *is* continues to be a subject of debate.

In 1936, Lord Raglan developed an erstwhile checklist for the Hero archetype in Indo-European literary traditions in his book *The Hero: A Study in Tradition, Myth and Drama*.[8] This was based loosely on the work of myth ritualists such as James Frazier, whose work *The Golden Bough* is still used today. Some of these markers for a heroic figure include the following:

1. The Hero's mother is a royal virgin,
2. his father is a king, and
3. often a near relative of his mother, but
4. the circumstances of his conception are unusual, and
5. he is also reputed to be the son of a god.
6. At birth an attempt is made, usually by his father or his maternal grandfather to kill him, but
7. he is spirited away and

8. reared by foster parents in a far country.
9. We are told nothing of his childhood, but
10. on reaching manhood he returns or goes to his future kingdom.
11. After a victory over the king and/or a giant, dragon, or wild beast,
12. he marries a princess, often the daughter of his predecessor and
13. becomes king.
14. For a time he reigns uneventfully and
15. prescribes laws, but
16. later he loses favor with the gods and/or his subjects and
17. is driven from the throne and city, after which
18. he meets with a mysterious death,
19. often at the top of a hill.
20. His children, if any, do not succeed him.
21. His body is not buried, but nevertheless
22. he has one or more holy sepulchers.

As one can see, the categories, although conforming to some of the heroes, seem arbitrary, until you start applying them. For example, Herakles only matches 17 of these points, whereas Oedipus aligns with 21. Additionally, these classifications tend to center only on men, but some qualities could, and should be applied to women. Finally, as we all know, many of the classical heroes exude super-human like qualities, great strength, giftedness, invincibility, none of which are necessarily covered by this list.[9]

How do we define the superhero? Is he a masked avenger dressed in tights, who fights crime and protects the weak, armed with some secret super power, an arsenal of cool gadgets, a fleet of hot cars, and sought by equally hot women? Unlike ancient epic warriors concerned with *kleos*, or personal glory, our modern heroes need to be selfless, righteous, and seek social justice on behalf of the weak and oppressed. But there are some echoes of the epic hero. Qualities such as a noble or strange birth, performance of great deeds and the quest are still used in developing the superhero. They are still warriors, fighting crime and monsters of all types. Tropes such as the arming scene, the descent into the underworld, destiny, and the return are all still used today. The difference is that today we as a culture tend to make them fit our own worldview.

The Hero's Code

Throughout the course of the book, you will frequently hear me refer to the "warrior's code," or the "hero's code," so I shall define those terms

An Attic black-figure amphora, dating to 500–480 BCE, depicts the duel between two epic heroes, evoking the oral traditions of Homer. On the left appears a low-crested warrior, brandishing a figure eight style shield upon his arm. He levels his spear at his opponent, a high-crested warrior bearing a round shield, who has fallen. Terracotta 23.4 × 15.5 cm (9³⁄₁₆ ×6⅛ in.) 86.AE.78. The J. Paul Getty Museum, Villa Collection, Malibu, California, Gift of Milton Gottlieb.

here. Epic warriors lived by a strict code of honor that they could invoke both on and off the battlefield, a moral compass if you will, a way of ordering and understanding their world, like myth itself, but most importantly, it created a cross-cultural *koine* that extended across the Mediterranean. For example, in Book 2 of the *Iliad*, when the Lycian hero Glaucus and Argive Diomedes collide on the battlefield, Glaucus mentions he is the grandson of Bellerophon. Diomedes responds in kind by claiming his grandfather, Oeneus was a friend of Bellerophon. Instead of continuing their duel, the two warriors lay down their arms and exchange armor, rekindling this friendship, thus demonstrating the custom of *xenia*, i.e., "guest-host relations."

Diomedes is a fantastic character and a poster boy for the warrior code. For example, Agamemnon frequently harangues him. Yet he always manages to weather the storm of opprobrious taunts, keeping his cool, and remembering the hereditable hierarchy with the high king, or *wanax*, at the top. Achilles, clearly, has a much harder go at this. His vanity, mercilessness, and temperamental nature frequently places him at odds with his king, and thus likewise the code. Another crucial tenet of the warrior code is honoring the dead. Stripping a body of its armor is seen as defilement and must be repaid in kind. Another is venerating the gods, one's ancestors, and one's community. Honor in Homer's world is everything. Losing one's nerve and composure, therefore, is viewed as a shameful act, even when coerced by the gods. The warrior Ajax, for example, driven to madness by the gods, attacks a small herd of sheep thinking them his comrades. When he realizes his mistake, he is unable to live with the shame and commits suicide by throwing himself on his sword.

Ultimately, the tale of *Iliad* is one of heroes and kings, a colloquy about war and warriors and one that would have a profound and lasting effect on later Greek identity. Archaic drinking cups buried with the dead provide subtle glimpses of Bronze Age warfare, and many more recall scenes similar to those in the *Iliad*. Funerary assemblages also resemble those mentioned in the funeral games to Patroclus. The remains of ancient palaces and the impassioned stories of Homer gave rise to hero cults and a new warrior *koine* that took hold in the Mediterranean. In essence, Homer's heroes were the ancient equivalent of the modern comic book hero.

Comic book superheroes, like the successive stories of ancient Greek heroes, have evolved to match the trends and values of their society. They became more inclusive and dealt with issues that confronted each new generation. Those familiar with the Golden Age of comics, for example, will recognize a huge shift to the Silver Age, as characters like Superman and Batman went from throttling villains to reflecting on how to find more peaceful solutions to bring justice to their cities. Instead of personal glory, modern heroes seek glory for the greater good. And just like the warrior *koine* of the past, modern fans of superheroes live vicariously through the exploits of their heroes. They collect stories about them, attend conferences, and even dress up, or cosplay them. Ask anyone who has attended Comic-Con: hero cults are alive and well in the modern Western world.

One of the most familiar tropes of epic, ancient or modern, is the traditional arming of the hero. This is the point at which the hero chooses his/her arms and armor before embarking on their journey or racing out to meet their destiny. Inarguably, the *Iliad* reaches its dramatic peak in Book 19 with the famous arming of Achilles. Much to the dismay of the Trojans, Thetis delivers newly fashioned armor to her son, armor that kindles his rage. How he arms himself is particularly interesting. First, he straps on greaves for his legs. Next comes the corselet for his chest, followed by sword and shield, the helmet which Homer describes poetically as though a star, and finally, the spear. So resplendent is our hero after arming himself that he is even compared to Hyperion, making him seem blazing and godlike. The same convention appears again and again throughout epic. The arming of Paris in Book 3 (lines 30–338) and Agamemnon in Book 11 (20–28) likewise play out the same way, with greaves and corselet. Odysseus also has an arming scene in the *Odyssey* (22.122–125), ironically only *after* attacking the suitors. Arrows spent, he places his bow against the door, straps a shield about his shoulders, and a well-wrought helmet bristling with a plume of coarse horse's hair. The armor, while offering protection, also provides Odysseus with an alter ego: warlike Odysseus.

This arming of the hero is a tradition well at home in modern culture. When Superman races off to save the innocent, he dashes into a phone booth, removes his everyday glasses, loosens his tie, and exposes his emblematic S for Superman. Likewise, Bruce Wayne descends into his cave, arming himself before heading off to battle. In almost every film, Batman is shown with a personal armory, replete with arming scenes. In Tim Burton's classic 1989 film *Batman*, our hero gazes upon the empty suit hanging in a vault before slipping on the cowl and cape. He is transformed. The scene is repeated in *Batman Returns* (1992) and is even somewhat satirized in films like *Batman Forever* and *Batman and Robin*.

Iron Man takes this arming scene to an all new level. In the 2008 film *Iron Man*, Stark suits up. Taking the pose of the Vitruvian Man, he is fitted and riveted with armor that he takes for a ride like one of his flashy, high-end sports cars. In 2010's *Iron Man 2*, we drool over the portable suit, which Stark carries in a suitcase. In the *Avengers* (2012), after Stark is tossed from a window, J.A.R.V.I.S. launches a suit that saves him from falling to his death. In *Avengers: Infinity War*, with a mere tap of his finger, Stark can instantly don the suit using nanotechnology.

At its core, the suit of armor not only represents protection for the hero but a mark of his or her identity, a practice that extends as far back as tribal society and the smearing of war paint.

The suit, however, is not the only thing that makes the man. As we see, when Patroclus dons the armor of Achilles, he may deceive some at first, but ultimately it does nothing to protect him. It is the warrior underneath. In *Spiderman: Homecoming*, for example, Stark demands Peter Parker return the suit he made for the young hero. In a scene reminiscent of Patroclus and Achilles, Parker claims he just wanted to be like him. "I am nothing without this suit," Peter claims, to which Stark replies, "If you are nothing without the suit, then you shouldn't have it." Here Stark indicates that there is more to the man than his suit. There is a code of ethics and beliefs just like those of warriors past.

Who Is This Homer, and What Is Epic Poetry?

Who is Homer? Surprisingly, for as greatly admired and universally acclaimed as he is, we know exactly flapdoodle about the man himself; the original bard, by and large, remains a mystery. Nevertheless, the many-storied singer of tales has been claimed by many lands. His birthplace may have been Chios, Ionia, Athens, or some even claim him to be of Egyptian descent. Nobody knows for sure. When did he live? No one knows exactly—anywhere from the eighth to the early seventh century BCE. Was he blind, did he sing out of tune, have halitosis? Was he male or female? Was he even a person at all or a tradition of poets and oral recitations? Does it really matter? Like modern day fans of superheroes, ancient listeners yearned to hear stories of Hector, breaker of horses, and Achilles, greatest of the Greek heroes. Ultimately, his or her tales have lasted the test of time, because something about them reaches us at a very primal level. Myths and their heroes unite us.

What most modern audiences are surprised to discover is that most epics were actually sung and to the tune of something called dactylic hexameter. It is a style of poetry that has six feet and varying tempo. Each foot can either be a dactyl, i.e., a long syllable followed by two shorts, *dum-diddy*, or a spondee, that is two longs, or *dum-dum*. Often a dual rhythm is employed. One beat is set by the meter, while the other is set by the bard. In modern terms, one might think of hip-hop, rap, or even Eminem.[10]

Oral Tradition vs. Epic Vision

One might say that the comic book has its roots deep in the oral traditions of the ancient world. Whether cylinder seals from ancient Babylon depicting superhuman heroes battling implacable beasts or heroes and warriors dancing around the belly of a Greek vase, such examples of visual culture are vital to our understanding of epic tradition, for they, too, generate narratives all on their own. Consider the famous *Tabula Illiaca*. Dating to the Roman Imperial period, this collection of 22 miniature marble reliefs inscribed with images from the Iliadic cycle is what we might consider the Roman equivalent of a limited edition series. The scenes are drawn predominantly from the *Iliad*, but also from the *Aethiopis*, the *Little Iliad, Ilioupersis*, and the *Odyssey*. Scenes from the Theban Cycle and Labors of Heracles are also featured.

Perhaps the most gratifying example is the famous *Tabula Iliaca Capitolina,* discovered near Rome at Bovillae in the late 17th century. Deliciously exuberant, it boasts a virtuosity seldom seen in Western art. Measuring a mere 25 cm × 30 cm, this small but astoundingly detailed stone slab brings the world of Homer to life visually by weaving together a pastiche of several critical scenes from the Trojan epic. The viewer then fills in the missing bits in between each scene, connecting the dots so to speak, in order to complete the narrative.

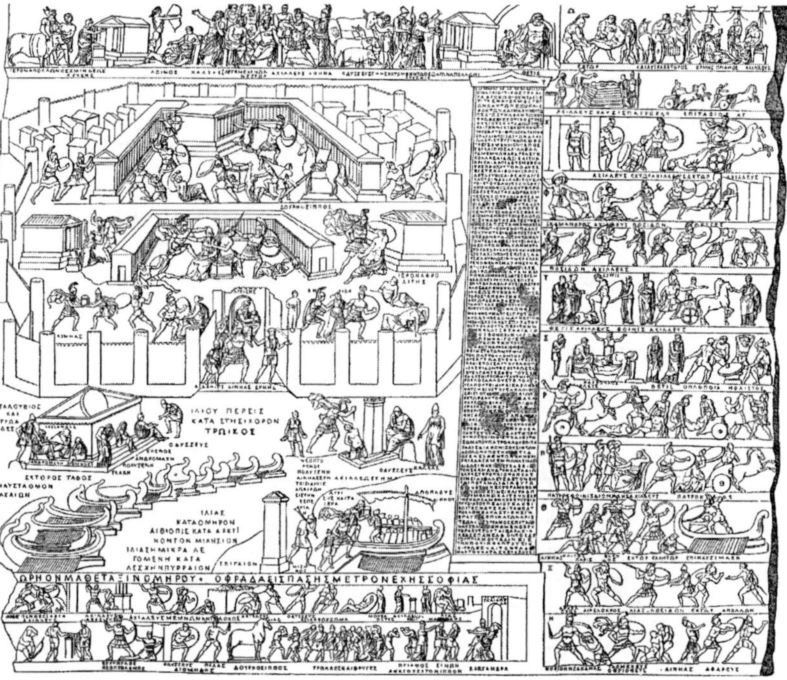

A visual guide to the Trojan epic cycle, the famous *Tabula Iliaca Capitolina* presents pivotal moments from the *Iliad*, *Ilioupersis*, and *Aethiopis*. The limestone slab offers multiple ways of viewing: bird's eye, action-to-action, but also left to right, and bottom to top. Currently held at the Capitoline Museum in Rome, Italy. (This line drawing is reproduced from *An Atlas of Classical Antiquities* by Theodor Schreiber. London: Macmillan and Company, 1895, 176–179, plates XCII and XCIII.)

At the upper left, scenes unfold from Book I of Homer's *Iliad*. From left to right (like a comic strip) we catch sight of the Trojan priest, Chryses, as he propitiates the god Apollo with sacrifice. Next, Apollo fires a plague-bearing arrow into the Greek camp, followed by the council of the Greeks and Achilles leaping forward to kill Agamemnon. As tensions mount, Odysseus appeases Apollo with a sacrifice, while Thetis pleads with Zeus to save her son Achilles. The action pauses there, interrupted by an enormous column bearing a partial transcript of Homer's text. It then picks up again along the right side. Paradoxically, the progression of events unfolds not from top to bottom but from bottom to top, a bit like Trajan's column.

The center of the piece provides a bird's eye view, capturing the final tragic moments from the *Ilioupersis* and the Fall of Troy. Within a courtyard we catch a glimpse of the Temple of Athena and the abduction of

Cassandra by Ajax, who is dragging her by the hair. Below and right, a Greek soldier emerges from the top of a wooden horse, lending the scene its context. Throughout, archers and men with shields add to the chaos of the scene. Directly below, framed by a second portico, we stumble upon a chilling scene as the blood-thirsty warrior Neoptolemus (Pyrrhus) impiously sacrifices Priam on an altar, in view of his wife Hecuba, who is being dragged away. This vignette would have struck a major chord with Roman audiences, because it is a pivotal scene from their own national epic, Vergil's *Aeneid*. During the sack of Troy, when Aeneas flees, he looks back with horror as Neoptolemus slays the young prince Polites in front of his father, Priam, before murdering the old king himself.[11] The scene changes the way Aeneas sees the world. Dominating the piece, and just below this, is the figure of Aeneas. He appears dead center at the gates of the city devotedly bearing the figure of his father Anchises upon his shoulders and leading his son Ascanius by the hand from the ruins of the city. Hermes acts as guide to the pious hero. Meanwhile, in the background, his wife Creusa, hiding her face, sadly falls behind. Beyond the gates, we find the Tomb of Hector and a line of ships that lead the viewer to a scene of Neoptolemus sacrificing Polyxena. A dejected Odysseus looks on while below we find Aeneas, at a later moment, boarding a ship bound for Sicily.

Just below, and rounding out the narrative, are two bands populated with scenes from the *Aethiopis* and *Little Iliad*. Achilles can be seen slaying the Amazon queen Penthesilea, Thersites, and Memnon before finally succumbing to one of Paris' arrows, while his mother Thetis, stricken with grief, turns away. Directly below, within its own frieze, we find scenes from the *Little Iliad*. There is the death of Paris, Odysseus and Diomedes carrying off Troy's prized Palladium, and the fateful welcoming of the wooden horse, full of Greeks, into the city.

Like the divine smith Hephaestus hammering out the shield of Achilles, our artist has created a masterpiece in miniature, encompassing an entire world within a single letter sized slab of stone. The tablet not only blends elements of both literary and artistic styles, but at the same time offers a complex view of the Trojan cycle. The real thrill for the scholar is being able to understand how to decode that view. In his book *Understanding Comics: The Invisible Art*, Scott McCloud lays the groundwork for looking at modern comics and their psychological effect on the viewer. Despite being modern, and hardly definitive, McCloud provides structure for building new approaches. While Romans applied their own *way of looking* and drawing meaning, we are ultimately looking at how pictures and words relate to one another. We can, for example, observe which symbols and scenes chosen encapsulate certain themes, the sequential effects each one has on a viewer and even on themselves in the overarching narrative.

One approach McCloud discusses is the concept of closure. Put simply this is the idea of how a viewer reconciles or makes sense of what happens from one scene to the next, again *connecting the dots*.[12] He outlines five major types. The first example, *moment-to-moment*, shows the main character from one panel to the next with little action. In this instance, there is little closure needed by the viewer. *Action-to-Action* highlights a main character through a series of panels completing several actions. *Subject-to-subject* shows two subjects sharing a common space over time. *Scene-to-scene* involves different panels, with different settings and times, but that are part of the same narrative. One useful comparison of this may be found in the old American western. Imagine if you will a scene with two holstered men facing off, sporting cowboy hats with hands about their waists. The next scene shows a clock tower, with hands pointing straight up toward noon. Finally, the scene dissolves to show a grave with a hat on top of it. Most of us would probably come to conclude that a duel had occurred, and someone had lost based on the symbols of hats, high noon, and a grave. Obviously, greater effort is required by the viewer to fill in what is happening between the scenes depicted in our tablet, but the idea is still the same.

Clearly, the placement of the *Ilioupersis* at the center of the viewer's gaze highlights its importance, as does the slightly larger figures. These catch our eyes first. It stands to reason then that larger must mean more important. The scenes, all part of an over-arching narrative, progress from top to bottom in chronological order. To use McCloud's template, which I think is quite relevant here, the series of panels vary between *action-to-action* and *scene-to-scene*. The choice in scenes helps the viewer order the various epics. Even if one couldn't read the text, the inclusion of the wooden horse within the city walls and taking of prisoners both point to events occurring after Homer's epic. We must also note that the artist paid particular attention to rendering the city gate, on Aeneas (Brilliant, 1984), as he appears multiple times, and the opening up of space once he gets outside the city. The space is less constraining, signaling perhaps for Aeneas there is hope, while for the Greeks, who seem to be dejected, gathered around the tomb of Hector or watching Achilles' son Neoptolemus continue his violent deeds, there is no hope at all. Taken as a whole, there is a single landscape, but it contains multiple scenes from the epic that occur at different times—Aeneas, for example, appears three times. The point of the work then is not necessarily to express realism. It is instead a didactic work highlighting certain scenes and heroes, ones perhaps that bespeak of Roman values. It begs the question, where is the artist turning for his models?

Some scholars such as Kurt Weitzmann have attempted to answer this very question. He places this work within the greater discussion of literary traditions, papyri, and their influence on art. Contrastingly, Michael Squire argues that such pieces may have been directly influenced by Roman wall painting. The House of Octavius Quartio in Pompeii, for example, boasts a central wall panel with scenes from the first Trojan War. The first Trojan War? Ah, yes. Contrary to popular belief, Paris' libidinous blunder was not the first to stir war between the Trojans and the Greeks. Tensions had crystallized after a visit from Herakles. Apollodorus, a Hellenistic writer, and the most widely credited source, claims that Priam's father king Laomedon had left his daughter Hesione as a sacrifice to Poseidon. Herakles, joining Jason on his expedition for the Golden Fleece, does what he does best, and heroically offers to rescue the girl in exchange for the sacred mares of Zeus in the king's possession. Laomedon agrees but later reneges on the deal. Herakles promises to bring war in exchange for this dishonor. The painting captures the classic scene where Herakles confronts Laomedon.[13] Directly below this appear smaller scenes from the *Iliad*: the famous encounter with Priam beseeching Achilles for the return of Hector's body, for example.[14]

While all of these theories prove provocative and exciting, none of them truly explain the origins of the *tabula*, its audience, or how it should be read. The *tabula*, for example, uses labels underneath the figures and Greek letters to signify specific scenes, like the ordering of books, suggesting that it does not necessarily draw exclusively from visual culture or literary tradition, but a distillation of both. Even if the viewer can't read it, they can scan it and get the gist.

Ultimately, the *Tabula Iliaca* represents a complex narrative, which does not strictly adhere to literary tradition. In the scene with Hector's ransom, for example, Hermes appears in godlike form rather than in human disguise, as Homer relates. Here, we must realize the limitation of the artist and the medium. Without Homer's account, those looking to identify Hermes might mistake him as a mere mortal, if the artist rendered him so. Labeling him should suffice, that is unless you are trying to appeal to an audience that is perhaps either semi-literate or unfamiliar with Greek. The inclusion then of recognizable traits, such as the traveling hat (*petasus*) or winged sandals (*talaria*) of Hermes, is like depicting a superhero with a giant S on his chest. You can recognize the figure based on a culturally predetermined set of visual cues and semiotics. McCloud's approach demonstrates that one can bridge present narratives by identifying how parts relate to the greater whole. It is, however, not the only approach.

Squire compares the *tabula* to an ancient version of "Where's Waldo," wherein one can play games with finding certain characters. At the very least what we find is a creative interplay between similar scenes, e.g., Thetis beseeching Zeus, juxtaposed with Priam beseeching Achilles, suggests a possible connection to the viewer. This same idea can again be found in the center wall painting from the triclinium of Quartio in Pompeii, where Herakles approaches an enthroned Laomedon, while below Priam approaches an enthroned Achilles. The combination of these two scenes suggests an overarching theme of the turning of fortune in favor of the Greeks. Such examples demonstrate a continuum of possible *readings*—a way of engaging with the narrative more than once and perhaps finding new personal narratives. In this way, the visual depiction of the epic is not necessarily meant to be read *panel-by-panel*, like a comic strip, but rather with greater variability, with scenes serving as talking points, and the piece itself an example of visual virtuosity.

While McCloud and Squire offer tantalizing approaches, without context, neither can provide an authentic Roman perspective. We are merely left grasping at straws. That being said, they do provide different ways for us to think about how the ancient viewer *might* have seen the epic cycle, and the hero, without the aid of a text. We may then recognize that the *Tabula Iliaca*, for the Romans, was a cohesive visual guide to the Trojan cycle. While it may look like a comic, it serves the purpose of reminding us that there are multiple ways, ancient and modern, to find closure thereby unlocking the code of visual narrative.

Theoretical Framework: Semiotics, Comics and Film

Now comes the part you aren't going to like very much: theory. The word itself is liable to either inflame some sort of visceral and violent reaction, like the throwing of this book across the room (please don't) or lull one into a sudden but interminable coma. So, if you want to skip ahead to the individual chapters, please feel free to do so, but, if you're in for the long haul, read on. Writers view with much trepidation the prospect of introducing theory to their discussion. No one likes it, but it is often necessary to take a definable approach so that others might be able to duplicate or follow your line of thinking. You wouldn't wander off into the woods without a map, now would you? Neither should research be undertaken without a good theory or model. One of the most laudable theoretical models, in my humble opinion, is semiotics.

What is semiotics, and how do we define it? Ferdinand de Saussure, not necessarily the person you would want to *invite* to a cocktail party, but someone you might *bring up* at a cocktail party, once described language as a system of signs, *words*. These words have both a linguistic and conceptual value. The French literary theorist Roland Barthes argued that *myth* was also a system of communication, which he called meta-language:

> Speech of this kind [i.e., myth] is a message. It is therefore by no means confined to oral speech. It can consist of modes of writing or of representations; not only written

> discourse, but also photography, cinema, reporting, sport, shows, publicity, all these can serve as a support to mythical speech.[15]

The staggeringly brilliant author and semiotician Umberto Eco once claimed: "Semiotics is concerned with everything that can be taken as a sign. A sign is everything which can be taken as significantly substituting something else."[16] His point is well taken, in that the field of semiotics is ambiguous at best, as one might interpret everything as carrying meaning. Of course, as a post-modernist and to illustrate his point, Eco peppered his own prose with continuous layers of symbolic ambiguity. Well aware of the intrinsic value of literature in expressing meaning he stated: "To survive, we must tell stories."[17]

Today we continue to define the boundaries of semiotics, looking for meaning conveyed through body language, gesture, words, charged language, and visual illustration.[18] For example, the stars and stripes on heroes' costumes often stir feelings of American patriotism. Intrinsically, though, all of these things are engrained in our *habitus*. For example, as we shall see, the personification of America, Columbia, bridges the gap between the ancient Amazon and the modern American one. Chandler sums it up as follows: "Semioticians study signs not in isolation but as part of semiotic 'sign-systems' (such as medium or genre). They study how meanings are made and how reality is expressed."[19]

Consider the ancient Greek hero Herakles. In ancient depictions, he is shown with his emblematic club and lion skin cap, a trophy from his encounter with the Nemean Lion. Such symbols become codified and appropriated by those wishing to mimic his story and qualities. A portrait bust of the emperor Commodus, for example, depicts the despot not as he was but how he wished to be perceived with the same lion skin cap and club. The meaning, we can only assume, is one of strength and perhaps hints at a semi-divine nature. Superman, likewise, has his cape and emblematic "S" on his chest, Captain America his shield, Wonder Woman her magic lasso. Once the story is told it becomes part of our cultural repertoire.

There are, however, certain semiotic differences allowing for multiple readings. What do I mean by this? Note that I make a careful distinction between emblem and symbol. While a symbol may carry a general meaning, an emblem seems more specific. In our previous examples, emblems are resigned to a specific type of character. While Superman's S might be considered emblematic, the cape is a more general symbol of the superhero. Nevertheless, it is the combination of each that allows an audience to recognize the character as Superman. Likewise, while a lion might indicate royalty or perhaps strength, the lion combined with a club may indicate to an ancient Greek or Roman the hero Herakles.

Now consider for a moment the ancient observer, as he or she struggles to make sense of a character in a wall painting with a winged hat and sandals. Initially they may recognize him as Hermes, the messenger of the gods, but the inclusion of angry gorgons and the absence of a caduceus, suggests instead the hero Perseus. Now, while there is a distinction, this is not to suggest that one symbol is divorced from the other. They are intrinsically linked. One versed in classical myth, for example, cannot see Perseus without thinking about Hermes, who loaned Perseus his emblems. It is the unique combination of symbols (winged sandals + winged hat + gorgons) that makes something emblematic (= Perseus ≠ Hermes).

Symbols, on the other hand, are more general. In some ancient depictions, for example, a torch might indicate a dark place or night, whereas the inclusion of both a moon and the sun may indicate a cycle. Such readings are culturally proscribed, but they are neither simple nor stagnant. Over time, symbols become multi-vocalic, building their own unique repertoire of meaning. Symbols and emblems have a life of constant discovery and rediscovery, and they are always changing. Even from the first utterance, the story changes for the audience who perceives the words of the poet, then applies their own meanings. Even though both poet and audience share a certain habitus, a certain cultural archive, the resulting dialogue involves an individual's personal interpretation. Think of the childhood game telephone, after someone whispers in the ear of another, the listener attaches their own meanings. Thus, the story of Troy, which survives today, stems from an oral tradition, a dialogue, centuries in the making.

A semiotic approach looks at forms of representation, i.e., film, as a system of visual symbols, such as the meaning of a cape, a mask, or a sword. What are the most prominent *signs* or myths in modern comic books? How are costumes of certain heroes, for example, treated in the Avengers series, versus, say, the X-men? Is there an emphasis on uniformity or individuality? In terms of film, semiotics looks both at the symbols in film as well as the film as an entire narrative, how characters interact, the events that unfold, and the recurrence of certain themes. How do films draw on mythic symbols, subvert or re-write certain myths, and redefine the paradigm of the epic hero? How do films and the comic books they represent diverge? Beyond the obvious difference that one is just visual (comics), while the other is both visual *and* aural (film), for the comic book medium, endeavoring to sum up the entire contents of the story in one single image for, say, the cover is of the utmost importance. The same could be said about summing up the content of a movie with a trailer or even a movie poster. With digital media, we encounter email campaigns, social media advertising blitzes, tantalizing Twitter feeds, and barrages even in the grocery store (who doesn't want to try Spider-Man string cheese?)—the images follow you everywhere you go.

This is not so different from the visual culture of the ancient world. Grave goods honoring the deceased and recovered from both Greece's Mycenaean and late Geometric periods, for example, abound with scenes of warriors and warfare. The now famous Pylos Combat Agate, discovered in the grave of the Griffin Warrior, and dating to the 15th century BCE, captures a scene of two warriors fighting over the body of a fallen comrade, summoning for some the epic clash of Hector and Achilles over Patroclus. Adorning the cups and vases of Greece's late Geometric are scenes of warriors marching off to battle, ships sailing the wine dark sea, and charioteers participating in funeral games. The symbols of the Homeric hero, it seems, became an industry producing phenomena. In lieu of historical accounts, art historians forever struggle to contextualize such works. Were these echoes of epic narrative and heroes in the style of Homer to accompany the dead on their journey, or actual accounts of Bronze Age battles? While we are left pondering such questions, the koine that followed Homer had the collective knowledge, the "software," to decipher these images imparted through oral and visual culture.

Long after Homeric heroes had gone to the houses of dust, their stories continued to survive throughout antiquity, told and retold for centuries, a medley of different oral traditions, always finding life again, each time in slightly different armor. This same storytelling tradition is alive and well in the modern day—in the comic book artist, filmmaker, and video game designer. These modern impresarios have picked up the mantle of Homer,[20] turning to myth and mythic archetypes to frame their storylines. But do such archetypes necessarily carry the same meaning, the same visual representation they once did, or are they distinctly different? What's the significance of the similarities and differences in terms of cultural construct? Without giving too much away, the basic premise of this book is that regardless of time or culture, we all need a hero to be able to cross the boundaries of the civilized world when we cannot, to live those dreams we wish to live, to die and return a hero, which is why we keep returning to the mythic archetype and reinventing it, because it works. How we reinvent the hero, however, is equally compelling and worthy of further study, for it holds up a mirror to our own modern society upon which we can reflect.

Introduction

Over the past few years, comic book heroes have increasingly earned the attention of classical scholars, inciting a dialogue about the nature of the epic versus the modern-day hero. Epics such as the *Iliad* provided the Greeks with a deep sense of their heroic past.[1] Reinventing the epic in modern comics and cinema continues that time-honored tradition, allowing readers to connect to the same timeless past. Good stories speak to us on a primal level but almost in a whisper. We have to look and listen closely. There is something we can recognize—a bit of ourselves in the hero, and sometimes in the villain—and like the ancient Greeks, many of our modern heroic tales tend to center around the theme of mortality and what it means to be truly human. With every retelling of the epic tale, something new is added, but many of the underlying themes, such as war, friendship, identity, and rage remain the same. Are we simply recycling ancient archetypes? In his ground-breaking book *The Hero with a Thousand Faces*, Joseph Campbell posits just that: all hero narratives derive from a single monomyth:

> *A hero ventures forth from the world of common day into a region of supernatural wonder: fabulous forces are there encountered and a decisive victory is won: the hero comes back from this mysterious adventure with the power to bestow boons on his fellow man* [23].

While we can all agree that Western culture may have inherited certain archetypes from Greek and other ancient mythologies, one must assiduously consider how modern society adapts these archetypes to fit a modern context and the significance of what we abandon from the paradigm.

The starting point for this book then is the premise that the development of the modern comic hero can be traced back to its origins in ancient myth by focusing on semiotics. The chapters in this book are not designed to offer a definitive approach but rather an invitation for reflection.

Chapter I, "Captain America: An Achilles for the Modern Age," focuses on nostalgia, the bond of friendship, and survivor's guilt manifested in both Achilles and Captain America. In the beginning of the chapter, however, I detail and define what makes Achilles and Cap super soldiers. In essence, though Achilles is born of a nymph, a figure of some divinity anyway, he is dipped into the River Styx by his mother to become immortal ... well, almost. His famous heel is the one spot on his body vulnerable to attack and mortality. Captain America, on the other hand, is entirely mortal, yet the super serum administered to him as a part of the secret government program, *Project Rebirth*, makes him more than human. Steve Rogers morphs into the soon-to-be-legendary Captain America.

Regardless of their incredible strengths, both Rogers and Achilles experience the devastating loss of a close comrade. How these feelings reveal themselves varies greatly. Achilles projects the loss of his best friend Patroclus outward toward any Trojan soldier that crosses his path, although he is like a heat-seeking missile toward Patroclus' killer, Hector. Captain America, on the other hand, internalizes Bucky's loss by self-blame and immolation. While the result of their compatriots' deaths is similar, namely, to force the hero's hand into returning to battle, the two reactions seem as far apart as one could get. This difference says more about our beliefs as a culture than necessarily about the nature of grief itself.

Larger than life, these heroes also wield weapons far beyond those of mere mortals. One in particular, the shield becomes a distinction. Crafted by the divine blacksmith, Hephaestus, the shield of Achilles was designed to stun and amaze with its unique features—one might even call it a piece of ancient "tech." Likewise, Captain America's shield represents a marvel of modern technology, and although Tony Stark's (Iron Man's) father fashioned the shield, the material it was made of was not of this world. Vibranium, an extraterrestrial alloy mined from a meteorite, makes the shield completely infallible and its bearer safe from any Earthly harm. In essence, Achilles and Cap both use shields, which offer seemingly divine protection.

Divine aid aside, what distinguishes them from their fellow soldiers is a sense of exclusion. They are, like so many heroes, loners. For one reason or another, they just don't fit in. After Captain America is found and brought back to life from his icy fall, he finds that he must learn to navigate to a brave new world. Although he still appears young to others, his body and mind are both mired in the past. With his friends gone, wracked by feelings of guilt, loneliness, and haunted by post-traumatic stress disorder, he struggles to find his place not just in the civilian world, but also in a completely different society than when he was last conscious. Rogers represents that nostalgic link to America's perceived innocence and to traditional values, when life as a whole was simpler. He thus tends to be inflexible, often over-simplifying much of what he views around him in the strange world he now inhabits.

Achilles, likewise, is a man out of time. Dishonored by his superior officer, Agamemnon, he goes into self-imposed exile, refusing to re-join the battle at Troy, and leaving the Greeks without their strongest champion. When he returns, the war has dramatically changed. While one may argue that Achilles' imprisonment is self-imposed, I would argue that Agamemnon's breach of proper behavior befitting a king forces Achilles out of the limelight in order to preserve his own heroic virtue. From such comparisons we can see that the model of the modern superhero draws heavily from that of the Homeric hero, allowing us to make comparisons (and sometimes contrasts) that can be richly rewarding and allow the modern viewer to interpret this and other heroic figures as the multi-layered, complex social phenomena that they are.

Many such stories and comparisons exist. In Chapter II, "Wonder Woman: Echoes of the Amazon Warrior," I discuss the long-held love affair with the exotic warrior known as the Amazon as it pertains to the character of Wonder Woman and American culture, addressing such topics as the body, identity, sexuality, language, and of course classical perceptions. I begin with a discussion of the traditional Amazon warrior, which is not at all a simple task, chiefly because there are three distinct trajectories: (1) real Amazons, who were warrior women of the Eurasian steppe, (2) mythological Amazons, who cut off a single breast to be better archers and hated men, and (3) modern comic and cinematic versions of the Amazon. I give a brief discussion of who some of the mythological Amazons are and their qualities, which make them most like the comic book heroine, Wonder Woman.

Penthesilea was the mythological warrior queen of the Amazons, who, according to Homer, falls in love with Achilles as they battle at Troy. Textual references aside, Penthesilea is a popular iconographic symbol in visual culture of the age, appearing in a variety of media including vase paintings and temple friezes. Her physical representation in many of these instances appears more masculine than feminine: she often sports pants, a sword or spear and a shield, and sometimes a hatchet as well. More often than not, she bears the mark of Otherness, dressed in Phrygian clothes and animal pelts. It is precisely this foreignness that makes the Amazon warrior even more terrifying to the Greek male; not only is the adversary foreign, but she's a woman fighting on the same field as men.

As a point of comparison, but also contrast, I then move into my discussion of the modern Amazon warrior, chiefly Wonder Woman. Like Penthesilea, Diana, the Amazon who will become Wonder Woman, is a child of royalty from the far Eastern reaches of the known world (the Black Sea). Initially, Diana is chthonic. She is born from the earth instead of the sexual union of male and female. In this sense, Diana is magical, if not necessarily divine. Later comic book stories portray her as the scion of Zeus, king of the Olympian gods, and her mother, Queen Hippolyta. Like Penthesilea who is the descendant of Ares, the Greek god of war, she appears thus semi-divine. When U.S. Army intelligence pilot Steve Trevor crash lands on her home island she receives the hero's call. After recovering, Steve is sent back to the world of men with a warrior companion, Diana, hereafter referred to as Wonder Woman.

Wonder Woman's garments and weapons, however, are quite *unlike* Penthesilea's. They epitomize male-dominated society. Her creator, William Marston, though wishing to create a strong female role model, inadvertently perpetuated our phallo-centric world by giving his Pygmalion-style creation the same accouterments that draw the male gaze anyway: bustier, slimming girdle, and revealing suit.[2] Further, her use of the lasso to tie up her opponents promotes the heroine as a dominatrix, fulfilling deep-seated male fantasies of being dominated. Wonder Woman has been sexualized, given power to thwart or even remove male power, but she is not able to be actively or overtly sexual. Even when she encounters romance, it is well within the hetero-normative behavior of male society. The tone of the comic, while attempting to appeal to a different audience, namely, young women, is the epitome of the monosexual paradigm.

Xena, however, is different regarding the performance of her sexuality. This could be primarily due to the time period of her popularity, namely, the 1990s as opposed to the 1940s comic book world of Diana Prince. Unlike Wonder Woman, Xena explores her sexuality, taking male lovers, such as Borias, Marcus, and Julius Caesar, but also, many assume, female lovers such as her companion Gabrielle, although this is not as explicit as most lesbian love affairs on screen. Instead of the emphasis being on sex, it is on friendship, companionship, and loyalty. These are the same values ancient Greeks seem to express about ancient Amazons, but it may also be that the Greeks superimposed their own concept of same sex male friendships. Nevertheless, this single point of ambiguous sexuality not only imbues Xena with a certain degree of authenticity, it causes us to question the true nature of "real" Amazon society, especially since we have so little knowledge about the organization of the female warriors of the Eurasian steppe.

For many, Wonder Woman represents the rebirth of a modern Amazon warrior, and yet, Wonder Woman is still depicted through the male lens. She is the ideal woman, but she is still a stranger in a man's world, much like the ancient Greek views of the Amazons. The character draws heavily from a history deeply rooted in Greek mythology and the mythologizing of early America. Yet for Diana to be a true Amazon and break the bonds of masculine servitude, she needs to exist in a strictly Amazonian world, fashioned by a female and perhaps even a strict feminist perspective. Wonder Woman must break the chains of fetishism and instead grab the reigns of real instead of idealized female values.

Chapter III, "A Mind for War: Odysseus and the Iron Avenger," examines the mastermind of war, the tactician who survives by his wits and thus juxtaposes the wily Odysseus and Marvel's billionaire playboy Tony Stark. The chapter discusses several main points, which illustrate the comparison best: their role as inventor, their character as "playboy," and their similar *nostoi*, or returns home to a pliant yet fiercely independent, strong female figure. To begin, I examine the character of Odysseus as an inventor. Most regard Odysseus as the mastermind behind the Trojan horse, but he also devises several cunning plans for he and his men to escape from the man-eating jaws of Polyphemus, listen to the Sirens' intoxicating song unscathed, and even to slip through the tight grip of Calypso, a goddess who wanted to keep Odysseus for her own husband, by building a small raft from raw materials on her island of Ogygia.

What casts Tony Stark as an Odyssean figure, likewise, is his penchant for inventiveness. He, too, is able to assess a crisis and improvise tools and weapons to aid in his own escape. In the first *Iron Man* film, after being ambushed by terrorists, Tony is taken hostage and kept prisoner deep within an underground cave. Injured by shrapnel in the attack, he first has to save his own skin by building a mini arc reactor that powers an electromagnet in his chest keeping the deadly shrapnel from reaching his heart. To escape his captives, he then builds a protective suit made from spare iron parts and hides himself inside. This episode seems like a perfect conflation of Odysseus' Trojan horse and Cyclops vignettes.

Both heroes, though quite interested and well versed in relations with the opposite sex, have a unique relationship with one special woman. This woman, for both Tony and Odysseus, is an intellectual match and steadfastly loyal. Odysseus' journey back home from Troy introduces several paramours: Circe, Calypso, and Nausicaa. With Circe, Odysseus sires at least one if not two children during his one-year stay with her, and he stays with the sea nymph Calypso for seven years. He avoids marriage with Nausicaa, because by this time, he realizes he finally has the means to return home to his wife, Penelope. Tony Stark is a self-proclaimed playboy, so his lovers number far more, yet his Penelope, his steadfast and loyal match, is Pepper Potts. In the final Iron Man film, Stark confirms that Pepper is the only woman about whom he ever dreams. Yet these strong female co-leads have their own unique wiles, plots, plans, and victories, which I discuss more in depth.

For both Odysseus and Tony, the return home isn't just about Penelope or Pepper, though it is in large part. Part of the heroic paradigm is that both must return home from their far-flung journeys. For the Homeric hero, the return home (*nostos*) is the only way his story can be told, and stories are all that we are ... especially in the Homeric world. In a world without technology and 24-hour news, the only way a story is told is by the people themselves; his return is his *kleos*, his glory. Why fight wars and monsters if you don't live to tell the tale and get the props? Both heroes are certainly glory hogs.

Yet along with that glory is the very real responsibility of taking on battles no one really wishes to fight. In the film *Avengers: Infinity War*, New York is attacked by Maw and Obsidian, henchmen of Thanos sent to retrieve the time stone. Bruce Banner warns Tony that Thanos and the war are coming. He needs to call Steve Rogers for help in reorganizing the *Avengers*. Despite their recent estrangement, Stark agrees. Fate, however, intervenes, and hitching a ride aboard the enemy's ship, he is whisked away from earth to the distant planet of Titan, to fight a war he doesn't necessarily want to fight but is bound by duty to do so. This scene echoes Odysseus' initial departure from Ithaka and his dearest Penelope to fight a war in which he has no desire to participate. In both examples, the hero returns home to his beloved to lavish in the tales of their glory and their own heroism.

Chapter IV, "Unstoppable Rage: The Incredible Hulk and the Concept of the Greek Berserker," tackles the ever-elusive topic of divinely inspired rage, the berserker, and overstepping social bounds. The most lucrative examples I have chosen are Achilles, Diomedes, Ajax, and the Incredible Hulk. For many readers of Homer, Achilles is wrath incarnate. The fact that the poet begins the epic of the *Iliad* with the word for rage, *menis*, is a clear indication not only of what the epic is about thematically, but also how it manifests itself in many a hero. For Achilles, his rage is seemingly unique, owing to the terrible loss of his lifelong friend, Patroclus, in Book 18. When his rage is finally unleashed, it sets his enemies to flight as he slaughters innumerable Trojans in Book 21, mercilessly tossing their bodies into the river for the animals to consume, rather than allowing them proper burial. Seething with anger and revenge, Achilles chases Hector three times around the walls of Troy in Book 22 until Athena, the divine agent of much havoc in the epic, stops Hector and likewise encourages Achilles to move in for the kill. This divinely inspired rage overtakes Achilles, who then desecrates and defiles his opponent's now dead body, a breach of heroic code.

Yet Achilles is not the only Greek hero to "go berserk" on the battlefield. So too does Diomedes. Equally virtuous, he too represents the paragon of heroic excellence. A greater contrast, however, there could not be, for Diomedes, unlike Achilles, exhibits an incredible amount of self-restraint in his rage. For example, instead of chasing Hector after he killed Patroclus, Diomedes actually heeds Nestor's advice to return to camp. Though he wavers, in the end Diomedes' good sense prevails over his ego proving his heroic nature. Moreover, on one occasion when Agamemnon calls him cowardly and a mere shadow of his father, Diomedes resists the urge to banter with the warlord and utters not a word proving the better part of valor is to just remain silent and walk away.[3] Nevertheless, Diomedes is not immune to the contagion of battle rage. The difference, however, is that Diomedes is not avenging the death of a close friend. Instead, he is incited by the goddess Athena, who instructs him to only attack certain gods. So fierce is Diomedes' rage that he manages to wound the goddess Aphrodite before going head to head in battle with none other than Ares, the god of war himself. When he comes upon the god Apollo, however, he quickly backs down. Honoring the heroic code, he does not match himself with the gods (and hence does not act with *hubris*).

Another rage-filled hero worth mentioning is Ajax. Strongest of the Achaeans, his downfall and death are intrinsically tied to his madness, brought on by the perceived slight to his honor. After losing a contest with Odysseus over the now deceased Achilles' arms, Ajax, who had been previously unbeatable, is now unable to reconcile his defeat. According to some traditions, he secretly plots to murder his own army, but is thwarted by Athena, who drives him mad. Instead of his comrades, he exacts his revenge on a herd of livestock, a shameful act. Faced with dishonor, Ajax plants his sword into the earth, a symbol of his heroism and manhood, and in one desperate, final attempt to exert control and demonstrate his adherence to the heroic code, throws himself atop it.[4]

Madness befouls many an epic hero. One of the most famous examples of divinely inspired rage may be found in the tales of Herakles. In Euripides' *Hēraklēs Mainomenos*, we find the ever-resentful Hera dispatching her agent Iris to drive the young hero mad. In this madness, he imagines he is killing Eurystheus, the architect of his labors, and his offspring. Blinded by this vision, he storms through the palace, murdering instead his own wife and children whom he mistakes for his enemies. At the point of killing his father, Athena intervenes, knocking him unconscious. As in the *Iliad*, it is Athena who can both incite and quell a hero's rage.

Awakening, Herakles finds himself fettered to a pillar, the bodies of his dear ones massed around him. Rather than blaming the gods for his madness, he blames himself. Contrastingly, the chorus argues that Hera is to blame (*Hēraklēs Mainomenos*, 1311–1312). Ultimately, Herakles must face what he has done, and his shame is too much to bear. He is guilty of one of the most taboo and horrendous crimes one can commit in civilized society, the murder of one's family. Tarnished by shame, like Ajax, he contemplates suicide.

Shifting finally to the tales of the Incredible Hulk, I focus on the more tragic side of rage and its aftermath. Before he was the Hulk, Dr. Bruce

Banner was a physicist working on a project involving gamma radiation. During a test, he is accidentally exposed to his own creation and ends up turning into the Hulk, a creature triggered by the adrenaline brought on by intense feelings of any kind, but especially those of rage.

In the stories that inspired Stan Lee such as *Frankenstein* and *The Strange Case of Dr. Jekyll and Mr. Hyde*, the wholesome scientist who merely seeks knowledge tends instead to misunderstand his own experiments as well as the limitations of human perception. The major protagonists all exhibit intense emotions just beneath the surface, feelings that ultimately coerce them into crossing the line of what is socially acceptable. While the Hulk follows in this vein, his rage is not brought on by war but by anger itself. Yet Hulk's madness is not divinely inspired but neither is it strictly human. The gamma ray energy Banner is exposed to is an extraordinary event and far beyond what most people typically encounter in our daily lives, a lot like what Homeric heroes encounter when a god or goddess take the field of battle.

If rage is inspired by the gods then, like the Hulk, epic heroes lack agency over their own anger and destiny. They can blame the gods instead of themselves for stepping beyond the heroic code. Also like the Hulk, Homer's epic heroes didn't necessarily want to go to Troy and experience the frenzy of battle and its incipient rage, but instead they find themselves right where Fate had ordained. Achilles is overtaken by his anger much like the Hulk. He transgresses the behavior of the warrior code by defiling Hector and refusing him the proper burial. The Hulk and Achilles become rage incarnate.

Chapter V, "The Heart of the African Warrior: Memnon and Black Panther," spirits us away to the land of Wakanda drawing comparisons and contrasts between the epic King Memnon and Marvel's Black Panther in the hopes of engendering a discussion on race, identity, and power in the ancient versus modern world. We begin with the Homeric hero Memnon the Trojan's "hail Mary" warrior from the East (South?) and a study of the character for those readers unfamiliar with him. While his cameo in Homer's epic is indeed short, his story was compelling enough to the ancients to earn his own epic, the *Aethiopis*, a work that survives today only in fragments. These fragments, however, offer the portrait of a hero cast in the Homeric mold, bound by the same heroic code, despite coming from a different culture.

Like Achilles, Memnon is the son of a goddess, and hence semi-divine, although he derides Achilles for his mother being a mere nymph, whereas Memnon's mother is Eos, the more stately goddess of the Dawn.[5] Additionally, both are equipped with divinely wrought, otherworldly armor forged by the god Hephaestus and granted superhuman powers. In this we find similarities with the modern superhero known as Black Panther whose suit and claws are comprised of vibranium, an element born from a meteorite.

Memnon and Black Panther are also scions of nobility, and in true heroic form, their exterior beauty is a marker of this as well as their lineage and adherence to the heroic code. Both heroes are clad in the "skin" of a leopard/lion/cat, which is typically associated with Africa (Ethiopia or "the East" for the Greeks). They are both men of few words and not overly prone to boasting. In nearly every way, Black Panther and Memnon seem to be reflections extending across time.

At this point in the chapter, I pursue the themes of race and power reflected in a recent film, *Black Panther*, a new and much needed narrative, which not only recognizes traditional African themes, but also shows African culture as on par with or even surpassing the cultures of Europe and the West. The fact that this is even a question for modern audiences is a bit of a conundrum, really, because to the ancient Egyptians, the Nubians were the fiercest of warriors and represented a serious threat to their sovereignty. Beyond the borders of Nubia to the South lay the mysterious Land of Punt, a commercial mecca rich in exotic trade goods and rare animals. It was also a place long believed to have been the origins of the Egyptian gods and ancestors. Some scholars debate that the Land of Punt was actually Ethiopia, Memnon's native land. It is a place, therefore, steeped in history, wealthy, and powerful, never having been colonized by anyone—Hittites, Egyptians, Sumerians, Akkadians, Phoenicians, nor Greeks.

Black Panther's native land of Wakanda represents an enigmatic world similar to Punt. In the MCU, it is the richest, most powerful nation on earth, which likewise has never fallen beneath the yoke of European colonization. Its wealth stems from natural resources, specifically vibranium, which the political powers of the world desperately seek, a theme seemingly stripped from modern headlines and the very real modern crisis of conflict diamonds. Filmmakers place Wakanda in the best possible light, often times glamorizing African origins, but also creating a new mythology that focuses on the value of technology and the difficult issues of social justice.

In Chapter VI, "He Who Commands the Sea: Proteus, Scamander and Denizens of the Deep," I dive into the topic of the aquatic warrior, ancient Greek sea deities such as Scamander and Proteus, and how they compare to comic book figures such as Aquaman and Namor. I begin by trying to understand how the Greeks anthropomorphize a part of their natural world by creating a sea with a literal life of its own in characters such as Proteus. Though the Greeks often confused or conflated Proteus and Nereus, what matters is that they are both shapeshifting, omniscient, liminal sea deities, who draw their power from the water that surrounds them. These creatures are usually depicted as monstrous hybrids, sired by primordial entities that are more like manifestations of nature rather than anthropomorphic deities. Some artistic depictions even show them to be hybridized physically—part man, part sea creature or fish. Others take on the form of water itself.

Some, such as the river god Scamander, a venerable deity of the Trojan royal line, act as a moral mirror. For example, he asserts that Achilles' rage is polluting the river itself as he continues to heave the corpses of his opponents into its waters. Achilles' actions interfere with the natural order of Scamander's watery realm. His actions are keeping Scamander from reaching the sea. They also hint at an economic crisis: if the river cannot meet the sea, trade ceases to take place. Thus, the anthropomorphized river Scamander shows a different kind of consciousness, one that, unlike Achilles, respects and preserves the code of the warrior. In this way, Scamander might be considered an embodiment of the epic hero.

Such warriors also inhabit the watery depths of the Marvel and DC Universes. Marvel's Prince Namor, perhaps the "first" aquatic mutant character in the comic book realm, strongly parallels the ancient god Proteus. Like Proteus, Namor is a half-human hybrid—the son of a mortal sea captain and an Atlantean princess named Fen. His physical attributes and his dual heritage as both human and Atlantean render him an outcast of both societies, and like his Greek predecessors, he remains a liminal figure. Namor also uses his powers to manipulate water and sea life to protect his world from invaders. Not to be outdone, DC responds to Namor with an underwater hero of its own, Aquaman. The son of a human and an Atlantean, he too lives on the fringes of both societies up until the point where he reclaims his birthright as king of the oceans.

Namor and Aquaman continue a tradition of aquatic born warriors that extends as far back as Homer and perhaps even further. Their strengths and abilities show that even today, our modern sensibilities are not only fascinated by but also have a deep respect for and even fear of the sea. Its vast depths conceal unending abundance but also constant danger for the ancient mariner.

Modern adaptations of the sea-based heroic archetype merge the strengths of both land and sea. The same hybridity that beleaguers both Namor and Aquaman symbolizes for a modern audience a balanced warrior. Instead of confronting and battling nature, like Achilles, these heroes have a deep respect for the sea, so much so that they often embody it. They are fierce protectors, like the best of Homer's epic warriors. Their hybridity and inner conflicts, however, make them recognizably human, allowing us to identify more closely with their daily struggles.

Chapter VII, "Double Trouble: Divine Twins in Ancient Epic," lends insight on the fascinating topic of twin warriors as they appear in ancient epic and the comic book universe. In viewing the anomaly of twins in ancient texts and art, we can begin to understand the distinct advantages and disadvantages of having a twin and how this resounds in modern comic book twins as well.

Cross-culturally and even sometimes cross-linguistically, twins usually are shown as like-minded yet often binaries that embody opposing forces, like mortality and immortality, dusk and dawn, day and night. In so doing, they represent for many a beginning and an end, or cycle. This is certainly the case with Greek Castor and Polydeuces (Pollux), Herakles and Iphikles, the Indic Aśvins, and even the Hero Twins Hunahpu and Xbalanque of Mayan mythology. In the comic book world, there are two sets of twins I will look at more closely: the Wonder Twins Zan and Jayna and Scarlet Witch and Quicksilver. In every case—both ancient and modern—the twins draw their power from one another. In the event of the demise of one twin, the other either is rendered powerless or spends his/her time in constant pursuit of immortality in some form to bring them back together again.

Inarguably, in mythology twins carry a certain degree of power. At a time when infant mortality was relatively high, twins represented a miracle of nature. Beyond this, identical twins carry additional mystique in that each represents a living, breathing mirror of the other, an *alter ego* in every sense of the phrase. Twins arguably share a unique bond. In the rare instance that they are apart, they still seem to work in tandem, often alarmingly similar in their intentions and even, in some instances, seemingly sense the other's thoughts and feelings. When one suffers mortal pain, the other often feels it as well. This erstwhile telepathy certainly creates an intimacy that cannot be duplicated in any other instance, but it also creates an overwhelming vulnerability, for the loss is not necessarily the loss of a sibling, but the loss also of the self.

In Chapter VIII, "Defending the Epic City: Gotham and Troy," our narrative extends beyond the idea of the hero in mortal form and instead considers the city itself as a character of importance. Cities such as Troy are typically seen as merely the backdrop for the epic hero. We often neglect the fact that the city possesses a character all its own. Soaring battlements, imposing gates, and shimmering halls, the storyteller breathes life into a city so that, like the epic heroes, we remember the place where the encounter occurs. The epic city can be dark and brooding or a utopian fantasy, but make no mistake, cities are vibrant, ever moving entities, rising and falling and rising again. Metropolitan and chic, cities like Troy could certainly be seen as the Gothams of the Bronze Age, replete with the requisite luxury and moral turpitude.

Beginning with a deeper exploration at Homer's Troy, I train our lens on the walls of the city—their materiality and origins—to see them for what they really are: liminal zones which can be protective to those in need and an equally vulnerable place of attack for those seeking to breach them. Through the course of investigation, several questions come to mind. Why do we anthropomorphize and engender cities, and to what degree do the actions of an inorganic, unmoving entity impart identity to its citizens? Despite the challenges, very real connections between Homer's Troy and DC's Gotham City can be made. Both are protected by heroic royalty (Hector and Batman/Bruce Wayne), both cities' battlements have seen their fair share of war, whether from within or without. In the end, the city as character gives rise to its own demise by harboring both heroes and villains alike.

Chapter IX, "Swift and True: Tales of the Epic Archer"—recounts the tale of the epic archer—Paris Alexander, Philoctetes, and Ajax as the ancient predecessors of superheroes Hawkeye and Green Arrow. Often viewed as a second-string hero or merely a sidekick, these ancient equivalents of the modern sniper nevertheless provide a vital balance to the primary protagonists and the narrative itself. I would argue that the same ineffable tension between archer and front-line soldier exists in both the Homeric and modern comic book worlds. The archer, who often turns the tide of battle by a single swift action from afar, nevertheless is viewed with some trepidation, as if somehow his motivations are masked when he doesn't engage in hand-to-hand combat.

Here we revisit Homer, first viewing Paris and Pandarus, two Trojan characters who leave something to be desired as far as their heroic nature. In fact, their expertise with the bow tends to cause consternation rather than relief, as they are seen as cowardly and distinctly un-heroic, not just because they are archers but because they avoid direct conflict.

One possible explanation I entertain is that the undercurrent of distaste for the archer probably is owed to the cultural practice of the royal hunt. The hunt in and of itself is not despicable in the Homeric mind-set, but to kill a human opponent as one might an animal in a hunt, however, radically modifies the heroic paradigm. While the archer might appear to have the high ground (often quite literally), the very vantage point of the bowman often gives him an unfair advantage. Far from a mere quibble, such characters suggest a subversion of the social hierarchy. As the gods are to humans, so we are to animals, and shaking that archaic worldview from its hinges, the archer is at the very epicenter of the paradigmatic shift. Also, one must consider that the Greek world is, at the time of Homer's actual recording of the text, waking from its archaic slumber, sloughing the dream-like nature of Homeric warfare and instead trying on for size the newer, more modern phalanx-style fighting. Inasmuch as hand-to-hand combat wins the day in Homer's *Iliad,* the archer is an even older, more venerable figure, who has more in common with tales of giants and monsters of mythological *genus*.

Such traditions live on in DC's Green Arrow and Marvel's Hawkeye. Green Arrow, whose real name is Oliver Queen, is a pampered aristocrat. On a sailing trip, his villainous assistant strands Queen on a deserted island. Once there, our protagonist must find any means necessary to survive, and as fate has it, that means was a bow. While the island may seem like a prison to Queen, it is an actual prison to a local tribe, which is being enslaved by other island miscreants. In joining the underdog's fight for freedom, when Queen returns to the life he had before that watershed event, he changes from the self-centered, rich fop into a dynamic, crime-fighting advocate, defending those who need it. Those versed in epic will certainly see Queen's story as a shadow to the tale of Philoctetes. Philoctetes, like Queen, is an aristocrat abandoned on an island by those he trusted, in this case, his fellow Achaeans; armed with only a bow and his wits, he straddles the line between life and death. Like Philoctetes, and all heroes, Green Arrow finds his purpose in his return, his *nostos* back into his world, playing the role destiny allots him.

Hawkeye, on the other hand, does not come from privilege. An orphan, he joins a traveling circus where he trains in acrobatics and masters the bow. Always taking the high ground, Hawkeye assesses the situation from a distance, and like the god Apollo, shoots from afar. Despite his unique talents, however, Hawkeye is not destined to lead; in fact, archers never seem to hold the primary role either in ancient epic or in modern heroic stories. In the case of Hawkeye, one wonders if the ancient epic paradigm is actually binding him from a leadership position among the Avengers. His "programming," if you will, is such that he is neither noble nor receives divine aid, so this perhaps precludes him from wearing the gold and instead relegates him to a more subservient, silvery role as a side-kick.

In Chapter X, "God Among Us: Hero as Man and Superman," I reflect on the qualities of the divine, semi-divine, and otherworldly hero, who is forced by fate to live among mortals. Delving into the histories of Superman and Thor, I focus on the elements of Otherness, exile, and disguise, and how each of these, when combined, assembles an arsenal for the hero to complete his or her journey of self-discovery. Finally we shall look at their stories on a more macroscopic level, indicating their real purpose as savior figures, discovering exactly how this paradigm has clear roots in the oldest of the world's story-telling traditions.

By viewing Superman as a veritable twin of Achilles, I follow the well-trod path of the heroic paradigm, set out by Otto Rank, Lord Raglan, and of course, Joseph Campbell. Born of nobility, he flees the place of his birth, landing upon distant shores, and is raised in secret by strangers. Surviving his fate, he lives, he loves, and endures the lure of temptation to become a savior figure to his adopted homeland. Such stories hold an intrinsic value, for not only do they draw to the surface mythic paradigms deeply embedded in our own modern psyches, they also provide a conduit to the heroic realm. They are Everyman. They are one of us, and because we see our own humanity reflected back in them, we are reminded of how much more we can actually achieve and become; they provide us hope. We all struggle with our identities and the frequent conflict between what we are at our core and who everyone else perceives us to be. Unlike Superman or Thor, however, we have neither undercover identities nor superhuman abilities. Instead we seek refuge in a fantasy world where the hero *can* simply because it is his very nature to do what we *cannot.*

In Chapter XI, "Wind Walkers and Winged Warriors: Hawkman, Falcon and the Sons of Boreas," we turn our eyes to the skies to discuss the sons of Boreas and their modern equivalents Hawkman, Falcon, and symbolism of the winged hero. Early examples of winged heroes and gods hail from the Near East. There we find a fine line indeed between man and god—so fine in fact that there is no clear division between them. Contrastingly, Greek myths make clear distinctions between those who have a right to bear wings and those who should not.

I next consider the motif of wings and divinity in Homer, starting with Homer's repeated use of birds in similes. The application of wings, whether in metaphor or through magical transformation elevates the subject to a higher plane, both literally and figuratively. Birds are not bound by the strictures of human existence. Naturally imbued with flight, they can escape their current situation or plight. In some cases, the gods themselves transform into birds in order to flee the earth. In short, wings have the power to bring one closer to the gods.

Some characters are born with wings as a part of their physique, for example Zetes and Calais, the semi-divine sons of the Wind God, Boreas. These winged Argonauts serve as essentially protector figures akin to the *genii,* or *apkallu,* of the Near East, and are best known for routing the dreaded Harpies, disgusting winged creatures that befoul all that they touch. Other mythological figures take to the air on borrowed wings. One such example is the hero Perseus, son of Danae and the god Zeus, even if it is Zeus-by-rainstorm. Given winged sandals, in some accounts by Hermes and in others by nymphs, he uses them to cross great distances, defeating the gorgon Medusa and escaping from danger. Wings, however, are a technology fit only for the gods, and Perseus, realizing his mortal limitations, must return them in the end.

This is not the case with the hero Bellerophon. Initially the goddess Athena aids Bellerophon in capturing and taming the winged horse

Pegasus, which he enlists to defeat the fire-breathing chimaera, leaving him sitting on top of the world. Eventually his *hubris* gets the better of him. Using Pegasus, he charts a course to the home of the gods themselves, Mount Olympus. This bold move does not go unnoticed, and Zeus strips him of his power, demonstrating once more that humans are not supposed to have the abilities of the gods, especially the ability to fly. A similar fate awaits Daedalus' son Icarus, who misuses his father's grand invention—wings held in place with wax—by flying too close to the sun.

Turning to the winged heroes of comic book lore, I examine the specimens of Hawkman and Falcon. After discovering a mysterious crystal blade made from Nth metal, archaeologist Carter Hall falls into a coma and recalls a previous life in which he was an Egyptian prince killed by a priest of the god Anubis. When the archaeologist awakens, he uses the same Nth metal to create a pair of wings, allowing him to take flight and adopting the moniker Hawkman. Beginning in the Silver Age, Hawkman is re-written as an alien from the world of Thanagar. He still has his golden wings, but in this incarnation he appears more otherworldly, more semi-divine.

Falcon, on the other hand, is wholly human. The gift of his wings, whether from his S.H.I.E.L.D. prototype jetpack or the gift from Wakanda's Black Panther, allow him to fly under the divine aegis of protecting the innocent and aiding Captain America and the other Avengers against planetary threats such as Ultron and Hydra. Does Falcon ever exhibit *hubris* that might warrant having his wings snatched away from him? Not yet, but then again who knows what will come next for the winged warriors of the comic book universe....

Chapter XII, "Dangerous Beauty: Helen of Troy and the Femme Fatale," takes a brief detour from our primary focus on male heroes, to invite a reassessment of the dangerous beauty of Helen of Troy and the trope of the *femme fatale*. Throughout most of the book, I look at how Homeric warriors harmonize with the "heroic code," and how shockingly similar they are to most modern day superheroes. Here, at the end of things, I attempt to apply the same code to Helen, Silver Swan, Black Widow, and Poison Ivy. Are these female heroes? In many ways Helen is both the perfect example and simultaneously the most troublesome. If, however, we consider some of the key characteristics of the epic hero, Helen passes the test. The product once more of nobility and the gods, she is born from unusual circumstances—that is if you consider being born from an egg unusual. As the daughter of Zeus, Helen can't help but be a prize beyond compare. As a result, she is kidnapped on several occasions, most notably by Theseus, but returns to the city of her birth, only to disembark once more for the windy shores of distant Troy. Supernatural aid comes from none other than the goddess of sex herself, Aphrodite. To be sure, for the purposes of paradigmatic categorization, Helen appears every inch the hero(ine).

Comic book tradition is rife with examples of the *femme fatale*, either as a reflection of male fear of powerful women or the deviant desire to be dominated by such strong women. Black Widow, Cat Woman, Mystique, and Electra all inspire fear and remain shrouded in mystery and magic. Of all these, however, the closest match to the figure of Helen is of course DC's villainess Silver Swan.[6] Even her name, Helen Alexandros, demands the attention of the intertextually aware reader. This formidable adversary of Wonder Woman was a ballet star, who was apparently more of an ugly duckling before she strikes a deal with Mars for a more trademark beauty suited to the world of dance and performance. In her final performance, she fails to do as Mars demands of her in return for her beauty, and the Silver Swan falls away, leaving only Helen without her beauty behind.

A similar example appears in Natalia Alianova Romanoff, codenamed Black Widow. Beguiling and beautiful, this super spy and former KGB agent turned S.H.I.E.L.D. operative uses her charms to disarm her opponents before moving in for the kill. In the film *Avengers*, Romanoff and Barton (Hawkeye) have a unique relationship that isn't initially explained. Later we come to understand that Barton had been sent to eliminate her, but somehow he couldn't quite go through with it. The audience is never made privy to his reasoning, but it isn't a stretch to suggest that her beauty may have played a role in changing his mind. Even in the comic book tradition, Romanoff uses her feminine wiles to cozy up to Tony Stark in an attempt to infiltrate Stark labs and learn more about his technology. In both film and comic book universes she employs her power to manipulate men into carrying out her will. Even when she appears helpless, she is not; Black Widow is never a victim.

Throughout the entire book, a subtle theme weaves its way through each of the chapters, tying them together like a tapestry upon the loom: that is the role of Fate in the evolution of the epic hero. Therefore, finally in Chapter XIII, "The Hand of Fate: The Infinity Gauntlet and the Moirai," I conclude by taking a step back to consider the forces of fate and free will, and how these ultimately affect the development of the hero and the hero's quest. Despite the clear shift from mystic prophecies and meddling gods of Homeric lore to the scientific precision and logical plotting of the modern-day superhero's universe, destiny and personal responsibility are still powerful agents that make or break the heroes behind the armor and under the cape.

Now, without further delay, let us begin our journey in a universe not so very far away…

I

Captain America

An Achilles for the Modern Age

Achilles. It is a name that has survived the ages. Born to a goddess and equipped with armor and a shield forged by the gods, he is what we typically think of when we think of the epic hero. Greatest among the Greeks, he is also one of the most complicated of Homer's characters—loyal, brave, but also dark, brooding, and vengeful. At the end of the day he is, despite all his divine gifts, human and flawed, encumbered by his own combustible personality and *hubris*. In the *Iliad,* Homer relates that following a bitter dispute with Agamemnon over his war prize Briseis, Achilles retires from battle, returning only after the tragic death of his closest companion, Patroclus. When he re-emerges, he unleashes an onslaught so terrible, it causes both Trojan and Greek armies to shudder as he descends into an endless storm of bloodlust, madness, and revenge.

Anyone even remotely familiar with Homer's *Iliad* will undoubtedly recognize striking similarities between the hero Achilles and the modern comic book hero, Captain America. Both are an army of one, reclusive, and prime examples of the Other. Formidable strategists, they are imbued with almost superhuman powers and abilities, equipped with seemingly magical technology that sets them apart from their compatriots. Young and beautiful, they also develop close friendships with their male companions who die in battle, resulting in deeply rooted feelings of resentment and personal responsibility.[1] Similarly, both heroes are removed from the theater of war, returning to deal with issues of loss, abandonment, and post-traumatic stress. The aim of this chapter is to offer a new reading of Marvel's Captain America as a modern-day Achilles, but show that his development coincides more closely with modern issues of war, heroism, and *nostos*, or the hero's return home.

The First Avenger

Captain America has many of the same qualities born in the epic hero. Courageous and brave, he is willing to lay down his life for his country and those he loves, fighting on the front lines with his fellow soldier, but he is equally proud, stubborn, and self-righteous. Like so many heroes of old, his journey is a transformative one. Born Steve Rogers, a scrawny but scrappy kid from Brooklyn, he is appalled by the atrocities of the Nazis in Europe and endeavors to enlist in the American Army. Rejected due to his gangly physique, he nevertheless catches the eye of the no-nonsense General Chester Philips, who arranges to have him join a secret government program called *Project: Rebirth*. Injected with a super-serum, Rogers is transformed into a soldier imbued with incredible strength, agility, and endurance.

Donning his iconic costume of stars and stripes, Rogers meets and befriends a young soldier named "Bucky" Barnes while stationed at Camp Lehigh. Inevitably, Bucky discovers Rogers' secret identity: he is Captain America. Bucky, who is younger than Rogers in the comic, soon becomes his partner, and together they battle Nazis, villains such as Red Skull, and the masked and mysterious Baron Zemo. In the final days of the war, Zemo steals and launches an experimental drone armed with explosives. Racing against time, Rogers and Barnes strive valiantly to disable it. Tragically, the plane explodes mid-air and both Barnes and Rogers are believed to have been killed in action, cast into the freezing waters of the North Atlantic. By a strange twist of fate, Rogers' body is found floating in a block of ice nearly 20 years later. Revived, he enlists with the Avengers. Afterward, he has to learn to deal with a world and a war that has continued without him. We also learn of Captain America's deep feelings of guilt and unbearable grief over the death of his friend Bucky. In the Marvel Cinematic Universe, during an attempt by Cap and the Howling Commandos to capture Armin Zola, Bucky falls from a train plunging into an icy river below. Believed dead, he is later reborn a different type of super soldier.

The Super Soldier

Both Captain America and Achilles are "super soldiers": strategists, skilled in leadership, unsurpassable in the art of hand-to-hand combat; they are second to none on the battlefield. While Captain America is not technically *superhuman*, he is the best any of us could ever hope to be. The super-soldier formula has imbued him with superior human powers: agility, speed, and incredible endurance. Achilles, though semi-divine, does not appear to have any superhuman abilities either. He's just a badass. To

Interior panel from *Captain America Comics* #1 (1941) with Dr. Erskin injecting Steve Rogers with the super serum formula. © 2009 Marvel Characters, Inc.

safeguard him, his mother, the nymph Thetis, dipped him into the River Styx, but only up to his heel. This single flaw makes Achilles as mortal as the rest of us. Throughout Homer's retelling of the Trojan epic, we see that Achilles possesses incredible strength and stamina. In Book 19, readers learn of a type of super soldier serum. Athena pours nectar and ambrosia, the food of the gods, into the chest of Achilles, thereby preserving his strength and perseverance.[2] His physical aptitude, however, does not translate into emotional adeptness. He is still vulnerable to the same feelings of loss, anger, and revenge: in fact his emotions may indeed measure up to his larger than life appearance.

To some Achilles is a hero, to others the antihero. Homer did not necessarily see his characters as wholly right or wholly wrong, neither all hero nor all villain, but a more realistic combination of both. So how should we judge Achilles? The story of Achilles is the story of a soldier caught up in the storm of war, who must wrestle with his own fate as well as the fate of his fellow men, and his own personal virtue as well as the virtues of the prevailing system of honor. Young, rebellious, and proud—think of him as the Bronze Age James Dean—he is loyal to and cares deeply for his comrade Patroclus. Nevertheless, he is ultimately flawed, often swayed by anger and revenge. As Homer muses in Book 23, "the youth are quick in temper but weak in judgment."[3] Too often the young hero lets his anger get in the way of the greater good, and actually enjoys killing (not necessarily a terribly valuable life skill). Achilles is a liminal hero. He doesn't belong, because to belong would cease to make him a hero. Born from a Nereid, he is raised outside society, by the centaur Chiron, the personal trainer of heroes, but also inhuman. He also comes across as the classic Mama's boy, as his mother presents him with a new shield crafted by the gods, nay by Hephaestus himself. It is the near modern equivalent of showing up to the high school prom in a flashy new Mercedes.

The Shield

The shield is the quintessential mark of the epic hero and certainly of Achilles. It represents the favor of the gods and the hero's connection to them as exhibited in the famous ekphrasis scene in Book 18. With his armor having been stolen by Hector, Thetis, the mother of Achilles, implores the lame but skilled craftsman Hephaestus to construct a new suit and shield for her son, who is destined to die young but glorious. Amidst the thundering hammer falls and plumes of black smoke, the divine artificer agrees. Recalling the earlier kindness the sea nymph had paid him when she rescued him from the sea, he promises that it shall be a work like no other, a marvel to any who look upon it.[4]

> And on the fire, he placed hearty bronze and tin and precious gold and silver; and afterwards he set on the anvil-block a great anvil, and took in one hand a massive hammer, and in the other he took the tongs. First fashioned he a shield, great and sturdy, adorning it cunningly in every part, and round about it set a bright rim, threefold and glittering, and therefrom made fast a silver baldric. Five were the layers of the shield itself; and on it, he wrought many curious devices with cunning skill.[5]

From Homer's description, readers can gather that the shield is extremely large and strong—an amalgam of different metals and not all of them from this world. Homer also intimates that it is a source of technological wonder, imbued with "curious devices." One has to wonder what the poet means by this. Are these powers of protection we cannot quite see or does it have something to do with the narrative quality of the piece itself, for he then launches into the decorations that appear on it, a glorious reverie of different scenes and characters.

At the center of the shield's cosmogony stand two cities. One celebrates marriages and feasts, while the other quails beneath the storm of war. Hephaestus includes scenes of cycles, such as a field being plowed, a vineyard with grape pickers, a contest between two lions over a bull, and a threshing floor filled with dancing youths. All of these stories are encircled by the great arms of the sea. Incredibly, Homer describes some of these

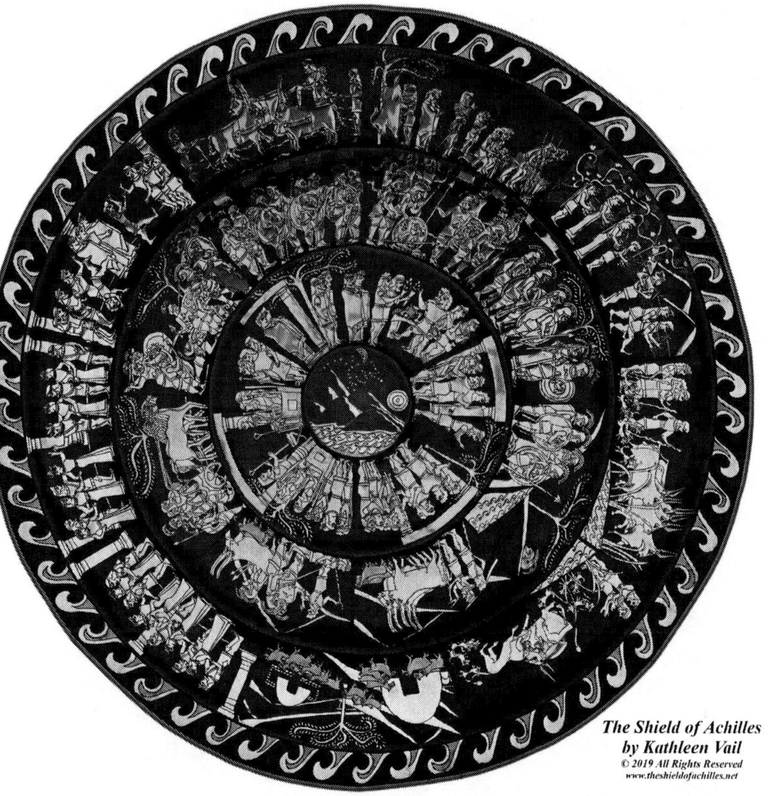

A medley of figures at peace and at war teem to life in Kathleen Vail's modern recreation of the great shield of Achilles. *Reconstructing the Shield of Achilles* by Kathleen Vail. Story Merchant Books, 2018. See also her excellent blog, theshieldofachilles.net.

vignettes as if they are in motion. Figures are dancing and singing as if they had the power to mesmerize the viewer or leap right off the shield itself. In this sense, the stories upon it seem startling real. It is thus a self-narrating work of art, one that can spin its own tale, or biography, through visual culture.

When completed, Thetis descends from Olympus to deliver the newly fashioned gift to her son:

> Thus speaking, the goddess placed the arms in front of Achilles, and they all rang loudly in their splendor. Then shuddering seized all the Myrmidons; neither did any man dare to look thereon, but instead they shrank in fear. However, when Achilles saw the arms, then rage filled him all the more, and his eyes blazed forth in a terrible way from beneath their lids, as if flame; and he was delighted as he held the glorious gifts of the god in his arms.[6]

First, it is important to recognize the close personal connection Achilles has with this piece of visual culture. The shield exists to serve him, and him alone. Only he can wield it. At some points it seems almost cursed; for example, on the heels of Achilles' death, the warriors Ajax and Odysseus contend for the greatly coveted arms and armor. While Odysseus emerges victorious, Ajax, embittered, is driven mad by the gods and throws himself on his own sword. Odysseus likewise receives a bad turn, and is kept from reaching home while the shield mysteriously vanishes. We may take this to mean that to Homer, only the nobility, and perhaps even more limitedly, the descendants of the divine, are able to utilize let alone decode the meaning of such visual culture. Yet this is not just any piece of visual culture but a status symbol; like owning a BMW, there are certain luxury features that are designed just for the owner. This shield may indeed have contained physical features that made it "coded" just for Achilles.

Next, to everyone else, the shield has the ability to generate sound on its own accord, and one that creates a deep sense of dread. Even the Myrmidons, Achilles' shock troops, shrink from its presence, perhaps because it represents a technology hitherto unseen.[7] We may take this to mean that they, being of lower social status, do not know how to read or use the technology. Achilles, however, is able to see something in the imagery, and it is something that fills him with both rage and delight. Homer also relates the shield's power to create synesthesia. It *rings* aloud with splendor. Perhaps this is one of the "curious devices."

The ekphrasis scene itself, it seems, is an attempt by Homer to match traditional oral poetry against the encroaching visual culture from the Near East ... and perhaps even to best it. Cypriot bowls, for example, with bands of figures and animals may have found their way into Homer's world. One must note that the artist, Hephaestus, and even Daedalus (whose threshing floor at Knossos is given a nod in the design of the shield) receives the attention of the poet, perhaps because he is able to essentially miniaturize an entire cosmos and capture it on a shield. So too does the epic poet, who suspends and controls the narrative to indulge in a fleeting glimpse of material culture. The fact that the shield is organized into circles suggests that Homer's Greeks viewed things in cycles, e.g., seasons, epic cycles, the ocean encircling the land. When we think perhaps of the banded figures girding the bodies of vases that were deposited on graves, we do well to remember that in viewing those narratives, one had to move likewise in a circle. Rituals involving circumambulation may have had a dizzying or disarming effect and might even have enacted a spell.[8] Whether or not Achilles' shield was imbued with actual magic, we know its materials were not of this world.

Captain America's only weapon is his trademark shield. Its round shape and patriotic star along with its colors—red, white, and blue—recalls the freedom and good old-fashioned American values for which Cap is known as well as the rounded shields of the classic warrior. A unique blend of power and technology, it too instills in his enemies a deep sense of wonder and dread as it screams through the air. Virtually indestructible, its aerodynamic design allows Cap to launch it as a projectile weapon, but it acts more like a boomerang, or Thor's hammer—always returning to its master. In the comic tradition, while attempting to recreate the fabled adamantine for the war effort, its creator, Dr. Myron MacLain, develops an alloy and uses it for the shield. Unfortunately, he was never able to replicate his experiment.[9]

In the films, it is an amalgam of different metals, including steel, yet it was also created from alloys harvested from a meteorite, which comes to be known as *vibranium*. Like Achilles' shield, therefore, Captain America's is literally one of a kind and out of this world. Surprisingly, this is a common theme pervading many world mythologies. King Tutankhamen, for example, was buried with a dagger made from a meteorite—described extraordinarily as iron *born of the sky*. The lance of Mars, the Roman god of war, housed in the Regia, was also extraterrestrial in nature, as was a brass shield that Plutarch claims fell from the sky during the reign of Numa, a gift from the god Jupiter.[10]

Achilles' shield is the absolute latest in Bronze Age technology. In stark contrast, no pun intended, Captain America's shield represents a bygone era. In *Avengers: Civil War*, Tony Stark reveals that his father helped to construct Cap's shield.[11] We might take this to mean that a little bit of Tony's father is imbued in the shield, and by extension, Steve Rogers, who in a way acts like Tony's foster father. It is no wonder then that the two are destined to come to blows. It is often the heroic paradigm that in his quest to become the hero, the son must supplant the father, whether Oedipus, Luke Skywalker, or Tony Stark. Here, the two fight over how to lead the Avengers. While Captain America believes humanity is the future, Stark believes its only salvation can be found in technology. Then again, he can't help but feel it, for technology is literally a part of him, something near and dear to his heart.

For the Greeks, the shield represents many things. It is a blessing from the gods, a technological marvel, and the panacea for winning the war, but it is also a mirror of the outside world. For Captain America, the shield is his calling card. With its iconic stars and stripes, it is also a doublet for the American flag and stands as a symbol of protection, for the shield after all is a defensive weapon. Cap frequently hurls it to disarm his enemies but rarely to kill them. In a similar way, the Hoplite shield is woven with others to form a defensive wall, which cannot be broken.[12] Every hoplite relies on the shield of his brother.

Brothers in Arms

Camaraderie is a governing theme throughout the *Iliad*, embodied most prominently in the friendship of Achilles and Patroclus. Though the topic has long held the interest of scholars, the exact nature of their relationship has somehow continued to elude us. For example, what does the term πολὺ φίλτατος … ἑταῖρος (*poly filtatos … hetairos*, "his dearest companion") really mean?[13] Were they "just friends," or were they in fact lovers? Nowhere in Homer's text is it indicated that Achilles and Patroclus were actual lovers.[14] That they had to be lovers and not the closest of friends is a gross assumption, but not necessarily one made only by modern scholars. It furrowed the brow of many an ancient author as well.

Phaedrus, for example, in the *Symposium*, sees them as lovers, although he too argues that Aeschylus in the lost work *The Myrmidons* misrepresented their relationship. Because Achilles is younger, beardless, and more youthful than Patroclus, he must be the *eromenos* (beloved), rather than the older *erastes* (lover, protector). Xenophon, however, in Chapter 8 of his *Symposium*, has Socrates argue that the two men's relationship was merely platonic, that it was simply one of devoted comrades in arms. To die for a friend was viewed in his time as most honored by the gods. Here one must exercise caution, for the idea of male bonding based on classical ideas of *paiderasteia* should not necessarily be applied to a Bronze Age culture. Furthermore, Patroclus and Achilles are also related by blood. According to Pseudo-Apollodorus, Patroclus is the son of Menoetius and Polymele, one of the daughters of Peleus.[15] Menoetius gave him to Peleus, after Patroclus killed a young boy in anger. He then grew up alongside Achilles. If we accept the idea that Patroclus is older, he may be akin to a brother-like figure. Achilles' anger, then, is for the loss of an older brother, but I think it safe to say that having grown up together makes their bond as fellow soldiers stronger, like Bucky and Cap.

What is necessarily wrong with the idea of a strong male bond that is not sexual, especially when it comes to military service? When researching this book, I reached out to combat veterans and was a witness to some remarkable revelations. Many emphasized the intense familial bond they have, calling each other "brother." This fraternal bond is stronger than pre-enlistment friendships. Nothing brings men and women together more than the "big suck," when you are in the theater of war and facing death together. You would do anything for your unit family. You have been to hell and back together.

Another consideration is the importance of speaking the name of a fallen comrade. A soldier once told me a hero never dies as long as his name *remains spoken*.[16] Ironically, this comment came from a man who has never read Homer. Nevertheless, this sentiment lies at the very heart of the epic tradition. Achilles goes off to war to secure his *kleos*, his glory—to make sure his name is always spoken. It is also the reason why Odysseus struggles to return home: to make sure his name is remembered. Sadly, unlike Homer's soldiers, many modern soldiers mourn the loss of their fallen comrades alone. Some people travel to monuments to remember someone or pour a shot of booze for their fallen friends, often writing their name on a napkin and leaving the drink untouched. Jonathan Shay talks about when soldiers rotate out as individuals, it is harder to deal individually with PTSD. In Homer, brothers mourn fallen brothers together. Perhaps this is why there is a higher incidence of PTSD and suicide today rather than in the Bronze Age.[17]

Whether it is Bucky and Cap or Achilles and Patroclus, there is undeniably a different type of bond between soldiers struggling in the thick of battle. This is glaringly apparent in the films *Captain America: The Winter Soldier* and its follow up, *Captain America: Civil War*. In the first film, Captain America discovers Bucky is alive but brainwashed into working as an operative for the criminal organization, Hydra. In *Civil War*, Cap rescues Barnes, discovering from him that Hydra has an army of similarly brainwashed super soldiers in cryo-stasis. Not wanting to wait for authorization, Captain America goes rogue and joins Bucky on a mission to save the winter soldiers, enlisting the aid of Falcon, the Scarlet Witch, Hawkeye, and Ant Man. Followed by Tony Stark, who has assembled his own team, they soon find that Zemo has killed the rest of the winter soldiers. It is inadvertently revealed that Bucky was responsible for the murder of Stark's parents. This leads to a heated battle with Captain America again defending his comrade in arms against Iron Man. In the end, Cap and Bucky seek asylum in Wakanda with Barnes agreeing to return to cryo-stasis until he can be fully cleared of his brainwashed programming.

Often the motivation for Captain America is clear—to save his friend—but Bucky also represents a living connection to his former life. With the death of Peggy Carter, he now only has Bucky. There is a trust between them, even when at odds, that they will see each other through anything, as Cap says, "to the end of the line." To clear Bucky's name is to properly honor him as a soldier. Likewise, Achilles enacts the proper rituals, ensuring Patroclus is properly honored and remembered. He holds competitive games, lights the pyre, and mourns. It is important to note that while Cap seeks to *avenge*, that is seek justice for his fallen comrade, Achilles seeks *revenge* by inflicting pain on any and every Trojan in his path.

A Living Legend

Another important dimension to the character of Captain America is a sense of nostalgia or being out of sync with time. After his body is retrieved and brought back to life, Cap finds himself a living legend in a strange new world, a world that has left him behind. Wracked by deep feelings of guilt, loneliness, and post-traumatic stress he struggles to find his place while secretly longing to return to the past. In many ways, Cap's struggle to find balance mirrors the kinds of feelings modern soldiers experience after returning from war.

While Achilles' absence from the battlefield is only a matter of days, Captain America's spans several years. Nevertheless, in the case of both heroes, their worlds have changed dramatically. After Achilles goes into self-imposed exile, Hector and the Trojans wind up dominating the field of battle. Agamemnon concedes he will return home, to which the warrior Diomedes, who elects to stay behind, reminds him of his duty. Nestor advises Agamemnon to consider that Achilles going AWOL is the cause of the current downturn. The king extends gifts and council to make reparations. Odysseus praises Achilles in his exordium but then also reminds him of his patriotic duties. Nevertheless, Achilles refuses. It takes the devastating death of his companion in Book 16 to finally entreat him back into the fray.

At the beginning of the *Avengers* film, S.H.I.E.L.D. commander Nick Fury approaches Captain America who is venting his rage on a series of punching bags. Plagued by flashbacks, he takes out bag … after bag … after bag, declaring, "I went under, the world was at war; I wake up, they say we won. They didn't say what we lost." Fury, like Odysseus, admits mistakes were made but tries to convince Rogers to return. "Trying to get me back into the world?" Rogers quips. Fury responds, "Trying to save it," appealing to Rogers' sense of patriotism. Being asynchronous also leaves Captain America feeling vulnerable and alone. With the loss of his war-time love interest Peggy Carter and Bucky Barnes, the last remaining traces of his previous life are gone. Cap, however, is not the only one displaced. The Hydra scientist Armin Zola has also survived, his brain transferred to a super-computer located at Camp Lehigh. In *Captain America: The Winter Soldier*, Zola reveals that Hydra has been behind the chaos in world events, slowly infiltrating S.H.I.E.L.D., before announcing they are both "out of time."

Achilles' exile also makes him asynchronous. Patroclus, for example, has to bring him up date on current events. While one may argue that Achilles' imprisonment is self-imposed, I would argue that Agamemnon's rebuke forces Achilles into exile in order to preserve his heroic virtue. The same might be said of Captain America. If he had not been lost, there are chances that his virtue may have been comprised, for although America after World War II was viewed as an altruistic ally, the 70 years of failed American politics would have taken their toll.

Both heroes return to battle at a time when the world needs them most, during a time of great moral decline. In the *Iliad*, Agamemnon eschews the way a *wanax* or high king is supposed to act. He is un-heroic and often un-virtuous. Diomedes reminds him of his duty. The Achaeans require that the traditional epic warrior, fresh from his hibernation, win the battle, for it ratifies their value system. The same sort of process occurs in the *Avengers*. The world needs Captain America's unique sense of traditional virtue in order to combat Hydra, because it verifies American values at a time when they are in decline.

In *Captain America: Civil War*, Rogers' values are put to the test. Following the deaths of innocents in Sokovia, the United Nations has imposed a set of accords for the Avengers. Like the death of Patroclus, it is a dose of real loss of life that causes armies to stand down. The Avengers are divided. Rogers, however, remains resolute. He is reminded of the words of his late friend Peggy Carter: "It is your duty to plant yourself like a tree, look them in the eye, and say 'No, you move.'" It is the same question the Avengers have been struggling with the entire time: to follow the crowd and what is popular or follow one's own free will. Rogers represents free will and that nostalgic link to America's perceived innocence and traditional values, when decisions appeared simpler. He thus tends to be inflexible, often over-simplifying political situations, seeing them as black and white, rather than various shades of gray. This recalls for many the hero Achilles, who, in the Embassy scene in Book 9 of the *Iliad*, ultimately refuses compensation from Agamemnon for the loss of Briseis, a prize of honor. For Achilles, there is no price for impugning this honor, but he does not see the deleterious effects of his actions on his fellow soldiers. He only sees his own wounded pride. Perhaps, it is Ajax who sums it up best, when he tells him his anger has made him too proud.

Loss, Guilt, Revenge

Once thawed from his icy slumber, Captain America awakens in a fugue state, swinging, screaming, "Bucky! Look out!"[18] It takes the combined effort of both Thor and Iron Man to restrain him. Calming down, he eventually comes to grips with the events. "He is dead—he is! And nothing on Earth can change that!" he admits to himself. For the next few years, Bucky serves as a constant reminder not only of a bygone era but also of Cap's inability to save a comrade for whom he felt responsible. In the film version, *Captain America: The First Avenger*, after Cap is disarmed, Bucky picks up his shield. Like Patroclus donning the shield of Achilles, however, he is unable to fend off an attack and a blast sends him reeling from the train. Cap tries to rescue him, but fails, and watches helplessly as his friend plummets into an icy river below. He is momentarily overcome by grief. The next time we find Rogers, he is drinking at a bombed-out bar. The irony for Cap is that the super-soldier serum prevents him from becoming intoxicated. He must find another way to mourn. Cap blames himself for the death, but Peggy argues that Bucky died for what he believed in, for Cap.

The death of a friend often is a call to arms for the epic hero. Bearing the scars of his loss, Achilles stands apart from Agamemnon, because for him it is about camaraderie. It also bespeaks of the archaic tendency to romanticize the Bronze Age hero and celebrate the individual soldier, rather than preserving the Bronze Age power structures with the *wanax* at the top. Compare this to post World War II America. Did the country necessarily require rage and individualism, or camaraderie, optimism, and patriotism? Most would argue the latter. Nothing, of course, is ever that simple. What we really need and even what we merely think we need are not always transparent, and as American foreign policy and culture changes, so, too, do our needs as a society. Symbolically, Captain America reminds us of a golden bygone era, of simpler times, but he also represents the future. If Homer also stands at the dawn of a new age, the 9th century BCE, then Achilles represents the *novus homo*, the new man, rather than the traditional epic hero. Achilles says to hell with the *wanax* and the whole system of government the existence of the *wanax* entails, and instead says, "I am Achilles, and I do whatever I want!" He returns because of his friendship with Patroclus rather than a sense of duty or any adherence to structures of power and rank.

Bucky, like Cap, remained on ice, until 2004 when he resurfaced as the Winter Soldier. Pulled from the ice, Bucky was reprogrammed by the Russians to be a Cold War spy. When the two friends finally reconnect, both in the comic and in the film, Cap recognizes his friend, but the Winter Soldier replies, "Who the hell is Bucky?" The rebirth of Bucky represents an interesting twist. No longer is Cap mourning his friend's death but his life as a brainwashed agent. Years later in the comic tradition, after Cap is killed, it is Bucky who must mourn the loss of his friend. His rage is slightly different.

Interior panels of the *Avenger #4* (1964). Thor and Iron Man struggle to restrain Captain America after awakening from his icy slumber and recalling the death of his close companion Bucky. © 2009 Marvel Characters, Inc.

After being taken out by a sniper's bullet, Cap is hauled off to the hospital leaving Bucky to search for the killer. After encountering the villainous Crossbones, he is still unable to locate the person responsible, whom he believes to be Red Skull. While the Avengers mourn the death of Cap at his funeral, Bucky mourns his friend's passing in a bar, watching it on the television. When someone in the bar claims it is a disgrace to bury him in Arlington, Bucky crushes his glass and starts a fight.[19] After seeing Tony Stark speaking at the funeral, Bucky directs his anger toward the new director of S.H.I.E.L.D. and Red Skull. At one point Bucky threatens to kill Crossbones, grabbing him by the throat, to which Red Skull remarks that Captain America would never kill anyone in cold blood.[20] Eventually, Bucky and Stark reconcile, and Stark reveals that Rogers' last wish was for Bucky to carry on the mantle of Captain America, which he does.[21]

Passing of the Mantle

Another recurring trope in the MCU is the legacy of the hero, or the passing of the mantle. One of the most remarkable and poignant examples can be found in *Captain America: Winter Soldier*. In one scene, Rogers visits his own exhibit at the Smithsonian where he reflects on his service and his friend Bucky. The mannequin with his suit stands larger than life, adding to the legend of Captain America, while the man Steve Rogers looks on. There is a stark difference between the man and his myth. Many such scenes also occur in epic. In Book 2 of the *Aeneid*, for example, after stumbling upon scenes of friends in the Trojan War, Aeneas likewise is forced to relive the pain of his encounter and the loss of his friends.

Moments later, Rogers is recognized by a young boy wearing the Captain America shield on his t-shirt. The boy represents a new generation enamored with the legend and again underscores Rogers as a man out of time. In *Avengers: Endgame*, after returning to the past to live out a normal life with Peggy Carter, an old Rogers returns to 2023 and hands over the iconic shield to Falcon. When he asks Falcon how it feels, he replies, "Like it's someone else's." In Book 16 of the *Iliad*, Patroclus begs Achilles, who has withdrawn from the battle, to wear his armor and carry on the fight. Achilles agrees, but only so long as he saves the Greek ships from being burned. While not long term, the scene from Homer represents the classic passing of the mantle, which we still draw on today.

Judging a Book by Its Cover

The cover art for the first issue of *Captain America Comics* is a celebration of both American propaganda and classical imagery. The debut issue, designed by the late great Jack Kirby, shows Captain America coming face to face with Adolf Hitler in a secret bunker. At the center is the Nazi leader. Stunned, he reels backwards, as Cap delivers a powerful blow with his fist and deflecting a storm of bullets with his shield. Hitler betrays pain and emotion, while Captain America appears stoic. It is the epitome of the Greek classical style only in comic book form. For example, compare the sculptural reliefs of titans and giants depicted on the altar of Pergamon with their twisted expressions of anguish and pain, while the gods, devoid of emotion, cast them into Tartarus. Moreover, Cap's hat bears a pair of tiny white wings, recalling again classical depictions of Hermes, messenger of the gods.

Donning his red, white, and blue costume, Cap is a living, breathing representation of America and patriotism. Speaking of which, instead of his trademark round shield, at first he brandishes an engrailed 19th century type heraldic shield adorned with three white stars at the top, and a series of stars and stripes below it. This type of shield closely resembles the one wielded by Columbia, the personification of America. What stands out to the viewer is the stark contrast between Cap's colorful regalia to the dull brown and military green of the Nazis, casting him as vibrant and alive. Blazoned across the top is the title of the comic, *Captain America*, with a banner of red, white, and blue stripes replete with stars. At the bottom is a caption for Cap's young ally, Bucky, who salutes the viewer, and begs the

A panel from the north frieze of the Great Altar of Pergamon (164–156 BCE), currently held in Berlin at the Pergamon Museum (Inv. Winnefeld 23.1–4), captures the vigorous confrontation between the Olympian gods, who appear strong and stoic, and the Titans and Giants, who show signs of anguish and pain. Photo credit: bpk Bildagentur/Photographer: Johannes Laurentius/Art Resource, NY.

viewer to do the same. It is political propaganda at its best, but it is also infused with classical symbols.

The second issue features Captain America smashing through a window into another secret Nazi lair. This time, he bears his emblematic round shield. Hitler, who again betrays his emotions, is shown reeling backwards. On the table in front of him is a globe with North America marked out with a Nazi flag. Bucky, tied to a chair, looks on helplessly. The cover for issue 3, designed by Alex Schomburg, is an explosion of color. It centers on the blonde Betty, who, tied up, is about to be shot through a massive cannon. Captain America appears in the upper right, swinging his trademark shield and sending a Nazi flying. On the other side of the cannon we see Red Skull laughing maniacally as he ties up Bucky.

As these few examples illustrate, Captain America almost always appears in a pose of action, and almost always with his shield. Like Achilles, Cap will be intimately tied to this particular weapon. Notice that he uses it as a shield, a defensive weapon, and his hands, rather than high tech weapons and guns to subdue his opponents. This demonstrates his willingness

Interior panel from *Captain America Comics* #2 (1941) features the title character, storming a secret Nazi lair with his iconic shield. He sends a surprised Hitler reeling backwards, landing in a waste paper basket. Art by Jack Kirby and Joe Simon. © 2009 Marvel Characters, Inc.

to get the job done by simple means and through hard work. He appears to always be in control of his emotions while his enemies grimace, shout, and howl—betraying some sort of emotion—as he subdues them. Again, this stems from a classical tradition of imbuing Greek gods, athletes, and heroes with stoic or emotionless countenances. Many times, his closest friend, Bucky, appears along side him, but he always needs to be rescued. Like Patroclus, he is the *therapon*, or ritual substitute for Cap.[22] Cap is almost always colored in red and blue, the colors associated with America, attesting to his patriotism, and to the patriotism of anyone purchasing the comic, for the comic book serves as a portable work of art.

Conclusion

Many modern comic book heroes have their origins in the epic tradition, which we have inherited through cultural products and social practice, ideas expounded upon by Pierre Bourdieu in his 1986 work *Distinction*.[23] Whether initially recognized by the writer or artist, the template of the Homeric hero is deeply ingrained in American culture, primarily as an artifact of inherited Western European educational systems, many of which valued Homer and the *Iliad*. Captain America represents for many of us a modern-day equivalent of the Greek hero Achilles, who struggles with the loss of his fellow soldier and friend and who finds his values at odds with a higher authority.

All of which forces us to return to the main question of epic: what does it mean to be a hero? The hero is ultimately on a quest for wisdom, to transform him or herself into something higher. For Achilles, it was moving from a one-dimensional character—stubborn, proud and erratic—to one who ultimately has to deal with real loss, and finally, empathy for the enemy and personal responsibility. Captain America's journey takes him into exile, self-imposed, to honor his friend, a nobler cause, but also to the cause of the free world. In seeking out the rest of the winter soldiers, he both wishes to protect the world from a new order that would limit one's ability to act, but also appeal to those soldiers who have been left behind. In the end, Captain America is a moralist of the highest caliber, but he, like Achilles, risks the cohesion of the Avengers/Achaeans, and the will of the masses he has agreed to protect. The *Civil War* film makes an interesting argument, one that may never truly be resolved, but it is the same kind of argument that has been in play since Homer.

II

Wonder Woman

Echoes of the Amazon Warrior

Bursting onto the comic book scene in 1941, the superheroine known as Wonder Woman has been one of the DC Universe's most popular and time-honored characters. An Amazonian princess from the island of Themyscira, Diana is a strong-willed, powerful warrior, who, despite her awesome abilities, some of which include god-like strength, bullet-proof bracelets, and a lasso of truth, always seeks a compassionate and peaceful resolution to her encounters with villains. Conceptualized by William Moulton Marston as the kind of woman who should run society, Wonder Woman has been a constant source of controversy. She stands both as a powerful beacon for feminist ideals, but also as a woman constantly finding herself in a submissive role, tied up by villains, and the object of the male gaze. Her place in American pop culture, though well earned, also may have been due to normative representations of exotic warrior women such as the Amazonian queen Penthesilea mentioned in Homer and further developed in the fragmentary text *Aethiopis*.

The purpose of the present chapter is to examine whether Wonder Woman fits the model of the ancient or modern conception of the Amazon warrior. Furthermore, what role do mythic characters such as Hippolyta and Penthesilea play in shaping our western conception of powerful woman warrior, and how does this lay the groundwork for the later reception of DC's breakthrough Wonder Woman? Finally, how does Wonder Woman embody feminist theory? Does her character help or hinder our interpretation of the Amazon warrior today?

The Traditional Amazon Warrior

When we contemplate the nature of the Amazon warrior we must first acknowledge that a great deal of what we know is the product of Greek mythic traditions and imagination. No group ever referred to themselves specifically as *Amazons*. It is a term of otherness, created by Greek writers and historians, such as Herodotus and akin to similar phrases like Ἀνδροκτόνες (*Androktones*), "destroyers of men." Brutal and savage, the Amazons of Greek myth were a force to be reckoned with. The match of any man, they lusted only for war[1] excelling at horsemanship and archery, going so far as to slice off at least one of their breasts to become better archers. Cast as the foil to the Greek hero, they killed any man who wantonly wandered into their realm.[2] Homer, who is the first to mention them, calls them ἀντιάνειραι (*antianeirai*), which has been interpreted by some as enemies, but more convincingly the "equals," or "peers of men."[3] From the beginning then, for a society ruled by men, Amazon women were seen as a threat to the status quo and thus have been demonized. From such a crucible arises the modern Amazon warrior, embodied in characters such as Xena and Wonder Woman, who alternatively reflect modern views of feminism, gender, and power.

Real Amazons, if we can even call them that, were probably based on the Scythian warrior women known to have inhabited the Eurasian steppe, of whom we know so little about.[4] Were they matrilineal? Did they fight alongside men? Historical and archaeological evidence helping to elucidate these points continues to elude us. We do know that they were buried with weapons, as were women in pre–Roman Italy and Greece, but did they even use them? Who is to say that these do not represent family heirlooms rather than individual weapons actually used by the person interred with them? Regardless, they were certainly renowned for their equestrian skills, though they were hardly man-hating monsters.[5] One could also easily see Spartan women as exempla of the real-life Amazon warriors. Such women, in their youth, were trained to be the equals to their brothers—this included learning to ride a horse and throwing a spear.[6] They believed that strong men could only come from strong mothers.[7] This incited ridicule from some like Aristotle who claimed Spartan men were dominated by their wives.[8]

There has been much debate about the origins of the mythic Amazons. Herodotus believed they originated in Asia Minor along the banks of the Thermodon, while Diodorus contends they came first from Libya and later migrated to Asia Minor.[9] Some claim they were the issue of Ares, god of war, and the nymph Harmonia, while others contend it was Ares and Otrera, the founder of the Temple of Artemis at Ephesus.[10] In time, Otrera supposedly gave birth to queens Hippolyta and Penthesilea.[11]

Hippolyta figures prominently in the Ninth Labor of Herakles, where the hero is sent to retrieve the Amazon's girdle for the despotic king Eurystheus.[12] In one version of the story, Hippolyta falls in love with Herakles and relinquishes the prize, but Pseudo-Apollodorus includes Hera, who

One of the most celebrated sculptural works, the Mattei Amazon, a Roman copy of a Greek original by Phidias, shows an Amazon warrior wearing a short chiton, and exposing a single breast, disputing the belief that Amazons removed a breast in order to become better shots with a bow. A lunate shield appears behind her right leg in the original at the Vatican Museum in Rome, but this replica resides at the Metropolitan Museum of Art in New York and does not include the shield. AD 1st/2nd c., Imperial Roman; Gift of John D. Rockefeller Jr., 1932; accession number: 32.11.4.

foments trouble. Appearing among the Amazons as one of them she quickly spreads the rumor that Herakles aims to abscond with their queen.[13] This leads to a bloody battle where in the chaos Herakles kills Hippolyta, seizes the belt, and like all Greek heroes, sails away into the sunset leaving a path of destruction. Other tales relate that she was kidnapped and given to Theseus. Becoming his wife, she is later rescued by the Amazons, which gives rise to the Attic War.[14] Yet others contend that when Theseus attempted to marry Phaedra, thereby casting Hippolyta aside, the queen mustered her Amazons, leading them to attack the wedding party at which time, she is killed. Still other traditions contend that she was killed accidentally by her sister, Penthesilea, in a hunting expedition.

Penthesilea

Walk onto America's streets today and ask anyone "Who is Wonder Woman?" I can guarantee you someone will trumpet an enthusiastic answer, but ask anyone "Who is Penthesilea?" and you will probably be met with a vacant stare. Although just as popular as Wonder Woman in her day, the mythical figure of Penthesilea, the warrior queen of the Amazons, has largely been forgotten. Daughter of Ares and sister to Hippolyta, she appears in Arctinus' epic *Aethiopis*. Surviving now only in fragments, the work highlights both her role and that of the African warrior Memnon, who arrive to offer aid to Priam in his most desperate hour. Arctinus claims she is of Thracian origin and displays great prowess in battle, the equal of any man. In the end, however, she is ultimately killed by Achilles, whose spear pierces both her and her horse.[15] In the aftermath, Achilles supposedly falls in love with the warrior maiden. This earns the ridicule of Thersites, whom Achilles slays out of anger.[16]

This momentous encounter, exquisitely rendered in a sixth century BCE black-figured amphora at the British Museum, captures the full intensity of the encounter.[17] The artist presents Achilles in his high crested helmet and short chiton springing forward, his spear wavering over the Amazon warrior, who recoils, bending on one knee—their eyes locked. What first grabs the viewer's attention is the fact that Achilles' helmet masks his emotions. We cannot really tell what he is feeling, but his eyes carry the look of battle frenzy. Contrastingly, Penthesilea is exposed. She is turning, perhaps in a manner of retreat, with her shield withdrawn and her spear hardly lifted. Furthermore, she is adorned in leopard skin, a sign of her foreignness. Eastern figures, such as Egyptian priests or the Olympian god of wine, Dionysus, wear such clothing. But if this were the only vase you ever studied, you might get the wrong impression.

A frieze from the Temple of Apollo Medicus at Bassae, currently held at the British Museum, is equally compelling. It presents a nude Achilles, without helmet, pressing forward with his shield. Penthesilea reaches out to him, unarmed. While their eyes are locked, the scene lacks the emotional intensity one comes to expect from lovers as per the conventions of classical sculpture. This stands in stark contrast to a scene reported by Pausanias on the throne of Zeus at Olympia highlighting the queen in her death throes, but supported by Achilles.[18]

Dating from 530–525 BCE, this stunning, black figure amphora by the Exekias painter shows the Greek warrior Achilles slaying the Amazon queen Penthesilea. The fully-armored and high-crested son of Thetis plunges his spear into the throat of his victim, who, dressed in a leopard skin and helmet, has fallen upon one knee. In the final moment, the two warriors lock eyes. © The Trustees of the British Museum/Art Resource, NY. (British Museum accession number: 1848,0801.1).

A Lucanian red-figure krater dated to the fifth century BCE represents another intriguing piece. It too shows the battle between Achilles, again on the left, and Penthesilea on the eastern right.[19] This time, however, the face of Thetis' son is exposed allowing the viewer to see his eyes and countenance more clearly. His spear sinks down, wilting, as his eyes fall upon the Amazon queen. In this rendering, the fleeing Amazon is shown in Phrygian style dress, a Phrygian cap, and shortened chiton with spots, although there is no evidence of an actual leopard skin. More importantly, she only has one breast, preserving the long-held belief that Amazons removed half a breast to be more proficient at firing a bow.

While the insinuation is for us that Amazons are willing to do anything to get the shot, there is also the ambiguity of her gender. The fact that Penthesilea is not only a ruler but also a warrior is both shocking and scandalous to a Greek (male, especially) audience. Her dress and demeanor are already unnerving, a woman geared for battle. Then there are her weapons.

Sometimes she is depicted wielding a spear, a male projectile weapon, but sometimes she wields an axe, hardly the weapon of a traditional Homeric hero. Most carry a spear, or maybe a sword, but rarely an axe. While it may appear exotic to some, it has a symbol whose roots run deep in ancient Greece.

In Minoan culture, the double axe, or *labyrs* was also a symbol typically associated with ritual sacrifice. Take for example the scene of ritual sacrifice on the Hagia Triadha sarcophagus, where a priestess pours a libation into an urn, underneath a pair of double axes. It was also associated with the Minoan goddess, a central figure and one that appears in a position of power. A gold seal ring discovered by Heinrich Schliemann at Mycenae shows a scene of epiphany with a goddess seated beneath the tree of life and a priestess with a double axe. Later in the classical period, we see Clytemnestra wielding the axe in a bastardized form of the same ritual sacrifice.[20] Greek men are accustomed to seeing powerful women such as Medea resort to poison or witchcraft in order to subdue their enemies. A weapon such as a sword or an axe, requiring face-to-face contact, thus stands as a sign of overt masculinity. The Amazon queen also bears a lunate shield, the mark of Thracian peltasts, a group seen as outsiders, living in small towns or organized into small tribal communities.[21] So not only is Penthesilea a threat to traditional Greek masculinity in her androgynous dress, weapons, and actions, she is also a terrifying example of Otherness to the Greek xenophobe as well.

As queen, Penthesilea led her troops into battle against the greatest assembly of Greek armies of all time. As a warrior, Penthesilea had no equal. Masked by war, however, she wields a weapon even greater than the sword: a beauty that disarms even warlike Achilles, who, lifting her helmet, falls in love. While her reasons for coming to Troy are ambiguous—the promise of gold or seeking redemption—her legacy has endured. While she represents a foil to the Greek epic hero, she remains an actual heroine of her own culture. For modern audiences, she is the epitome of the classic Amazon and *femme fatale:* a strong female leader who gets what she wants by any means necessary. While she may come from a far-off land, her skills and beauty locate her at the center of one of antiquity's most notable conflicts.

Atalanta

Amazons, however, were not the only female hobgoblins to haunt the hearts of ancient men. Another was the woman raised in the wild, a more local, familiar form of the female Other. Such is the case with the virgin huntress Atalanta. Abandoned on a mountaintop by her father who preferred a son to a daughter, Atlanta is discovered by a mother bear, who cares for her as one of her own.[22] Free from the shackles of a male dominated society, she becomes a fierce archer, hunter, and tracker who devotes herself to the goddess Artemis. In time, word of her incredible beauty and deft hunting skills reaches the ears of a young hero named Meleager, who lusts after her from afar. He invites her to join him on a quest to kill the Calydonian Boar, a fierce beast sent by the goddess Artemis to plague the kingdom. Included in the predominantly male hunting party are the twins Castor and Polydeuces, Theseus of Athens, Jason, Iphikles, and Meleager's uncles (sons of Thestios).[23] Atalanta's presence causes great consternation. Nevertheless, struck by her beauty, Meleager defends his choice and most fortuitously, too, for while several of the men are initially killed, it is Atalanta's arrow that draws first blood. Because of this, Meleager awards the beast's hide to her.

The act instantly stirs the wrath of Meleager's uncles. Claiming it unjust to award such a valuable trophy to a woman and additionally to put love before kin, they take it from her. Enraged, or perhaps driven by lust, Meleager slays them and returns the trophy to her. This might have been the end of it, if not for a prophecy given by the Moirae, claiming Meleager should live so long as a particular log burned in the family hearth. Grief-stricken over the death of her brothers, Althaea, Meleager's mother, tosses that log into the fire, bringing about the death of her son—tough love to say the least, but the tale shows how beauty can be dangerous and lead to one's destruction.

Alas, Atalanta's story does not end there. Later she is reunited with her father, who, we assume, is over the whole sure-wish-I-had-a-son-instead-of-a-daughter thing. He tries to get her to agree to marry, as any respectable woman should, even those raised by bears. Atalanta shrewdly agrees, so long as the one she marries can outrun her in a race. Hearing of her exploits and beauty, many suitors race for her hand but lose, death awaiting those who failed. Finally, it is Hippomenes, grandson of Poseidon, who eventually comes up with a plan. Armed with three golden apples given to him by Aphrodite, he tosses one in front of the maiden whenever she gets ahead. Eventually, through trickery, he wins.

The story of Atalanta serves at the very least to demonstrate that a woman who can stand on her own is valued more as a prize than for her own aptitude in ancient Greece. Fiercely independent, she is the match of any man. Although beautiful, she is not a *femme fatale*, for she does not use that beauty to manipulate men. Instead, she prefers not to marry and devotes herself to Artemis. Symbolically, Atalanta stands not just as a woman, but also the Other. Like the Amazon, she exists outside the world of men and thus is unused to their wiles and trickery. Her strength, agility, and shrewdness should instead be valued and honored, making her the kind of woman who should rule instead of being ruled, much like Marston's Wonder Woman. Yet the dynamo from Themyscira has a few other models in our own American history, which may have influenced some of her unique attributes.

The Modern Amazon Warrior

Columbia, Rebirth of the Amazon in America

They say great heroes never really die but live on in the story-telling tradition. This is why so many heroes, such as Odysseus, struggle to return home, so that they can tell their story. Sometimes these heroes are rediscovered and given new life. This is certainly the case with the Amazon. Some might argue that she was revived in visual personifications such as those of Jacques Grasset de Saint-Sauveur, who, in 1796, depicts a dark-haired America with a feathered-headdress holding a bow and quiver, bare-breasted and pictured with a beaver and tortoise.[24] In 1806, she receives a face-lift. Saint-Sauveur depicts her with the same bow and quiver, but with a spear, like Athena, dressed in a short chiton, sitting on a classical style architrave. In the span of a mere ten years, America becomes "classicized." We shift from a more "native" American look and natural feel to a somewhat sterile but very European style classicism. What causes this shift? Although an accomplished artist and world traveler, Saint-Sauveur had not necessarily visited some of the places he tries to actualize. In fact, he reflects the prevailing attitude of many missionaries at the time, of refashioning indigenous peoples in order to brandish the stamp of European progress upon the rest of the world.[25] So while initially depicting America as a noble savage, his revised copy in 1806 shows a subsequently civilized America, one making great strides towards progress.

Such classical models were then transferred to later depictions of America, such as Columbia.[26] By World War I, Columbia appears in a Greek style chiton, adorned in stars and stripes, like Wonder Woman, and interestingly wearing a Phrygian cap.[27] The figure is a classic beauty with blond hair. With arms outstretched and large eyes, she is a welcoming, attractive figure. In contrast, a poster by Vincent Aderente titled *Columbia Calls* shows the same Phrygian cap, wearing a traditional Greek style dress but holding a sword at her side, a symbol of power and righteousness. Such depictions may have been drawn from earlier political cartoons, such as the 1860 Currier and Ives engraving showing Columbia beating Stephen

Frontispiece to *Encyclopédie des voyages: América, 1796*, depicting the allegory of America, seated, who is shown bare-chested, wearing a feathered apron, bracelets, and crown, and holds a quiver and arrows. *Encyclopédie des voyages: América, 1796* by Jacques Grasset de Saint-Sauveur, courtesy gallica.bnf.fr / Bibliothèque nationale de France.

A classicized allegory of America dressed in a chiton, lion-studded sandals, carrying bow and quiver, and sitting on a classical style cornice. The image of a Western ship appears behind her. *Encyclopédie des voyages: América, 1806* by Jacques Grasset de Saint-Sauveur. Alexander Turnbull Library, Wellington, New Zealand.

Douglas with a whip. The figure of the beautiful woman, who can enforce punishment over men, even powerful men, certainly paved the way for comic characters such as Wonder Woman. If there was any doubt, take a look at early drawings of Columbia from the Columbia Records phonograph packaging. It shows Columbia with a starred bustier and striped skirt.

"Be Patriotic" poster by Paul Stahr, ca. 1917–1918, shows a woman with a striking resemblance to Columbia with her Phrygian-style hat, but this time she wears stars and stripes instead of classical dress and drapery. Lithograph poster; accessed via Library of Congress website: https://www.loc.gov/item/96515511/.

Wonder Woman, Diana of Themyscira

As lovely as Aphrodite, as wise as Athena, with the strength of Hercules, inarguably, one of the most exalted female superheroes of all time is Wonder Woman.[28] Hailing from the distant island of Themyscira (Paradise Island), a kingdom ruled by fierce warrior women, Wonder Woman began life as Diana, daughter of Hippolyta, queen of the Amazons. Like the Amazons of Greek myth, these women are distrustful of men, capturing a few unfortunate souls every 30 years in order to, well, replenish their numbers. Of course, once they had met their purpose, most of these men were killed. Some fortunate enough found themselves under the protection of Hephaestus. In early versions of the story, Diana's birth is chthonic. That is to say, she was created from the clay of the Earth by her mother Hippolyta.[29] Unlike Pandora, who was formed by male gods, Diana is created by female forces and like so many heroes, born of a royal virgin.

Columbia Calls—Enlist Now for U.S. Army, designed by Frances Adams Halsted and painted by Italian-born artist Vincent Aderente, shows Columbia with Eastern headgear but Western-style drapery in her dress. The style is certainly classicizing and entreats the youth of America to join the Army. C. 1916; lithograph poster, color; sheet 102.3 × 75.4 cm; accessed by the Library of Congress website: http://www.loc.gov/pictures/item/95506508/.

In her debut in All-Star Comics in 1941, Diana discovers a mysterious stranger, Steve Trevor, a U.S. Army intelligence pilot, who crashes on the island.[30] As she nurses him back to health, she slowly begins to fall in love with him. Once healed, Trevor wishes to return to the war. After learning of Trevor's fight against the Nazis, Hippolyta orders that he must be returned to the world of men, accompanied by an Amazon warrior who will aid him in his fight. A contest is held among the Amazons to determine their best warrior. Although her mother forbids her to enter, donning a mask, Diana secretly competes and wins. Her armor and her title, Wonder Woman, are a special gift from her mother. Joining Steve, she aids him in his fight against injustice, and adopts a secret human identity, working as a nurse and then a secretary.

Over the years, Wonder Woman has continually surprised readers with her myriad of weapons and abilities. Gifted with incredible memory, she is also an excellent equestrian, trained in hand-to-hand combat, tracking, telepathy, and medicine. She exudes superhuman agility, durability, speed and strength, the ability to fly, and at one point was gifted with immortality. Her primary weapon is the Lasso of Truth, a golden rope created by the divine smith Hephaestus that not only restrains her opponents but also encourages them to speak the truth.[31] Diana, as all Amazons, sports a pair of indestructible cuffs—the bracelets of submission—which she uses to deflect projectiles, and, which serve as a constant reminder of the Amazon's loathsome enslavement under Herakles. In the 2017 film *Wonder Woman*, they could also be used to create a massive energy wave that disables her opponents. Her trademark red star tiara is not only a symbol of her royalty, it can also be used, like Xena's chakram, as a boomerang.[32] When she wants to travel, she can fly autonomously or soar above the horizon in her invisible jet. In the most recent film version, Wonder Woman adds a sword, Godkiller, and shield to her arsenal.

It is not the first time we find her adopting such weapons. After the series *Crisis on Infinite Earths*, George Perez and Greg Potter bequeathed Diana an axe, a spear, sword, and shield. Many of these are highlighted on the cover of *Challenge of the Gods* (November 1987), and the New 52's *Wonder Woman* Issue #36. Recently she has traded up once again, wielding the sword of Athena in the film *Batman vs. Superman* and *Justice League*. The inclusion of the axe obviously has associations with classical Amazon models, particularly Penthesilea. The shield, spear, and sword, the panoply of the epic male warrior, also places Wonder Woman on par with her male counterparts. This re-arming of Diana may reflect the undercurrent of equity-feminism during the 80s.

Following World War II, Wonder Woman continued her relentless battle against crime and oppression. By the mid–1950s, during the Silver

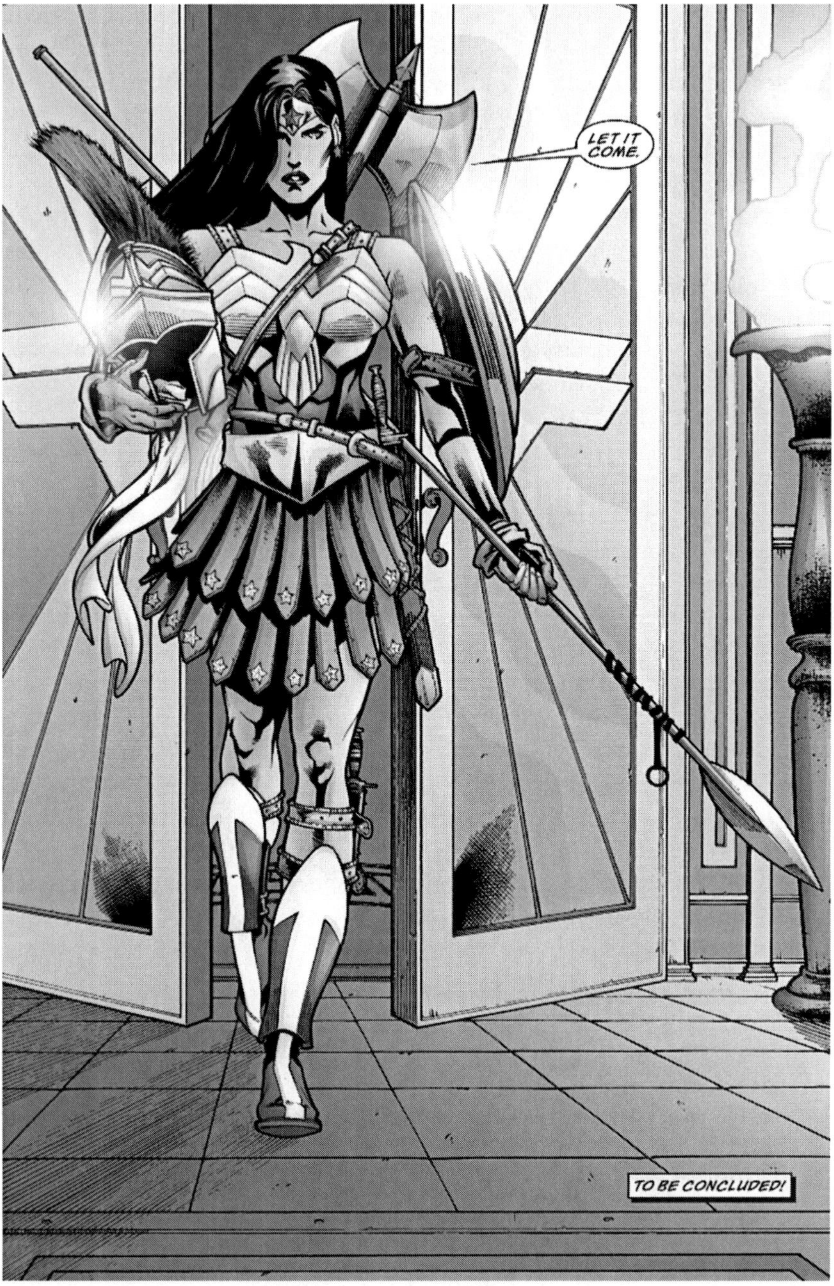

The superhero Wonder Woman gears up to battle against the villainess Medusa in *Wonder Woman* Vol. 2 #209, brandishing a spear, shield, helmet, and an axe behind her back. © 2004 DC Comics.

Age, she became one of the founding members of the Justice League. In the years that followed, the comics began to highlight her romantic side, and readers saw her settle down with her long-time beau Col. Steve Trevor. She becomes a housewife and mother to their daughter Hippolyte ("Lyta"), a storyline not reflected in the film series. Later in the 1960s she returns to the outside world to fight crime.

A seasoned warrior. A master tactician. A capable diplomat and a compassionate nurturer. A better understanding of Wonder Woman's mass appeal may be found in her qualities as a hero. Nevertheless, she is still a construct of a phallocentric, male-dominated society. Outside of her kingdom, she adopts the name Diana Prince, taken from a nurse she met, and whose identity she assumes. From the very start, her personality is one of contrasts. Her title "Amazon princess" says it all. She exudes traits of a fierce male warrior as well as a princess. Her name Diana, or in the Greek, Artemis, is taken from a goddess known for chastity and masculine qualities. Finally, the adopted surname, Prince, leaves her sexuality, but not her social status, ambiguous, like the traditional phallocentric Greek views of Amazon warriors. The fact that Diana has to hide her Amazon identity behind a somewhat masculinized name reflects the typical type of subordination feminists endeavor to dismantle.

Her creator, William Marston, though inspired to fashion a new role model of the kind of woman who *should* rule the world, nevertheless created a hypersexualized character, whose bustier, slimming girdle, and revealing suit stands as the quintessential focus of what filmmaker and feminist Laura Mulvey calls the male gaze.[33] Furthermore, her use of the lasso to tie up her opponents promotes the heroine as a dominatrix, fulfilling deep-seated male fantasies of being dominated. While Wonder Woman may have been sexualized, given power to thwart or even remove male power, she is not actually able to be sexual. Even when she has a romance, it is nevertheless within the norms of male society. To have sex, she must be married to Steve. The tone of the comic, while appealing to young women, is the epitome of the monosexual paradigm. Of course, Marston was writing in the 1940s, and although much has changed in our society, Wonder Woman is still the morally upright and strong figure that ostensibly should be running things on the planet, but from a male point of view.

Let us pause to consider whether a strong woman can also be sexually promiscuous. In many ways, it seems like Wonder Woman has been sterilized to fit Marston's ideal role model for women, but at what cost? For modern society, a woman who is both physically and sexually powerful, despite advances in feminism, seems too much to bear … which is why she fits the traditional Amazon model. While both Hippolyta and Penthesilea were fierce warriors, Hippolyta was punished for her desire for Theseus. Penthesilea, fierce in battle, turns the head of Achilles, who is distracted and acts dishonorably when he kills Thersites. In the ancient traditions, powerful Amazon women are punished. Within modern viewpoints, they are celebrated, though still fetishized.

Xena: Princess Warrior

One of the most popular re-imaginings of the traditional Amazon warrior is the character of Xena from the television show *Xena: Princess Warrior*. Ferocious in battle and an excellent equestrian, in many ways she is a modern mirror of Penthesilea and likewise searching for redemption for past aggressions. Moreover, her name literally says it all. Xena, from the Greek *xenos* means stranger, or outsider. She, like the classic Greek Amazon, represents the Other, a stranger from outside male dominated society. She dresses like a warrior, but like Wonder Woman, she is a bikini-clad beauty who appeals to the male gaze. Armed with sword and chakram, leather bustier, short leather skirt and boots, this Amazon is dressed to kill, but also to titillate. Compare this image, however, to ancient Greek depictions of Amazon women wearing Phrygian caps, male trousers, and carrying bows, shields, and hatchets, the same as their male counterparts; the discrepancies are obvious. The ancient Greek view aims for ambiguity. Amazons represent a danger for traditional Greek society, because the women dress like men. Most Greek women were resigned to certain areas of the house and the city, and certainly not allowed to participate in male-centric activities such as games and symposia.[34] Women who step beyond the house, dress and act like men, subvert male dominated society.

What makes Xena different is the performance of her sexuality. She is allowed to be bisexual, taking male lovers, such as Borias, Marcus, and Julius Caesar, but also, many assume, female lovers such as her companion Gabrielle. The relationship, however, hardly meets male standards of lesbian lovers. Instead, the emphasis is on friendship, companionship, and loyalty. These are the same values ancient Greeks superimpose upon the ancient Amazons. Xena is authentically ancient, precisely because of her sexual ambiguity. The Greeks wouldn't have understood our modern need to differentiate between "homo" vs. "hetero" sexuality—sex was sex. At least this is what we gather from the texts written by men, although there is some indication of a similar view held by women such as Sappho and some of the other fragmentary Greek lyric poets (Erinna, *et aliae*).

Conclusion

For many, Wonder Woman represents the rebirth of a modern Amazon warrior: strong, smart, independent, with the ability to hold her own in a male dominated world. Nevertheless, Wonder Woman is still depicted through an overtly male lens. She is the ideal created for women, by men, but she is still a stranger in a man's world, like the Amazons of old. The character draws from a long and rich history that has its roots deep in Greek mythology and the mythologizing of early America. For Diana to be truly free, to be a true Amazon and break the bonds of servitude, she needs to exist in an Amazon world, fashioned by a feminist perspective. She need not be fetishized but imbued with values that appeal to women that make her more real than idealized.

How would one apply a feminist lens to the character of Wonder Woman? In terms of gender and objectification, while she still dresses in a short skirt and bustier, she need not be depicted as such, and solely at the whim of the male gaze. With the recent increase in volume of the voices within and in support of the LGBTQ community, perhaps Wonder Woman's appeal needs to develop to include this fan base, especially since she is constantly having to hide her feelings to fit male expectations. This is not to say she needs to be gay, but to fully explore the human condition, such issues should be considered as a part of her world. For a while she was the only woman in the Justice League. Isolation, according to relational-cultural theory can be destructive to one's emotional development. Diana might need to explore deeper friendships with women, if not her fellow Amazons, more female super heroes.

We also need to redefine what it means to be a warrior, a leader, and a woman. This does not necessarily have only to do only with kicking a little villain ass. For a while we saw Diana struggle with real life issues as well, such as her role as a mother. While comics are largely treated as escapist fantasy, social safety valves, or mirrors for modern cultural injustices, we should not necessarily sacrifice these ideals in lieu of good character development. The world of the epic hero also retains a certain degree of escapism, but the heroes persist because of their human qualities. Heroes argue, lose face, die, mourn, enact incredible acts evil, yet they are often redeemable.

If we take a look at Wonder Woman's Rogues' Gallery, we find it predominantly populated with female antagonists: the ruthless Nazi spy Baroness Gunther, archaeologist turned super-villain Cheetah, the witch Circe, Dr. Poison, Dr. Cyber, Silver Swan, Hypnota, and the list goes on. Although a woman is featured as the superhero, having her only combat predominantly female villains upholds a system of inequality, where a woman can only rise to power and independence by avoiding male conflict rather than asserting herself as an equal. In the myths of ancient Greece, Penthesilea was the equivalent of Achilles. We need, therefore, to make Wonder Woman the match of *any* man. A modern Wonder Woman is not afraid to stand up to overt displays of male aggression. As a matter of fact, Wonder Woman attracts our attention precisely because she stands out in a male dominated world. What makes her strong, one might argue, is her struggle against chauvinism and the reliance on her own standards and values. To place her back in her own world also robs her of her hard-earned agency.

III

A Mind for War

Odysseus and the Iron Avenger

Deliciously deceptive and the hero of his own epic, Odysseus is renowned for his brilliance, cunning, and sagacious wit. It is often *he* to whom the Greeks turn for the voice of reason. It is *he* who convinces Achilles to return to war, *he* who is first chosen to fight Hector, and it is *he* who single-handedly turns the tide of battle in favor of the Greeks. To him we owe the ever-enduring trope of the Trojan horse and the proverb "beware of Greeks bearing gifts."[1] The *Odyssey* serves as a veritable resume of his cleverness: take for example the island of the cyclopes where Odysseus uses the underside of sheep to escape the cave of the monster Polyphemus, or the encounter with the sirens where he, in one of the best examples of ancient life hacks, fashions earplugs made from bees wax to drown out their seductive song for his men, while he listens tied to the mast of his ship.[2] Throughout Homer's epic, it is his inventiveness that seems to set him apart.

Often referred to as iron-hearted, or made of iron, Odysseus' inventiveness is a trait mirrored in the modern-day hero, Iron Man, aka Tony Stark.[3] Rocketing across the skies of the Marvel universe, the wise-cracking Stark often employs trickery and technology to win his battles. His mind is his greatest weapon. Trapped in the cave of his enemy, Stark builds a suit of armor from spare parts to help him escape, like the war-weary Odysseus who devises a plan to escape the cave of the cyclops. Eventually, Stark conceals himself inside the suit and flees the cave of his captors. In the original *Iron Man* film, Stark's journey mirrors conventional epic, especially the plight of Odysseus in the *Odyssey*. Like Odysseus, Stark is always trying to make his way home to a dutiful and loyal partner. Like Penelope, the character of Pepper Potts is not only patient but also wily in her own right. Both women are left in charge of the hero's assets while he is away, and both have to contend with threats to their respective kingdoms.

The aim of this chapter is to demonstrate that Odysseus and Stark share many of the same characteristics, including a penchant for τέχνη (*techne*), strategy, and, well, living free and loose. Iron Man also echoes many of the same epic themes present in Homer's *Odyssey*, such as technology, war, and homecoming, or *nostos*.

Attic black figure column krater, 525–500 BCE depicting the wily Odysseus fleeing the cave of the Cyclopes beneath the belly of a sheep. Terracotta 33 × 35.5 × 30 cm (13 × 14 × 11 13/16 in.), 96.AE.303. The J. Paul Getty Museum, Villa Collection, Malibu, California, Gift of Barbara and Lawrence Fleischman.

Genius Inventor and Master Strategist

Greek mythology is replete with examples of the artificer or inventor who employs his τέχνη (*techne:* art, craft, or guile) to win the battle. There is Hephaestus, the Κλυτοτέχνης (*Klytotechnes*), or master artificer of the Olympian gods, who forged the glorious armor of Achilles, and mortal Daedalus, creator of the famous labyrinth to cage the monstrous Minotaur. Among their rank is the wily Odysseus. Fiendishly clever, he is the one most often credited for devising the ruse of the Trojan horse, but his accomplishments continue beyond that.

Before the war, to get out of going to Troy, Odysseus feigns insanity, but is unmasked when his infant son Telemachus is threatened. When drafting Achilles, who cleverly had been disguised as one the daughters of the king of Scyros by his mother, Odysseus figures he can lure the hero out by hiding weapons among the gifts he brings to court. When Odysseus sounds a battle horn, while the daughters flee, Achilles leaps into action, grabbing the weaponry ready for a fight.

After the war, when trapped in the cave of Polyphemus, he hatches a brilliant plan of escape, first intoxicating Poseidon's son. Then, as the monster slept, he and his men would drive a giant pike they had sharpened into the monster's one eye, blinding him. Finally, using Polyphemus' sheep as cover, he and his men would flee the confines of the monster's cave. Equally masterful is Odysseus' plan when he stumbles upon the mesmerizing sirens' song—earplugs made from beeswax.[4] Technically, it is Circe's advice, but the hero seems to receive most of the credit for it. Next, to escape Calypso's island, Odysseus has to construct a raft—felling 20 trees, boring holes and connecting these with rivets, constructing a mast and yardarm, and a system of levers to help him lower the craft into the water.[5]

This giant pithos from the Workshop of the Calabresi Urn (Etruscan, active 650–625 BCE) shows Odysseus and his men hoisting the huge branch to blind their captor, the one-eyed giant Polyphemos. 85.6 × 56 cm (33¹¹⁄₁₆ × 22¹⁄₁₆ in.), 96.AE.135.a; The J. Paul Getty Museum, Villa Collection, Malibu, California, Gift of Barbara and Lawrence Fleischman.

Odysseus' penchant for assessing a situation and fashioning weapons and tools to aid his escape are on par with Tony Stark. In the comic book tradition, after his caravan is attacked, Stark finds himself a captive of the warlord Wong-Chu, who forces him to build weapons in a well-guarded cave. Meanwhile, the hero's brush with death has left a sliver of shrapnel in his chest, which is slowly making its way to his heart. Stark contrives the mini arc reactor whose primary purpose is to power an electromagnet that keeps that splinter of shrapnel from reaching his heart. To escape the cave, he forges a suit made of iron from spare parts, a Trojan horse of sorts, in which he hides himself. Throughout the films, the red and gold hero is always credited for his quick-minded inventiveness and never-ending collection of amazing suits, like the Mark XLII, that could be summoned on command. While Captain America gets his powers from a bottle, Stark's powers are self-made.

Stark fabricates a technological soldier out of metal for his friend, James Rhodes. Isn't it interesting, however, that we don't really ever think of Rhodey as a super soldier, too? He is an excellent pilot and solider, but it is

An interior panel *Iron Man* # 218 (1987) showing old bucket head testing his new deep-sea armor, another example of his inventive nature, as he tries to thwart an enemy plot to seize a toxic gas tank from the legendary *Titanic*. Written by Bob Layton and David Michelinie. Art & cover by Bob Layton. © 2014 Marvel Characters, Inc.

clearly the hybrid man and machine that makes Stark's soldier stellar. War Machine feels more like the reservist, though he joins the ranks during the Age of Ultron. Tony Stark is the star of that show, and Rhodes is just driving a copy of his suit.

Despite all his technology, Stark spurns the label of a soldier. He will put on the suit, but he refuses to take orders or surrender his freedom, that is until the *Age of Ultron*, when it is clear that his actions are responsible for the deaths of hundreds of civilians. Stark prefers to be the strategist, the armchair general. When he does join the fray, you'd better be certain that he's already got several plans. In the comic book tradition, for example, in addition to the arc reactor, he has devised a suit for almost every occasion: underwater, space, and suits imbued with stealth technology. In the films, his list of designs include the Iron Legion, J.A.R.V.I.S., the holotable, the Iron Man Gauntlet, Jericho, a Namo gauntlet, and a version of the Spider suit, just to name a few. His Hulkbuster armor is by far the *pièce de résistance*, armed with missiles, grappling hook, repulsors, and a jackhammer-like extended punch. Even if you take away the toys and tricks, you still have Iron Man, the mind behind the inventions.

One of the clearest advantages Iron Man has is access to J.A.R.V.I.S. (Just a Rather Very Intelligent System), an AI interface named after his father's butler, Edwin Jarvis. J.A.R.V.I.S. has access to security systems, can launch Iron Man's many suits of armor remotely, and often aids Stark in defeating his enemies by feeding him intelligence on surrounding terrain and potential threats, such as we see in the battle of New York and the Chitauri. J.A.R.V.I.S. can also take physical form. In the film *Iron Man 3*, he takes control of the Mark XLII suit and pulls Stark from the wreckage of his mansion. Because J.A.R.V.I.S. is typically without form, we might classify this AI as otherworldly, moving between reality and cyberspace. Like Athena providing advice to Odysseus or Telemachus, J.A.R.V.I.S. acts as though a force of otherworldly or even divine intervention, offering advice, removing obstacles, and providing insight the hero would not typically have on his own.

Man Vs. Machine

Man versus machine. It is a recurring theme in modern culture today. Films like Fritz Lang's *Metropolis*, James Cameron's *The Terminator* series, and Ridley Scott's visually stunning *Bladerunner* offer a frightening vision of the future, where man and machine are potential adversaries. This theme is also at play in the Iron Man comics and recent feature films. They say the suit makes the man. In Tony Stark's case, this is particularly true. The arc reactor powering his armor also keeps the life-threatening shrapnel embedded in his chest from reaching his heart. The suit and reactor are ever-present reminders of his vulnerability, his mortality. The suit is also the manifestation of his ego and alter ego. It reflects his inner genius, a mind for design. But it also allows Tony to transform himself into something more. Like the armor of Achilles, Iron Man's suit allows him to become superhuman, to become the image of the ultimate hero. The armor bestows power. In the first *Avengers* film, Stark remarks, "this little circle of light, it's part of me now, not just armor. It's a terrible privilege." In the scene, Stark is trying to convince Dr. Bruce Banner that the Hulk can be controlled, by relating his own struggle with power.

One of the most highly anticipated scenes for fans of the Iron Man films is the arming of the hero. In the film *Iron Man*, we watch intoxicated as Stark, assuming the pose of the Vitruvian man, first transforms into the Iron Avenger. His arming scene is like watching a modern-day assembly line. Robot arms whir and spin, equipping him with iron boots, greaves,

An interior panel from *Tales of Suspense* # 57 (1964) showing Iron Man arming himself and bemoaning his injured heart. © 2012 Marvel Characters, Inc.

gloves and a hood-like chest plate complete with a glaring headlight. Rivets and chrome, flashy yellow and red metallic paint, makes it all seem very beautiful as our hero transforms into a human hot rod. With repulsors embedded in his palms and a top speed of Mach 5, this hyper-velocity armor is enough to make the modern auto enthusiast's heart skip a beat. In subsequent films, there is a discernable crescendo, from portable suits disguised as suitcases, to AI powered suits that can move freely on their own, to nanotech that can arm a hero in a matter of seconds. It is hard sometimes to even tell where the line between man and technology end, and over time, one begins to wonder who is really driving, Tony or his alter ego, Iron Man.

Curiously enough, at first in the comic book series, Stark explains that Iron Man is his bodyguard, in order to protect his anonymity. Ultimately, the suit allows Tony to do what is in his nature, and the two become inseparable. Captain America presses the point in a moment of classic banter from the first Avengers film. "Big Man in a suit of armor. Take that off, what are you?" Stark snaps back, "genius, billionaire, playboy, philanthropist." The jab, however, gives the audience pause to reflect. Is Tony anything without his suit? Is he a hero or simply a self-indulgent genius with a flashy car? Stark has not fully earned his heroic stripes, even if he has all the sexy trappings in his shiny red suit. Stark's transformation from eccentric, philandering playboy to hero is a gradual one.

But at what point does he begin to grow a conscience? In the first Avengers film, it is no secret that Stark and Captain America are often at odds with one another. Cap finds Tony's self-absorbent behavior toxic to the team. Just before S.H.I.E.L.D.'s flagship is attacked, Cap confronts Stark: "The only thing you really fight for is yourself. You're not the guy to make the sacrifice play, to lay down on a wire and let the other guy crawl over you." To this Stark cleverly replies: "I think I would just cut the wire." "Always a way out," Cap fires back. "You know, you may not be a threat, but you better stop pretending to be a hero." It is more than simply a competence-porn scene between the two heroes. It plants the seed in Stark that has him essentially question his own heroic caliber.

Later, during the battle of New York, Stark gets the chance to prove his mettle. With a Chitauri invasion imminent, the World Security Council targets New York with a nuclear missile. Stark resolves to sacrifice himself. Intercepting the missile, he gallantly redirects it through the wormhole toward the Chitauri command ship as his suit begins to lose power. Facing certain death, he tries desperately to contact Pepper. Sadly, his message goes unheard. The missile detonates, destroying the ship. Amazingly, our hero survives, plummeting back to earth, just as the wormhole closes. Saved by the Hulk, who catches him, he lives to fight another day, but this selfless act is one that redeems Iron Man. He actually becomes the hero, because he finally is willing to make the sacrifice play. After his fall, he is born anew, with a new purpose, to develop a means to protect the Earth from future invasion, mirroring the heroic paradigm of death and return.

Stark's brush with death has left an indelible mark on the hero. As Pepper Potts poignantly observes in *Iron Man 3*, Stark has become obsessed with his technology. On the surface, he seems to know who he is, but does he? At the end of the second Iron Man film, Nick Fury informs Stark that while Iron Man would be a suitable candidate for the Avengers initiative, Tony would not. With this seed planted, as time goes on, we see him evolve into a hero. While the suit may allow Stark to reach new heights, it is his human logic and reasoning that are in charge. In answer to the question, who is ultimately in control, we need only look to the end of the *Iron Man 3*. With his suits destroyed, the shrapnel and reactor removed from his chest, Stark realizes that the suit does not necessarily make the man. It is the man inside. He reconfirms this when he states: "My armor was never a distraction or a hobby, it was a cocoon, and now I'm a changed man. You can take away my house, all my tricks and toys, but one thing you can't take away—I am Iron Man."

A similar exchange occurs in Book 9 of the *Odyssey* between Odysseus and the cyclops Polyphemus. After blinding the monster, Odysseus initially tells him that his name is Nemo, *No One*, thereby preserving his anonymity. After rescuing his men, however, Odysseus falls victim of his own *hubris* and cannot help but trumpet his own cleverness, you know, just for the yucks. He shouts back to the monster:

> Cyclops, if any mortal man should ask you
> about the shameful gouging of your eye,
> say that it was I, Odysseus, sacker of cities,
> son of Laertes who lives in Ithaka.[6]

That single disclosure is what seals his fate, for once Poseidon, Polyphemus' father, discovers this secret, he makes it his *raison d'être* to keep Odysseus from reaching home, to keep him from achieving his glory, or *kleos*. If he cannot reach home, he cannot recount his tale, which is the only path to heroic glory. For the epic hero, destiny is key to one's identity. To skirt this destiny, to claim personal autonomy over the gods is forbidden for the ancient hero. This is why Odysseus continues to conceal his identity until he has safely returned home and defeated all his foes. Iron Man's heroic "coming out" similarly exposes himself and his loved ones to danger. In *Iron Man 2*, his new celebrity status makes him the target of Senator Stern and the villain known as Whiplash. In *Iron Man 3*, Pepper is kidnapped by Aldrich Killian, the hand pulling the Mandarin's strings. Whether in Homer or the MCU, the revelation of true identity often paints a target squarely on the hero's back.

Billionaire Playboy

Monsters, storms, and witchcraft aside, Odysseus' return journey, or *nostos*, is also filled with perilous paramours. There is the Sea Witch Circe, whose name comes from the Greek verb *kirkoô,* meaning "to bind or imprison with rings." With her deep knowledge of potions and herbs, she transforms Odysseus' crew into mindless swine when they pull ashore on the island of Aeaea. Odysseus spends a year with her, siring children Latinus and Telegonus. Circe's powers are hardly subtle. They bespeak of emasculation of the male who is reduced to a simple beast.

Next in the line of forlorn lovers is Calypso, a powerful nymph dwelling on the island of Ogygia. Odysseus spends seven years with her as a captive in her cave. Robbed of his masculinity and agency, he becomes a mere plaything of a goddess. During that time, she also attempts to seduce him, wooing him with her song and attempting to transform him into an immortal. Eventually, Odysseus grows weary of her and wishes to return to his wife. With Athena and Hermes seeking his release, he eventually leaves the cave, builds a raft, and escapes. Finally, Odysseus washes up on the shores of Scheria only to narrowly escape betrothal to King Alcinous's daughter, Nausicaa. Such is the life of an epic hero. Finally, he returns home to his wife, Penelope, who through it all has remained ever faithful, running the kingdom in his absence.

Parallels abound with Tony Stark. Like Odysseus, Stark resides in a palatial world. Whether it's Razor's Edge, his beachside mansion overlooking the sea, or Avengers' Tower soaring high above the Manhattan skyline, the genius inventor is king of his own realm and has an abundance of inexhaustible resources at his command. Take J.A.R.V.I.S., for example: a highly sophisticated AI, based on his former butler, who aids Stark in his research by accessing data, allocating resources such as the robot powered Iron Legion, and granting access to the inaccessible. J.A.R.V.I.S. often acts as Iron Man's eyes and ears. Eumaeus, Odysseus' swineherd and friend, is an invaluable resource, who likewise carries vital messages and aids the hero in retaking his palace from the rapacious grasp of Penelope's suitors.

Perilous paramours? Stark has these as well. In the comics, Christine Everhart, a reporter for the *Daily Bugle*, investigates Stark Industries. She also appears in the film series, and questions Stark about the fact that his weapons are responsible for the deaths of innocent civilians. After being seduced by him, she wakes up the next morning only to find him gone. Pepper is there to hand over her clothes. Then there is Natalie Rushman, a.k.a. Black Widow, a S.H.I.E.L.D. operative who, disguised as a personal assistant is sent to keep tabs on Stark to see if he is ready for the Avengers Initiative. In *Iron Man 2* there is sexual tension between her and Stark. In the comics, Stark and Romanov are romantically linked as well. In *Iron Man 3*, Tony shares his bed with the brilliant scientist Maya Hansen, who sees Tony as having the potential to help her perfect her invention, Extremis, a nanotech form of genetic enhancement. Throughout the comics, Tony Stark dates an impressive array of talented young women: Joanna Nivena, Janice Cord, Marianne Rodgers, Natasha Romanoff, Whitney Frost (the crime boss Madame Masque), Janet Van Dyne, aka the Wasp, neurologist Dr. Su Yin, and Kathy Dare, just to name a few. Throughout it all, one woman has remained a loyal friend and confidant: Virginia Pepper Potts.

The Lover at the Loom: Penelope and Pepper Potts

Pepper Potts is Penelope reincarnated. For example, both enact the role of the dutiful wife, both are wily, and both rule the kingdom in their lover's stead. At the beginning of *Iron Man 2*, Pepper is made the head of Stark Industries, a role she takes on with all *gravitas*. As CEO, she protects the kingdom, like the epic heroine, allowing the hero to embark upon his journey. While billionaire playboy Tony Stark flirts with danger and takes part in a number of dalliances, they are never "the one." In due time, he comes to realize that Pepper is his true love. As Tony recounts in *Avengers 4: Endgame*: "when I drift off, I will dream about you, always you."[7] Stark's heartfelt sentiment is a modern mirror for the epic hero Odysseus, who after many failed romances realizes that his one true love is Penelope.[8] Odysseus pines for his soul mate in Book 5 of his eponymous epic. Calypso cannot seem to understand why: "that bride for whom you pine each day, surely she is not greater than I in form or stature."[9] To this Odysseus replies that while true his wife is less than immortal, he nevertheless longs for home.

Bold, brilliant, and beautiful, Odysseus' wife Penelope is in many ways just as exceedingly cunning as her husband.[10] Penelope is a strategist in her own sphere, wittingly conceiving the idea of allaying the advances of her suitors by weaving a shroud for Laertes, Odysseus's father. During the day she plies the loom, weaving her father-in-law's final garment, but by night she unweaves all of her hard work. The soul of Amphimedon claims that he was undone by her guile.

Call to Action, Wisdom Gained and the Return Home

The hero's call to adventure, which whisks him far away from his home, is a recurring trope not only to epic, but to tales of modern superheroes as well. In the film *Avengers: Infinity War*, New York is attacked by the henchmen of Thanos, Maw and Obsidian, who are sent to retrieve the time stone. Bruce Banner warns Stark that Thanos and the war are coming. They need to call Steve Rogers to help reorganize the Avengers. Despite their recent estrangement, Stark reluctantly agrees. Fate, however, intervenes. Hitching a ride aboard the enemy's ship, Stark is whisked away from earth to the planet Titan. His call to adventure mirrors many elements we find in Odysseus' departure for Troy. A war is inevitable; Odysseus knew it from the start as one of the participants in the Oath of Tyndareus. Bound by duty, he leaves his home and his beloved Penelope to fight a war in which he does not wish to participate. Similarly, to save the Earth and Pepper, Iron Man begrudgingly stows away aboard on a ship bound for the distant world of Titan, to fight a war he doesn't necessarily want to fight. Again, duty as an Avenger and as a warrior requires him to do so.

This call-to-adventure theme is replayed in *Avengers: Endgame*. After Thanos harvests the Infinity stones and wipes out half of the universe, Ant-Man, Captain America, and Black Widow devise a plan to travel back in time to change events and approach Stark for help. Stark, who has now married Pepper and fathered a daughter named Morgan, is resistant, however, a picture of the now disintegrated Peter Parker causes him to reconsider.[11] Reluctantly, he joins them on their quest, eventually traveling back in time and reuniting with his father, Howard. Howard, however, is unaware of his son's identity, since Tony assumes the alias Howard Potts as they carry on a conversation about life. This scene in particular recalls the meeting of Laertes and his son Odysseus, after the hero returns home.[12] Odysseus does not initially reveal himself. When Laertes begins to weep over the memory of his son, however, Odysseus finally reveals himself to his father and embraces him. In both cases, father and son are reconciled, although in the case of Stark, Tony never reveals his true identity, leaving it to his father to figure out. Clearly, Odysseus pities his father. He reveals himself, because he cannot bear to torment him. Stark, in contrast, is only looking to provide *himself* with closure.

One of the most recognizable father son relationships is that of Odysseus and his own son, Telemachus. With a father absent for nearly 20 years, Telemachus only knows of Odysseus through song. Striking out on his own, the young hero later discovers bits and pieces of what may have happened to him from his fellow soldier and king of Sparta Menelaus. When Odysseus finally returns, he is disguised as a stranger, laying low at the hut of his loyal servant Eumaeus. When they are alone, and Athena has lifted his disguise, Odysseus reveals his true identity to his son. The two embrace and begin devising a plan to recapture the palace. Their relationship is hardly unique in the Greek world. Sons frequently stayed at home while their fathers marched off to war. Telemachus is looking for a father figure, and Odysseus wishes to pass down his legacy, thus their reconciliation is a vital part of the fulfillment of Odysseus' quest. Odysseus has made it home, and his glorious exploits at Troy will always be remembered, so long as the suitors are removed. Their mere presence is a constant threat to Telemachus' birth-right, not to mention Odysseus' own *kleos*.

The father son relationship is also a governing theme in the MCU as well, and demonstrated in the relationship between Iron Man and everyone's favorite neighborhood web-slinger, Spider-Man, aka Peter Parker. On screen, they form a similar father-son duo, albeit by choice rather than blood. Stark plays the mentor and adoptive father to Parker, who lost his Uncle Ben *and* both of his parents. In the Marvel comic tradition, their relationship is strained at best, but in the MCU they are BFFs, two brilliant minds, but more like father and son.[13] In the film *Captain America: Civil War*, Stark, impressed by the young boy's tenacity, helps Parker become the hero he most wants to be by supplying him with his hero's mantle, a new spidey suit, and recruits him in aiding the Avengers. Likewise, Odysseus helps Telemachus in earning his heroic mantle, when he recruits him in the battle against the suitors. In *Spider-Man: Homecoming* Stark takes back the suit, briefly, when he thinks Parker has acted irresponsibly. Parker claims that he is nothing without his suit, to which Stark replies, "If you are nothing without the suit, then you shouldn't have it." Here again is another example of Stark's transformation, realizing that the suit really does not make the hero, but rather the actual man behind the mask and under the armor. In *Endgame*, when Stark travels back in time and finds Parker still alive, he embraces him as a son. Although Morgan Stark is Iron Man's daughter by blood, Stark sees Parker as the son he never had, largely because he notes a bit of himself in the precocious but big-hearted youth.

Parker, in many ways, will pick up the mantle of Iron Man after his death. In *Spider-Man: Far from Home*, S.H.I.E.L.D. commander Nick Fury bequeaths Stark's iconic glasses to Parker, which grants the boy access to the databases and the weapons stockpile of Stark Industries. Parker is still reeling from the death of his adoptive father, but he eventually heeds the hero's call. He uses Stark resources to construct himself a new suit and takes on the villain Mysterio. In this sense, he has literally accepted the mantle of his adoptive father, to continue the fight to protect Earth.

Conclusion

The story of Iron Man, like that of Odysseus, is the story of the gifted quick-witted strategist, who can think his way out of almost any situation. Other striking similarities exist. Both are non-soldiers, who begrudgingly head off to war. Both are also catapulted to the other side of the universe and must go through many trials on their way home to a loyal and crafty lover, but there are arrant differences as well. Odysseus, for example, never makes the sacrifice play. We watch him struggle, womanize, and mourn, but does he ever really change who he is? Ultimately, the journey of the hero should be a transformative one. Tony Stark, on the other hand, while starting off as an Odysseus-like figure, changes from a rebellious young man into a hero that has the courage to admit his mistakes, and to put his own life on the line for the sake of the greater good. In both the *Iliad* and *Odyssey*, we encounter epic heroes, like Achilles or Agamemnon, who act solely for their own benefit. So, while traditionally we tend to call these men heroes, they often act shockingly un-heroically. Their actions often lead to the suffering of others. Odysseus adopts a similar cavalier attitude, for he is willing to sacrifice some of his men to Scylla and Charybdis in order to find his way home across the Straits of Messina. Despite being transformed by his journey, one wonders, does Odysseus ever truly act heroic? He is cunning and brave to be sure, but does he fit the definition of an epic hero like Diomedes?

Iron Man conforms to the modern heroic paradigm. When confronted with the deaths of thousands of Sokovians, whom he endangered because of his egotistic quest to create Ultron, Stark must ultimately atone for his actions. In so doing, he begins to surrender some of that personal ego for the sake of the greater good. Transforming from the rebellious, self-centered youth, Tony becomes a more contemplative father figure. But does he really take the blame, or does he ascribe it to the whole team? For example, he goes so far as to guilt his fellow Avengers into signing the accords. Of course, this move is met with resistance from Captain America, who confronts Stark about keeping secrets and lying to the team. With the aid of Banner, Stark creates Ultron using stolen technology he could barely understand and gave birth to a monster. Then, he does it again in creating Vision.

In the end, however, it all comes down to moral versus intellectual virtue. Iron Man does become the hero he most wants to be, when he places his iron heart ahead of his iron head. After the events of the Infinity War, Stark returns home to start his life anew with Pepper and becomes a father. In so doing, he feels not only a personal connection with his daughter, but with his adoptive son, Peter Parker who acts like Telemachus calling Odysseus to continue his quest. Unable to accept the death of Peter, Stark reluctantly joins the Avengers in their second attempt to defeat Thanos, but recognizes that to become that hero, he must finally make the ultimate sacrifice. For Iron Man, it was not necessarily about the return home, and the solidification of glory we find commonly associated with the Greek epic hero. It is about fighting the good fight. In the end, Iron Man is a soldier, but a soldier with heart. He is willing to do whatever it takes to rescue his fallen comrades, proving that he and Captain America, though separated by a generation, fundamentally hold similar beliefs. Finally, like all heroes, Iron Man, the man who managed to always think his way out of a situation, must eventually face his own destiny and a threat he cannot overcome, except by means of sacrificing his own life.

IV

Unstoppable Rage

The Incredible Hulk and the Greek Berserker

> μῆνιν ἄειδε θεὰ Πηληϊάδεω Ἀχιλῆος,
> Sing, O Goddess, the rage of Achilles, Peleus' son
> —Homer, *Iliad* 1.1

Rage … unstoppable, blinding rage. It is a theme that predominates Homer's tale. Driven mad by the death of his closest friend Patroclus, the hero Achilles becomes a one-man killing machine, but he is not alone. This same madness poisons the hearts and minds of many an epic hero. Diomedes, for example, unleashed a terrible onslaught that claimed the lives of countless Trojans, and nearly two immortals. Likewise, the greater Ajax is driven to slaughter a herd of livestock, which his rage-induced madness makes him see as his human enemies instead, eventually leading to the hero's *aidos*, or fear of disgrace, and subsequent suicide.

What all of these characters have in common is that they have been overcome by a specific strain of rage, but what is it exactly, and how does our modern view of battle rage differ from that of the ancient Greeks? Are we talking about a state of mind akin to the berserker, spurred by the actions of war? How does it manifest itself in each of these characters? What are the similarities in our modern heroes' rage, the differences? Finally, are Marvel's Hulk and Wolverine modern-day examples of this Homeric type of rage? The purpose of this chapter is to delve into the psyche of Homer in the hopes of defining what we mean when we speak of rage as it affects the heroic temperament, and also how our modern-day super heroes may also illustrate Homeric rage. What does this say about us as a society and how we deal with great big emotions like rage?

Fire and Fury

Long have scholars contemplated Homer's emphasis on the word μῆνις (mēnis), typically defined as "wrath" or "rage." Curiously, it is usually reserved for the anger of the gods, for example Apollo,[1] as well as anger of the spirits of dead heroes,[2] injured parents,[3] or the vengeful "temper" of a people.[4] In the case of the epic hero, it is more than simply blood lust. It is almost an instinctual response to the tragic loss of a comrade, a need to avenge. It becomes an all-consuming force that allows the epic hero to achieve unimaginable acts of violence. Violence, however, was a way of life in Homer's world, and death always but a moment away. What links many of these episodes of uncontrollable rage is, ironically, the heroic code.

Homer's warriors live by this code, a set of conditions that guides his life both on and off the battlefield, to know one's place, and to live up to the expectations of the community. His honor depends on it, and honor for the warrior, was everything. So too was heredity, which is why Achilles and Agamemnon are fated to clash. Fear of shame and dishonor is also omnipresent. For Ajax, as we will see, the stain of shame, or *aidos*, is enough to lead him to take his own life. In many instances, however, anger, like one's fate, is attributed to the supernatural, i.e., the gods. Thus, it is very easy for the epic hero to commit an act of violence and later claim the gods *made* him do it, thereby eschewing personal responsibility for the act.

Here is where ancient and modern comic book heroes differ. Modern heroes shoulder the responsibility for their actions. Bruce Wayne, for example, blames himself for the death of his parents, and he spends the rest of his life fighting crime. Spider-Man, likewise, after letting a criminal escape who later kills his uncle, devotes himself to foiling crooks and protecting the innocent, adopting the motto "with great power comes great responsibility." When Tony Stark realizes his work is killing innocent people, he takes responsibility and changes his focus from arms dealer to philanthropist. Scarlet Witch, in *Avengers: Civil War*, is so traumatized when she inadvertently causes the death of Wakandan relief workers in the battle in Lagos, she withdraws from ever wanting to fight again. The focus on community rather than the individual hero forces modern heroes to take personal responsibility. Additionally, we have shifted from religion to science, thereby removing the *numen*, or godly presence, from the equation.[5] The modern-day super hero must own his or her own mistakes and problems.

The Wrath of Achilles

Twisted by rage and emboldened by divine armor, the hero Achilles rolls across the battlefield like an iron tank, swiftly and mercilessly dispensing dreadful vengeance and bitter death. Overtaken by his grief for Patroclus, he declares that he has no interest in food or drink, only in the destruction, blood, and the agonizing screams of mangled men. In Book 21, he slaughters innumerable Trojans tossing their bodies unceremoniously into the River Scamander for the animals to consume, rather than honoring the proper burial rites.[6] Elsewhere, in Book 22, Achilles finally confronts Hector, his friend's executioner. In this explosive encounter, Hector, like a startled foal, bolts, leaving Achilles to chase him relentlessly around the walls of the city. On the run, Hector is approached by Athena in the borrowed guise of his brother Deiphobus. She convinces the Trojan prince to stand his ground, which he does. Finally, standing toe to toe with his mortal enemy, Hector entreats Achilles to honor the warrior's code. To this Achilles sharply responds:

> There are no oaths between lions and men, and wolves and lambs are never like-minded.... Now, you will pay dearly for all my grief and for the friends you have slaughtered when *raging* with your spear.[7]

What stands out most for readers is that Homer introduces us to two distinct words: μένος (*menos*) and θυμὸς (*thumos*), both divinely inspired and human rage.[8] Is Achilles' rage divine? It is if you recall that Athena whispers in Achilles' ear that they will kill Hector together. Sure enough, after this Homer employs the word *meneos* instead of *thuon* to describe his anger:

> Achilles charged toward him, terrible *rage* filling his heart.[9]

Thus, we may assume two things: (1) frenzied rage may be god-induced, inhuman, and (2) this type of rage is clearly different than mortal rage.[10] Anger allows Achilles to dehumanize his enemy on multiple levels. For example, he calls Hector a dog and goes so far as to threaten to cannibalize him:

> Would that in any way wrath and fury
> might incite me to carve your flesh and eat it raw...[11]

The chilling scene is reminiscent of the *Thebaid* and the story of the Seven Against Thebes. In it, the Aeolian hero Tydeus, in a fit of madness, gorges himself on the brains of his fallen foe Melanippus.[12] So offensive is the act, that the gods instantly withdraw their promise of immortality to the hero.

Shortly after, Achilles' rage reaches its apogee. Fully aware of the weak spots in his own armor, which Hector now wears, he aims for the neck and plunges his spear into Hector's throat. Paralyzed, the Trojan is pinned to the spot. Achilles taunts him still, promising that dogs and vultures will make a meal of him, while Patroclus is given a proper funeral. It is not so much the dehumanizing harangue, nor even the violent way in which he dispatches Hector, which exemplifies Achilles' rage. It is what happens afterwards. Stripping Hector of his armor, he mutilates him by piercing his ankles and ties his body to the back of his chariot. Celebrating his vengeance, he then parades the corpse before the walls of the city for all to see, rather than affording him a proper burial, thereby denigrating the sanctity of death. Gruesome to say the least, but more importantly this act illustrates that Achilles lets his anger get the better of him. Violence in war was expected, and death was always a moment away, but vendettas speak to the very nature of the Homeric hero.

Another incredible exhibition of rage appears in Quintus Smyrnaeus' *Posthomerica*. Here we learn the story of Memnon, who loses his dearest friend to Antilochus, and who in retribution kills him. Nestor, Antilochus' father, entreats Achilles to avenge his son, which he does. The point is that such anger leads to an escalating series of vendettas, which ultimately turn the tide of war. In the case of Achilles, Patroclus' sudden and shocking demise draws him back into the fray, resulting in the death of Hector and the subsequent turn in fortune for the Trojans. For Memnon, the death of Aesop does the same. It draws him into the battle, and the resulting conflict unfortunately leads to his own death, but causes his forces, touted as the salvation of Troy, to flee.

Works of art representing these epic duels often afford us a clearer notion of rage. An extraordinary volute krater at the British Museum from the fifth century BCE captures the momentous encounter of the two heroes Achilles and Hector. Poised and ready to grapple, they are accompanied by their respective patron gods, Athena and Apollo. On the left, Achilles, with his visor raised, has a look of solid determination, while Hector, doe-eyed, lowers his spear. Athena, resplendent in her high crest and frilled aegis, firmly goads Achilles on from behind, while Apollo, armed with bow and arrow, turns to walk away. Despite the gravity of the scene, there is hardly any emotion at all, owing perhaps to the traditional sense of heroic stoicism.

Some vase painters, however, began to explore a few of the more intense emotions of the myth in their work. An archaic black figure amphora attributed to the Exekias painter in the British Museum is a perfect example.[13] It shows the two helmeted figures grappling. The cold, piercing, hypnotic eyes of a masked Achilles bear down on the Amazon Queen as he runs her through with his spear. Contrastingly, the barbarian warrior, overcome by her emotion, crouches, her mask drawn back leaving her vulnerable. Most chilling of all is Achilles' eye. While we may attribute this

Red figure volute krater by the Berlin painter (490–460 BCE) depicting Achilles and Hector engaged in combat. Behind Achilles appears the goddess Athena, while behind Hector appears a fleeing Apollo. The reverse shows Achilles fighting the Ethiopian king Memnon, with each one's mother Thetis and Eos looking on. © The Trustees of the British Museum/Art Resource, NY (British Museum accession number: 1848,0801.1).

to artistic convention, and the large dilated eye simply a way of making it stand out in a sea of shadow behind the hero's mask, the overall effect makes his eye appear bigger, dilated, indicating perhaps a fight or flight response or even rage. The overall effect leads the viewer to associate it with the evil eye found on Greek ships, an apotropaic device, or a mark of berserker rage. Some would argue that Achilles stands as a symbol of the precocious youth, who throws a temper tantrum whenever he doesn't get what he wants. He is a hero in training, on the quest, but not fully tempered by the heat of battle. His wrath then, may also represent violent, adolescent rage. It is a double-edged sword, for the Greeks have at their disposal a powerful weapon in Achilles, but it is a weapon that is ultimately uncontrollable.

Diomedes: The Quintessential Badass

Although Achilles has tended to garner the lion's share of attention, several heroes throughout Homer's epic exhibit equally unbridled acts of rage. Among them is Diomedes. Wise in counsel, courageous and bold, for many Diomedes is the quintessential epic hero. Despite being the youngest of Agamemnon's generals, he is both accomplished in battle and a natural born leader, commanding a force of 80 ships to the shores of Troy. That is third only to wise old king Nestor and Agamemnon himself. What is more, he beats Telamonian Ajax in a personal battle, wins every contest at the funeral games for Patroclus, and kicked the ass of just about everyone he came in contact with including Ares, god of bloodlust. Favored by Athena, he is one of the few heroes to survive the Trojan War and return home, and, according to some versions, to become immortal.[14]

Ensconced in divine armor wrought in the fiery forges of the god Hephaestus, Diomedes is a thundering bulwark, abounding in incredible strength and endurance. His abilities also include stealth and guile. His name, "god-like cunning," pretty much says it all, for it is he and Odysseus who lead a clandestine foray into Troy to steal the Palladium, the sacred statue of Athena prophesized to keep Troy unassailable. This is hardly the last tribute to Diomedes' *aresteia*, or excellence, either. In fact, it is just the beginning.

In Book 5, after wracking up an impressive kill list that includes Astynous, Hyperion, Abas, Polyidus, Xanthus, Thoon, Echemmon, and Chromius, Diomedes is finally challenged by Aeneas and Pandarus. Wounded by Pandarus, his anger finally erupts. The hero prays to Athena for aid.[15] Hearing his prayers, the goddess bestows upon him superhuman strength.

> Take courage now Diomedes to make war against the Trojans, for in your breast have I instilled the might of your father, dauntless such as the horseman Tydeus, master of the shield once had. The fog also have I whisked from your eyes in order that you perceive both god and man.[16]

Athena warns him to attack only certain foes. He may attack the Trojans, even Aphrodite, but he is forbidden to engage any other gods, for to do so would nullify the enchantment placed upon him. Now engorged with three times the fury, τρὶς μένος (*tris menos*), Diomedes rejoins the fight. Homer likens him to a hungry and wounded lion, whose fight or flight responses have not only been awakened, but also magnified.

A raging tide, Diomedes storms across the battlefield impaling Pandarus with his spear. He then manages to immobilize Aeneas, breaking his hip with a well-hurled stone. When Aphrodite appears to rescue her son, Diomedes lashes out at the goddess, slicing her arm and sending her wailing toward Olympus. Apollo swoops in. Despite being blinded by the god, Diomedes continues to fight, until Apollo warns him not to match himself with the immortals. The hero, again respectful to the gods and the epic code, subsequently disengages. In due time, he encounters the warlike

Ares. At this point, Athena grants the hero a reprieve, helping him drive his spear into the god's belly, nearly killing him.[17]

So terrible is the carnage that in the beginning of Book 6, Hector's brother Helenus convinces him to return to the city to arrange a sacrifice to Athena in order to propitiate Diomedes' relentless rage:

> She may ward off from sacred Ilium the son of Tydeus, that savage warrior, a strong counselor in fear, who indeed appears to have become the mightiest of the Achaeans. Not even Achilles did we ever dread in this way, that leader of men, who, they say, is born of a goddess; no, beyond all measure this man rages, and no one equals him in might.[18]

Curiously, the verb Homer uses is *mainetai*, which means "to rage, as in war." We may consider this akin to the term battle rage. Other examples of the use of this verb suggest a definition more like "to make mad with frenzy."[19] The second meaning suggests a madness initiated by the gods. For it is only with the aid of Athena and under her orders that Diomedes is able to subdue Ares. The Trojans, however, cannot see Athena. She is disguised under the invisibility helmet of Hades. Diomedes, therefore, appears to them to be attacking with his own rage, unaided by any divinity or mortal. Nevertheless, we the reader can see that he is filled with *enthusiamos* of Athena, who drives his chariot and even guides his spear. In this sense, his rage is godlike, thus living up to his name.

Despite his incredible abilities on the battlefield, Diomedes earns our admiration for his incredible restraint and adherence to the Homeric warrior code. Just as he and Glaucus, for example are about to come to blows, the warriors have an exchange where they learn that their ancestors once shared a pact of *xenia*. Surprisingly, they resolve to honor that friendship by exchanging armor rather than fighting. In Book 9, when Agamemnon vows to leave Troy because Zeus has withdrawn his support, it is Diomedes who rebukes him, pointing out that such behavior is unbefitting of a king. Instead of disparaging his commander verbally, Diomedes nevertheless shames him by volunteering to stay behind to continue the fight, alone. Finally, later on when he has Hector on the run, Nestor convinces him to return to camp, despite appearing cowardly. Though he waivers, he eventually shows that good sense wins out over ego.

Perhaps the most interesting passage can be found in Book 4. Here, Agamemnon showers him with petty torments, calling him a mere shadow of his father. Diomedes, however, resists the urge to engage:

> Such a man was Tydeus of Aetolia; how is it the son that he sired is worse than he in battle, though in the place of gathering he is better.
>
> Thus, he [Agamemnon] spoke, and mighty Diomedes having regard for the rebuke of the king, uttered not a word.[20]

True courage is knowing when and when not to fight. Diomedes knows this. The last we see of Diomedes in Homer's epic is the contest with Ajax, where he draws first blood, but he chooses not to kill his opponent, again, demonstrating a true hero shows restraint. In the *Little Iliad*, when Odysseus attempts to literally stab Diomedes in the back for the Palladium, Diomedes does not seek similar deadly retribution, for he knows Odysseus still has a part to play in the outcome of the Trojan conflict. Again, he uses good judgment—the mark of the restrained hero—rather than anger. The only time we see Diomedes lose control is with the immortals, and that is because another immortal is goading him. Athena exerts her divine influence over the mortal in order to both incite and calm his madness.

The Greater Ajax

Without question, one of the most tragic characters in the Trojan cycle is Ajax the Greater. Strongest of the Achaeans by far, not even he is immune to the power of divine madness. In the *Posthomerica*, after rescuing the body of Achilles, he and Odysseus clash over the highly prized armor of Achilles. After losing the contest for the armor, Ajax, who had been previously unbeatable, now bears a mark of shame. Embittered, he subsequently plots to take out the leadership of the Greek army. Driven to madness by the goddess Athena, he slays a herd of livestock (depending on the source, either cattle or sheep) instead of men.[21] As Quintus Smyrnaeus recounts in his *Fall of Troy*:

> Thus, he crowed, thinking that amidst the slain Odysseus lay clotted with blood at his feet. But in that moment from his mind and eyes Athena tore away the nightmare-fiend of Madness havoc-breathing, and it passed thence swiftly to the rock-walled river Styx...[22]

Let us consider for a moment the noun Homer uses, μανία (*mania*). According to the *Liddell-Scott-Jones* (the standard lexicon for ancient Greek), it means "madness" or "mad passion." It can also mean "*ethusiamos*" or "inspired frenzy." Once again, this conception indicates a state of mind precipitated by the gods.

Further on, Ajax bemoans his plight, but uses a slightly different word, λύσσαν (*lussan*), again meaning "rage" or "fury." Autenrieth, however, defines this term specifically as the rage associated with war.

> He groaned in misery, and in anguish wailed: "Ah me! why do the Gods abhor me so? They have wrecked my mind, have filled it with foul madness, making me slaughter all these innocent sheep!"[23]

Curiously, Pseudo-Hyginus in his *Fabulae* notes that Ajax, who was harboring rage, slaughtered the flocks in madness. Slaughtering sheep does not earn one glory in battle. Thus, Ajax goes down not as a hero but as a stifled, tragic warrior. The biggest question for readers is whether Ajax's rage gave rise to his madness, or was it Athena who orchestrated both his rage and the subsequent madness.[24] It is difficult to tell. What is clear, however, is that Ajax is crushed by the great injustice that has befallen him. To have acted heroically throughout the war only to find oneself fortune's fool seems justifiably unfair.

But what is a hero to do? His choice is to either blame the gods, or to blame himself. To blame the gods, however, flies in the face of the hero's code. It is hardly surprising then that Homer, in the beginning of the *Odyssey*, has Zeus declare: "Mortal men are now quick to blame the gods. They say that we devise their misery, but they themselves in their arrogance, bear grief worse than that which Fate ordains."[25] Thus, faced with dishonor and no recourse, Ajax plants his sword—a symbol of his heroism and manhood—into the earth and throws himself atop it. It is a desperate, final attempt both to exert his agency and to demonstrate his adherence to the code. If he brings shame, *aidos*, to his family, he must atone for it. For the reader this may seem an extreme act, but for Ajax, as for any Homeric hero, one's honor was everything. In the end, Agamemnon denies Ajax a proper burial, because of his act of terrorism. This speaks more to Agamemnon's character than Ajax's, for to let one event color ten years of loyal work seems peevish and petty. It also reflects the prevailing attitudes in Homer's time and before of the need for one to receive proper burial and be honored by the living.

Odysseus

Surprisingly, one of the most chilling examples of rage isn't in the war epic of the *Iliad* at all but instead in Homer's *Odyssey*. After disguising himself as a beggar and sneaking back into his own palace, in Books 21–22, Odysseus coerces his son Telemachus into ambushing Penelope's suitors, whom he intends to destroy. What results is a total blood bath. After locking them in a room, Odysseus begins to string his bow, a bow everyone now knows only Odysseus can wield. Slowly the suitors begin to realize their folly. While some take arms, others plead for mercy, but none is given as the hall is filled with their anguished cries and swift, pitiless justice. Afterward, Odysseus orders Telemachus to summon Eurycleia in order to identify the maidens who had stayed loyal and those who had sided with the suitors. Those who had been disloyal, he hangs—every last one.[26] His violent retribution has no bounds. Only when the families of the suitors come forth and he begins to slaughter them too does Athena step in to quell his rage. We have seen how Odysseus, once lauded for his counsel, has become a maddened killer, leading us to consider whether Homer's tales glorify the hero or are to be read as cautionary tales about battle trauma and PTSD, specifically the inability of the soldier to ever return to everyday life.

How do these and other instances in Odysseus' story help us understand the nature of berserker rage and divine-inflicted madness? In the altercation with the suitors, Odysseus, whose home and personal honor both have been threatened, aims to purge his house of the scourge upon it. He purposefully locks himself in the room with the suitors, which eerily suggests that he has no doubt as to his ability to be the last man standing amongst them. Like Bruce Banner, he knows his rage is terrible. By locking himself away like a cornered animal, Odysseus keeps the suitors from escaping but undoubtedly also induces his own rage, for at this point it is kill or be killed.

Despite the pleas for mercy, Odysseus only allots death. Homer portrays him as breathing fury, *menos*.[27] Odysseus is described at this point as a lion, returning from feasting on a felled ox. Again, we have the dehumanizing aspect of the enemy as prey and an inhuman, animal-like hero, a portrait of rage. Odysseus claims that the men were destroyed by the fate of the gods and their own misdeeds rather than by him. Here, too, the Homeric hero is able to justify his rage, because the gods enforce *xenia*, which the suitors have ignored. The generalized code of honor amongst men and especially warriors has been broken, and all bets are off as far as honorable treatment of one another.

The Madness of Herakles

Undoubtedly the most famous illustration of divinely inspired rage may be found in the tales of the mighty and much-loved Theban hero Herakles. All brawn and little in the way of brains, when it comes to heroes, Herakles is easily recognizable by his iconic club and lion skin hat and cape—a trophy from his encounter with the Nemean lion, whom he strangled with his bare hands, and thus a symbol of his raw, brute strength. The illegitimate offspring of Zeus, he was for the Greeks the greatest hero to have ever lived, a slayer of monsters, an explorer, a warrior, but constantly living under the ever-looming shadow of the storm god's wickedly jealous wife, Hera. His name, Herakles, literally means the glory of Hera, a constant reminder of Zeus's endless line of paramours.

In the end, however, Herakles is also a tragic hero. Driven mad by Hera, he kills his wife and children and seeks redemption in the form of 12 impossible labors. In Euripides' play Ἡρακλῆς μαινόμενος (*Hēraklēs*

Mainomenos), alternatively, we find the hero racing back to Thebes after the completion of his Twelve Labors, to deliver his adopted father Amphitryon, wife Megara, and his sons from the evil machinations of King Lycus. Lycus, having usurped the throne from Creon plans to murder Megara, his daughter and her children, in order to officially place himself on the throne. Arriving just in time, Herakles slays Lycus.

Hera, ever resentful of Zeus' philandering and wanting to bring shame to his golden boy, takes advantage of the situation and dispatches her agent Iris to drive Herakles mad. Blinded by rage he storms through the palace searching for Eurystheus, the architect of his labors, and his sons, but murders his own wife Megara and his children, mistaking them for enemies. At the point of killing his own father, Amphitryon, whom he thinks is Eurystheus, Athena in true *deus ex machina* fashion descends from Olympus to intervene. Striking Herakles in the chest with a rock she knocks him out cold.[28] When Herakles finally awakens, he finds himself chained to a pillar, the broken bodies of his dear ones massed around him, and laments. Surprisingly, he does not blame the gods for his madness but rather himself.

Contrastingly, Theseus, here his loyal companion, argues that the gods *are* to blame, and offers him absolution from *miasma*, or blood pollution.[29] He also offers him a home, money, and honor after his death. Theseus places the value of friendship above blood pollution. Here it seems Euripides is arguing that the heroic ideal no longer fits within the context of modern Athenian democracy.[30] When Herakles finally confronts the shame, or rather *aidos*, of what he has done, it is too much to bear. He, like Ajax, has acted dishonorably, and thus longs for death via suicide.

But it's not like Herakles didn't already have a short fuse. Notoriously, in one legend, he is said to have murdered one of his tutors, the great Theban musician Linus. The story goes that Linus tried teaching the young hero how to play the lute. When he was unable, perhaps because his heart was not into it, he struck Herakles. Enraged, the demi-god killed his teacher with the lute.[31] Those familiar with Jason and his Argonauts recall that he also murders the Boreads, Calais and Zetes, after they encourage Jason to abandon him and carry on with their quest instead of waiting for him to return with Hylas. It would seem that because of his short-temperedness, Herakles is easily swayed by divine madness.

It's Not Easy Being Green—Tales of the Incredible Hulk

When we think of rage in modern comics, one superhero stands out above the rest: the mean, green, fighting machine known as the Incredible

Above and opposite: Interior panel from *The Incredible Hulk Comic* #2 presenting a yellow eyed and roaring Hulk as he reduces a bridge in the small town of Faulkner to toothpicks. © 2013 Marvel Characters, Inc.

Hulk. Whatever you do, do *not* make Hulk angry. A one-man wrecking ball, Hulk smashes everything is his path, leveling buildings, and sometimes taking out other heroes. Created by the late, great Stan Lee and Jack Kirby in 1962, the *Hulk* is the story of a brilliant but reserved physicist, Dr. Bruce Banner, who is overseeing the test of his new gamma bomb at a military base in New Mexico. During the test, a teenager, Rick Jones, drives onto the base on a dare. Racing onto the testing grounds, Banner manages to save Jones, pushing him into an open trench. Banner succumbs to a powerful blast of gamma radiation. His act of self-sacrifice, unfortunately, transforms him into a monster, dubbed "Hulk."[32] Only later is it revealed that Banner's transformation is triggered by adrenaline brought on by intense feelings of fear, pain, and oh yes, anger.

The story may seem a familiar one. That is largely because its creator, Stan Lee, admits he was inspired by such classic tales as Robert Louis Stevenson's *The Strange Case of Dr. Jekyll and Mr. Hyde* and Mary Shelley's *Frankenstein*.[33] In *Frankenstein*, a young doctor, Victor Frankenstein, driven mad with grief over the death of his mother, throws himself into his work. Though his intentions were good, he takes it upon himself to cross the lines of modern society. Using science he gives life to a creature that is ultimately uncontrollable. Victor and the monster are separate, alter egos, but ultimately intrinsically locked in an eternal battle with one another. In Stevenson's novella, Dr. Jekyll is working on a serum that will allow him to repress his evil urges, but he accidentally releases the monster within instead of quelling it. Is it a man in the body of a monster, or a monster in the body of a man? The schism between man and beast is not so clear. The same is true of the Hulk.

In all of these stories, the scientist who is seeking knowledge and motivated by a sense of altruism somehow misunderstands the nature of his own experiments and the limitations of the human mind to perceive Nature in all its beautiful chaos. They are all driven mad, triggered by intense feelings, stress and emotion, crossing the line of what is socially acceptable, just like the epic heroes Achilles, Tydeus, and Ajax—characters we may call the berserker, men driven to mad frenzy by war. Contrastingly, the Hulk's rage is not brought on by war but rather by anger itself. It is that same anger that feeds his strength. One of Hulk's famous lines is "The angrier I get, the stronger I get!"[34] His rage is not divinely inspired, but it is not strictly natural either. The gamma ray energy Banner is exposed to is far beyond what we humans typically encounter in our daily lives. It is an extraordinary event, much like the interference of the immortals in the battles at Troy. In the end, the gamma bomb, which proved unpredictable, is a metaphor for the Hulk's transformation and rage, which is equally unpredictable.

Why do we find the Hulk's story so compelling? He is not by any means a traditional heroic figure. He doesn't wear a cape, and his heroic actions ultimately cause more harm than good. He is wholly unpredictable, which generally makes him a threat. Perhaps it is tragic irony. Banner never wanted to become the Hulk. He was a scientist, albeit conceited, but who, by and large, just wanted to do good, and at times, the Hulk wishes to be left alone, because he knows he cannot control his rage. The idea of uncontrollable rage is particularly appealing to adolescent boys, who, on the verge of manhood are learning to cope with more adult feelings, which leaves them vulnerable. The monster is visible and vulnerable. Young readers know that they have a friend and surrogate in the Hulk, for he can act out the rage they feel. They also have a model of what *not* to do, for the Hulk's ruinous rampages often outweigh the intended good. The Hulk is a sledge-hammer, when sometimes what is needed is a scalpel. Ultimately, the story of the Hulk is tragic rather than heroic. Even if his initial action of saving young Rick Jones was heroic, he cannot control the rage resulting from his experiments, from his manipulation of natural forces. He is thus punished for his *hubris*.

If wrath is sparked by the gods, then like the Hulk, epic heroes have no control over their anger. They can, therefore, blame the gods for stepping beyond the heroic code. Like the Hulk, none of our epic heroes necessarily wanted to lose themselves to rage, but found themselves caught up in the tangled web of the Fates. At many points in the Trojan epic cycle, Zeus imbues champions on the battlefield with god-like strength in order to fight like immortals, for example, Achilles and Memnon. Likewise, the Hulk's strength has no limits, and what is worse, the angrier he gets, the stronger he becomes.

The Hulk's telltale inhuman green skin and tearing out of his clothes highlights his break from the civilized world. In the Avengers films, the only thing that seems to quiet his anger is human touch from Black Widow. Like Athena to Achilles, Odysseus, and Diomedes, this beautiful but capable warrior can control the savage warlike beast ... or at least help him exert control over himself once again. Over time, the Hulk develops multiple personalities such as Savage Hulk, Gray Hulk, and Devil, some of which break off to become different facets of the single mind of Bruce Banner. It is the slow dismantling of the heroic figure, fractured in a sense by his surrounding society. In a similar way, Achilles, overtaken by his anger, breaks with the civilized world. He breaks with the warrior code by defiling Hector and refusing him the proper burial, and instead follows his own brand of justice.

One of the most persistent questions fans have is, does Bruce Banner retain the memories of what he does as the Hulk? Does he even remember his actions or their aftermath after his rage? This largely depends on the writer. Many times, Banner does not remember but awakens from his rage, clothes torn, disoriented and confused. In Marvel's *Tales to Astonish* Vol. 1 #66, Banner, who finds himself under attack in the ruins of a building, stumbles upon the body of a scientist, who sacrificed his life for the Hulk. It is only after discovering the body he suddenly remembers what happened. It is then, enraged, he becomes the Hulk once more. In *Tales to Astonish* Vol. 1 #68 "Back from the Dead," after he and Major Talbot escape Mongolian bandits, the Hulk seems to forget about Talbot, a long-time antagonist, and leaves him behind. In the film *Avengers*, during the battle of the helicarrier, Hulk falls asleep and wakes up in the rubble of a warehouse with no real memory of what happened. A security guard informs him that he probably used the building to shield others from his fall. In *Thor Ragnarök* the god of thunder encounters the Hulk on the distant world of Sakkar where the giant green beast has been living as a celebrity gladiator. During this time he has no idea how he arrived there, or what happened to the city of Sokovia. Memory loss, strangely enough, is one of the predominant signs of PTSD.[35]

Similarly, in Sophocles' *Ajax*, Tecmessa, the title character's war bride relates that after Ajax slaughters the sheep, he does not recall what he has done. When he returns to sanity, he commands her to reveal to him all that happened. Ajax is driven mad by Athena. His mind is overtaken by the gods. With the Hulk, however, one wonders whether we are dealing with an entirely different person, or simply Banner's Id, a splinter of himself. Banner describes the schism as if a car with two drivers at the wheel. Sometimes one overtakes the other. The fact that both Banner and the Hulk do sometimes remember the actions of their co-pilot suggests that both are present, but that one can overpower the other.

Wolverine

A brooding antihero with retractable claws and animal-like instincts, the character Wolverine is well known to Marvel fans. A founding member of the X-Men, Wolverine, aka James Howlett, is a man who often resorts to deadly force to subdue his enemies and is disposed to bouts of berserker-like rage, which are difficult to control. It seems only appropriate that his debut in the 1970s would be in *The Incredible Hulk*.[36] Wolverine's origin story is fraught with tragedy. Born in Canada, James witnesses the murder of his father at the hands of the family groundskeeper, Thomas Logan. It is this traumatic event that triggers James' powers. He grows a pair of sharp bone claws, which he uses to exact his revenge. Adopting the name Logan, he and his childhood companion Rose flee. In time, these same claws, however, tragically claim her life as well. Writers have even tied his rage to his claws, at one point creating "hot claws."

Wolverine's long-time nemesis is an equally vicious killer named Sabretooth, who often has been said to be Wolverine's father, although other writers hold it to be the villainous groundskeeper, Thomas Logan. Like Wolverine, he too has razor-sharp claws, great healing powers, and is prone to berserker-like rage. Every year, Sabretooth manages to track down Wolverine for an epic battle that brings either one or both of them to the point of death. While Sabretooth is treated as a cold-blooded killer, Wolverine always harbors feelings of guilt. His ability is both a blessing and a curse, for often when Wolverine acts out of self-preservation, innocent bystanders wind up on the slab.

Wolverine represents an amalgamation of different epic warriors. Like Achilles, he is often rebellious and a loner, but he adheres to a strict code of conduct like Diomedes. His failed romances and endless wanderings also tend to remind us of Odysseus. At one point he is even trapped by the group known as the Red Right Hand who, binding him in a magical circle, send him to the Underworld where he faces friend and foe alike. In the end, Logan is a reluctant and tragic hero, forced into service by the murder of his father.

Master of the Battle Cry

Chilling and raw, the fields of battle are often haunted by the terrible din of the war cry. Frequently a precursor to rage, the war cry serves to stir the emotions, to reach a state of frenzy. It is a common device found in both comic books and epic traditions. Before catapulting himself into battle, for example, the Hulk sends his enemies fleeing with a terrible, inhuman-like roar. In an extraordinary moment in the *Iliad*, after learning of Patroclus' death, Achilles, overtaken with grief, mars his face, tears his hair, and rends the air with a cry so powerful it summons his mother and her entourage of nymphs.[37] Later, after Iris' counseling, Achilles appears on the battlefield and screams so loudly that it sows great confusion among the Trojans and causes their horses to cower. Other Homeric heroes also bear the gift of the war cry. Menelaus and Odysseus, for example, can utter a shrill shout, while one of Diomedes' epithets is "Diomedes of the loud war cry."[38] Even Aeneas has his moment, shrieking with a terrible war cry when he gets caught up in the frenzy of battle.[39] Anchises' son, however, is neither in pain nor mourning. He uses the tactic to scare off those desiring to claim his hard-won booty.

The battle cry not only fills the enemy with a deep sense of dread, but it also empowers the hero with *thumos*, an ineffable spirit, that stirs and enlivens him to battle. At one point, Diomedes exclaims that Achilles will return to "the fight" when the *thumos* in his chest bids him and a god stirs him.[40] Here, it seems, we have a clear dichotomy of self-motivation versus divinely inspired motivation. The *thumos* may be sparked by the war-cry, by pain, grief, or anger, but it still seems to require an additional outside catalyst, namely a divine agent, to control it.

Often incited by attack, Wolverine's rage has been likened to the fury of Viking warriors or *Úlfhéðna*.[41] These warriors would don the skins of wild animals and enter into a trance-like state, making them impervious to wounds and seemingly invincible. For evidence, we often flee to the thirteenth century Icelandic text of the poet Snorri Sturluson who wrote that Odin's men bite down on their shields and howl, turning color, and engaging just about anyone in battle.[42] What causes these states is often a topic for debate: hallucinogenic plants, adrenaline responses incurred by the threat of imminent death, fight or flight. Who can forget the 2017 film *Logan*, when after being attacked, Wolverine takes down several armed foes, letting loose an animal-like scream?

While Homeric heroes only exhibit some of these traits, Jonathan Shay has made the very excellent link between the concept of berserkers and PTSD: "if a soldier survives the berserk state, it imparts emotional deadness and vulnerability to explosive rage to his psychology and permanent hyperarousal to his physiology—hallmarks of post-traumatic stress disorder in combat veterans."[43] This is clearly the case with Achilles, who, in Books 21 and 22, refuses any Trojan he slaughters proper burial rites.

Conclusion

Rage, in Homeric epic, is not necessarily blood lust, but a combination of stirred *thumos* and divinely inspired madness that transforms the hero. While it may be brought on by feelings of loss and anger, it can only be controlled by outside forces. There is a certain degree of ambiguity then among the ancient Greek poets and playwrights, for while the responsibility resided with the individual, authors such as Homer and Euripides clearly showed that the gods were ultimately to blame. The Homeric hero has but two choices: to accept the responsibility for his own actions or to blame the gods. Because blaming the gods does not fit within the parameters of the warrior code, the only option left for the epic hero is ultimately to blame himself. What links many of these moments is the loss of self-control, which allows the gods to take over. Similarly, feelings of pain and anger ultimately incur the Hulk's wrath. Occasionally, the only force of reason that can quell the rage, the *deus ex machina,* is in fact a *dea*—a woman, i.e., Black Widow or the goddess Athena.

On the field of war, when heroic conventions are ignored, rage is common. Achilles' rage may be the result of PTSD and actually acts as a safety valve for his fragile and grieving psyche, allowing him to come to terms with his friend's death. This grief-rage dichotomy isn't just present in Homer but also appears in later epic traditions as well, for example Vergil's *Aeneid*. While *menis* lacks a direct cognate in Latin, Vergil still manages to capture the Homeric essence of divine madness in Book 7. When the Fury Allecto, an agent of divine Juno, is unable to rouse the heart of the villain Turnus from his slumber, she drives a smoldering firebrand into his heart. Afterwards he awakens emboldened: *saevit amor ferri et scelerata insania belli, / ira super…*, that is, "the love of battle and vicious madness of war raged (in him) with anger above all else."[44]

The poet could have employed a number of different verbs, for example *irascor*, "to become angry." Instead, he chooses *saevio*, "to be fierce, to rage," because it is a rage also associated with animals. In a standard tripartite view of the world, this action places Turnus below gods and even men. This recalls scenes from Homer, such as when Achilles claims he will eat Hector, like a dog. A few lines later, Vergil compares his rage to a cauldron boiling, *furit*. Likewise in Book 12, Turnus begs his sister Juturna to allow him to rage, or else he will go mad.[45] In this, Vergil depersonalizes the rage, making it appear as though its own entity, having invaded Turnus, and he wishes to exorcize it before it drives him mad.

The question for us, as it was for the ancient Greeks, is whether rage is inherent in the epic hero, or is it brought on by outside forces. The Hulk keeps with this tradition. While Bruce Banner appears a mild-mannered scientist, his alter ego, the Hulk, is freed by a loosening of natural forces. Banner's act of saving a young boy was a heroic and instinctual response. Moreover, instinct is given power by the gamma radiation. It makes the Hulk unstoppable but also uncontrollable, and thus he becomes a tragic figure for audiences. Ultimately, only the gods, or in the Hulk's case the human hand of friendship, can calm the storm and stay the hand of the berserker.

V

The Heart of the African Warrior

Memnon and Black Panther

I must admit, my glowing friend, that I do prefer the company of lions and leopards! They're much more trustworthy than the predators one finds in so-called civilization![1]

Perched high above the jungle canopy, with ghostly glowing eyes and razor-like claws—Wakanda's crown prince, T'Challa, perhaps known better by his ceremonial title Black Panther, wages a tireless campaign, fiercely guarding his kingdom from the threat of ruthless mercenaries. When the character of Black Panther premiered in 1966, he was the first African superhero ever to star in in a mainstream comic.[2] Although originally only appearing in cameos, he earned his first feature run in *Jungle Action* #5. Hailing from the kingdom of Wakanda, a fiercely independent and yet uncolonized African nation, Black Panther possesses superior human abilities, excellent combat skills, and a vibranium weave suit that is literally out of this world. Yet, his journey—to live up to the ideal of his father and to ultimately discover himself—is the adventure of Everyman. Surprisingly, his story and abilities are also reminiscent of another famous African hero, Memnon, the ancient King of the Ethiopians.[3]

Of all of Achilles' foes, none were more a match in skill and fearlessness than brazen-crested Memnon. While only briefly mentioned in the *Odyssey*, the purported son of Eos was a much-celebrated figure throughout antiquity,[4] appearing in the lost seventh century BCE epic *Aethiopis*, attributed to Arctinus of Miletus, a student of Homer.[5] He also appears in Quintus of Smyrna's riveting *Posthomerica* and Philostratus' *Imagines*, depicted as the savior of Troy in their most dire time of need.[6] In antiquity, Memnon was not only the quintessential *African* warrior, but also the quintessential *epic* warrior, at least according to the Greeks. Though centuries have passed since Homer's tales, Memnon's importance to modern audiences cannot be stressed enough, especially when discussing the heroic paradigm in modern African American comics, film, and literature.

The aim of this chapter is to analyze the figure of Wakanda's crown prince, Black Panther, and to compare him to the epic figure of Memnon in order to incite a discussion on race, power, and national identity in the modern versus ancient world.

Stormy-Hearted Memnon

Africa has not only produced some of the world's most powerful warriors, but also great kings and queens who have left an indelible mark on human history, from Hatshepsut to Queen Amina, Ewuare to Shaka Zulu. This long-standing tradition of the battle-hardened African warrior even appears in Greek epic, embodied in the hero of Memnon. While those familiar with the *Iliad* will certainly have heard of Achilles, few actually know the story of Memnon. That is because he only receives a passing mention in Homer's account, but his is a tale well worth telling. A fuller account of the hero appears in the work of the ancient author Dictys Cretensis, who writes that the great warrior king arrived at the gates of Troy with an army of thousands, and that the advent of his sizeable cohort surpassed the hopes and dreams of King Priam. After his arrival, Priam

Achilles and Memnon appear on the belly of an Attic black-figure amphora dating from 530–520 BCE. The Metropolitan Museum of Art, New York; Purchase: Rogers Fund, 1921; accession number 21.88.76.

throws a massive banquet in his honor.[7] There, the two kings regale each other with tales of their campaigns. Memnon, however, remains humble in terms of his own accomplishments. "It does not seem good to boast prodigiously at the feast nor does it seem good to grant a promise, but instead relax at the dinner table in the great hall and devise suitable things…."[8]

On the following day, destiny takes hold, and Nestor's son Antilochos kills a close companion of Memnon's. Deeply pained, and mirroring Achilles's rage over Patroclus, Memnon avenges his friend by killing Antilochos. Nestor, stricken with grief, challenges Memnon. The king, however, out of respect refuses to fight the old man. Nestor then begs Achilles to avenge his son. Protected by armor crafted by Hephaestus and granted extraordinary godlike powers by Zeus, the two warriors clash. Fearless, Memnon taunts Achilles in the ancient equivalent of a game of dozens:

> Of birth divine am I, Eos' mighty son, nurtured afar by the lily-slender Hesperides, beside the River Okeanos. Not from you nor from dire battle, therefore, do I cower, knowing full well how far my goddess-mother transcends a Nereid, whose child you boast yourself to be. To Gods and men my mother brings light; on her depends the issue of all things, works mighty and glorious in Olympus made by which comes blessing unto men. But—thine—she sits in barren crypts of brine.[9]

Despite his boasts, Memnon loses the upper hand. Lifting his spear Achilles plunges it into the heart of his mortal foe. Blood gushing in sheets, the once proud and mighty Ethiopian warrior topples, his armor rattling in the dust, the earth wet with hot blood, and the tears of Dawn.

Memnon's appearance, however brief, completes a trope of the thrice delivered hero—Achilles faces Hector, leader of the far eastern Trojans, Penthesilea queen of the Amazons, and Memnon King of the distant Ethiopians—all representations of the Greek "Other"—to become the champion of the Achaeans and the ultimate warrior. Where value is measured on the battlefield, in the world of the hero, besting a well-matched opponent is everything.

For years, scholars have fiercely debated Memnon's origins. Some have suggested Ethiopia. Others contend he was Egyptian or even of Near Eastern descent.[10] Ironically, though traditionally viewed as an Ethiopian king, his journey to Troy does take him to Egypt then onto Susa, conquering both along the way. When he arrives at Priam's palace, he is said to have an army of thousands, composed of Ethiopians and Indians. While we can imagine a force of Ethiopians, Egyptians, and Sussans, a contingent of Indians seems a bit far afield … or is it?

In his *Imagines*, Philostratus describes Memnon as arrayed in the skin of a lion, and brandishing a spear.[11] Herodotus claims that the Ethiopians were noted for their spears and wearing leopard and lion skins.[12] Egyptian

The interior of an Attic red-figure kylix dating from 5th–4th c. BCE and attributed to the Douris painter captures the moment of tragic intensity when winged Eos, Dawn, gathers the body of her dead son Memnon. Louvre, inventory number: G115; Photo credit: Herve Lewandowski; © RMN-Grand Palais/Art Resource, N.Y.

priests were also known to have dressed in leopard skins, for example a lead figurine from the Kushite period at the Metropolitan Museum of Art.[13] A tomb painting of King Ay performing the opening of the mouth ceremony on the late Tutankhamen is likewise shown wearing a leopard skin.[14] Such skins, sent from Nubia as tribute, were highly prized for their rarity, and come to be associated with kingship, the priestly class, triumph over nature, and in some instances, even death. The panther or leopard, however, is also associated with the east, especially India and Dionysus. It is therefore possible that Greek writers are simply expressing that Memnon's armies come from vast unknown parts of the world: the far east and south.

Readers cannot help but note a number of striking parallels between Memnon and Achilles. Offspring of gods and semi-divine mothers, both warriors have divinity in their blood. Both are beautiful, lose their dearest companions, and leap into battle like a "lion."[15] Although only a metaphor, the lion nevertheless suggests a hunter, king of the beasts, and protector of

A leaded bronze figurine dating to the Third Intermediate Period–Saite Period (ca. 712–650 BC) from Egypt shows a Kushite priest wearing leopard skin, which can be noted crossing his chest and atop one of his shoulders. The Metropolitan Museum of Art, New York; Purchase: Edward S. Harkness Gift, 1926; accession number 26.7.1415.

the pride. For modern audiences, the lion can also be an apt metaphor for Black Panther. There are a number of notable differences as well. Memnon, already battle hardened, came to Troy to honor ties of *xenia*. Contrastingly, Achilles came looking for personal glory. Achilles serves a king, while Memnon is both warrior and king. This places them both within a certain warrior class, but also separates them in terms of social class; Memnon "outranks" Achilles in both cases.

Black Panther

Fans of the *Black Panther* comics and recent film will undoubtedly recognize a vague echo of Memnon in Wakanda's crown prince, T'Challa, especially in the epic battle between him and Captain America in the film *Avengers: Civil War*. When the two warriors clash over the Winter Soldier, Bucky Barnes, T'Challa scores Cap's indelible shield with his claws. This is because Black Panther's suit and claws and Cap's shield are both composed of vibranium, which comes from a meteorite. Like Achilles and Memnon, whose armor is forged by Hephaestus, Cap's shield and Black Panther's armor are evenly matched and likewise beyond this world.

Yet Black Panther doesn't just have divinely inspired armor like some of our Homeric heroes; he also has divine aid. Like Achilles or Memnon, whose divine mothers either help them directly or act as agents or intercessors with more powerful gods on their sons' behalf, Black Panther also has a goddess who looks out for him. In the comic, Wakanda's patron is Bast, derived from the Egyptian goddess Bastet, who takes the form of a cat or panther and also is known for acting as a guardian for the pharaoh. In the *Black Panther* film, T'Chaka informs his son T'Challa that when the meteorite struck Wakanda, a shaman received a

An interior panel from *Fantastic Four Annual* #5 (1963) depicts Black Panther as a peaceful but cautious protector. © 2016 Marvel Characters, Inc.

vision from the panther goddess Bast. We also see various Wakandans greeting each other with the phrase "Glory to Bast!" Bast makes a brief appearance in the film as a spirit guide, or psychopomp, a giant black panther who leads a warrior shaman Bashenga to the heart-shaped herb.[16] She also appears in the comic book tradition providing divine aid to T'Challa against the demon Mephisto.[17] Divine aid is a part of the Homeric and the comic book hero's make-up; you could say it's in their DNA.

Curiously, divine aid isn't manifested in the goddess herself; sometimes it appears as an instrument provided by the god/dess at just the right moment. Ah yes, here I allude to the heart-shaped herb, the source of Black Panther's powers, an herb which was revealed to the first shaman by the god Bastet, and grows only in Wakanda.[18] When consumed it enhances one's speed, agility, strength, vision, healing, and endurance. It also holds the power of self-regeneration.

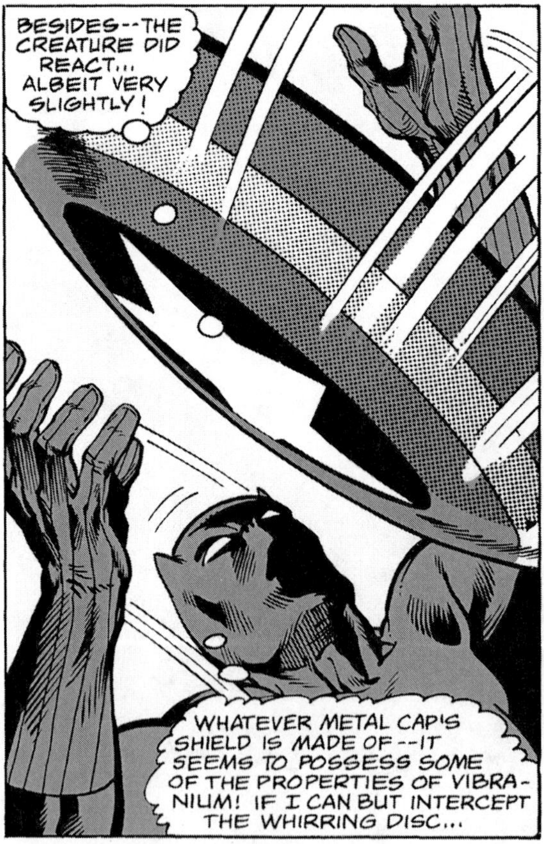

***Black Panther* # 15 (1977–1979) interior panel showing Black Panther seizing Captain America's shield. © 2016 Marvel Characters, Inc.**

Powerful herbs that grant heroes seemingly superhuman abilities also appear in Greek epic. In Book 10 of Homer's *Odyssey*, after Circe transforms and incarcerates Odysseus's men, Hermes, the winged messenger of the gods and patron of travelers, liars, and thieves, pays a visit to the son of Laertes. He forewarns him of Circe's power and recommends he ingest a magical herb, μῶλυ (*moly*), which will protect him against her enchantments.[19]

She will mix you a potion, and throw drugs into the

> food; but even so she shall not be able to enchant you, for the potent herb that I shall give you will not suffer it.[20]

The moly works, granting Odysseus the power to counteract the witch's spell. Other myths, such as that of Glaucus, mention herbs that arouse divine madness. These ultimately lead to metamorphoses and immortality.[21] Like the ancestral plane T'Challa visits after consuming the herb, Odysseus also connects with his ancestors in the Underworld after consuming the moly. All Hermes says is that the moly will protect him against Circe's enchantments, but it also could have protected him against other evils in the underworld. Odysseus, like T'Challa, emerges from the Underworld reborn, with new knowledge.

In the film, T'Challa consumes a rare mix of the herb. He then is buried alive. Afterwards, he enters a vision quest, where he gains insight from the heavenly realm. Therefore, when he finally emerges from his death-like state, he is not only physically renewed and enhanced, he also possesses divine knowledge. Comparisons may be drawn with the Sumerian king Gilgamesh, who embarks on a quest for a flower that will grant immortality. In the *Odyssey*, the hero Odysseus disappears from the civilized world and takes up residence, buried in a womb-like cave, on the island of Ogygia. Here, the sea nymph Calypso feeds him ambrosia, the food of the gods, to make him immortal. Afterwards, he is reborn, emerging from the rushing waters of the sea along the shores of Phaeacia, and delivered into the civilized world yet again by the young maiden Nausicaa whose advice allows him to curry favor with her parents, who provide the hero with a ship to return home. In these examples, the hero undergoes a death of the inner self, the Ego, only to emerge with new strength or wisdom—all with the aid of divine figures. Black Panther has earned his place alongside many Homeric heroes, because the age-old paradigm of the hero still holds today. Whether from Africa or Europe, the archetypes Otto Rank and Lord Raglan laid bare for us are still relevant and useful for "reading" the hero.

African Representation

The wide release of the 2018 film *Black Panther* was for many a much-welcomed watershed event, creating a new narrative, honoring traditional African themes, but also depicting African culture as self-governing, advanced, and noble. For those of us who study ancient history, however, particularly Biblical and Egyptian history, there was never any question of Africa's membership in the elite nation-states of the world. For the Egyptians, the Nubians were the fiercest of warriors and represented a serious threat that eventually took control and established dynasties of their own. Beyond the borders of Nubia lay the distant and mysterious Land of Punt, a country rich in exotic trade goods, spices, perfumes, and rare animals and long held to have been the birthplace of the Egyptian people, their ancestors, and the gods. Here, the Eighteenth Dynasty Pharaoh Hatshepsut, after a divine omen, led an expedition to establish new trade agreements. Some scholars debate that the Land of Punt was actually Ethiopia, Memnon's native land. It is a place, therefore, deeply rooted in history, wealthy, and powerful, never having been colonized by anyone—Hittites, Egyptians, Sumerians, Akkadians, nor Greeks.

Similarly, in the *Black Panther* film, Wakanda represents a distant utopia, a sort of land-bound Atlantis, steeped in history. In the Marvel universe, it is the richest, most powerful nation on earth. Its army of warriors is unmatched, and like Ethiopia, it has never been colonized by European powers. Its richness stems from natural resources, specifically vibranium, which is highly sought by several world powers. The theme resonates with many modern readers/viewers, as it mirrors many issues facing African nations today: for example, conflict or blood diamonds, i.e., diamonds mined in a conflict zone used to finance a warlord. The film places Wakanda in the best possible light, often times glamorizing African origins, but it also interweaves a new mythology that focuses on the importance of technology and tackles many difficult issues in social justice.

How are the two African warriors depicted in terms of visual culture? In antiquity, Memnon is often described as tall,[22] leader of a swarthy host,[23] and beautiful. Although later writers such as Philostratus tend to focus on the color of his skin, which he claims is not truly black, but has a tinge of red or ruddiness, the same author mentions his large body and long crop of curls.[24] Strikingly, there is a great deal of variation in visual culture in the treatment of the figure. For example, an Athenian red-figure kylix dating to the fifth century BCE at the Louvre displays Eos gathering the lifeless body of her son in her arms. Stripped of his glorious armor, Memnon appears with long curls, long beard, and pale like his mother, but essentially Greek.

Compare this with an amphora attributed to the Diosphos painter dated to 500 BCE. It shows the goddess Eos mourning her son, while Achilles, on her left flees.[25] Because the medium is black figure, both Memnon and Achilles are rendered black, as one might expect, while Eos, a goddess and a woman is shown white. Here, the color distinction is to signify gender, rather than race. Men are typically darker skinned, working in the sun, while women, typically resigned to the household are white. Finally, there is the 6th century vase at the Museés Royaux d'Art et d'Histoire, in Brussels. It shows a dark-skinned Memnon with traditional Africa features, with short, cropped hair and a beard, similar to earlier Egyptian depictions of the Puntite.[26] The warrior wears a filet, and is armed with a bow and quiver. What is interesting is that the artist has him flanked by two figures rendered in white slip, one with a Phrygian cap. Here, it seems the artist demonstrates his virtuosity of knowledge, in exoticizing Memnon and makes a clear distinction between forms of the Greek Other. While scholars continue to debate the identity of the historical Memnon, the literary figure is largely a collage of various historical accounts and assuredly the poet's own vivid imagination. Part of his appeal is that he exudes qualities of the epic hero, while his appearance and origins remain mysterious, distant, and thus enigmatic.

Misinterpretation of ethnicity and skin color is a particular challenge when studying visual culture such as this black figure amphora. Since the medium is limited, it is unsurprising that both male figures are shown black, and Eos, Memnon's mother, is rendered white—not just because she is a goddess, but simply because she is female. Attributed to the Diosphos Painter, dating to 500 BCE; The Metropolitan Museum of Art in New York, accession number: 56.171.25; Fletcher Fund, 1956.

In terms of modern comparison, T'Challa, much like his heroic predecessor, is also depicted as young, handsome, and bearded. Mask and armor aside, he tends to wear traditional Wakandan clothing. Honorable and respectful of elders such as his father, T'Challa also observes the traditional customs and ceremonies of Wakanda, particularly the code of the warrior. Like Memnon, he is a man of few words. While T'Challa represents the best of the African warriors, his nemesis Killmonger, a product of Western American influence, represents the worst. The problem here, as some have noted, is that Killmonger's character is totally unredeemable, perpetuating the racist image of the African American as unworthy. It is a difficult balance for filmmakers to remain true to the comic series, while also changing long held stereotypes of African Americans.

In keeping with African American culture, names and spoken language in Wakandan lore offer an important conduit in connecting to the traditions of the past. For example, in *Avengers: Infinity War* we hear the word *yibambe*, the isiXhosa word for "hold fast" chanted before the Wakandans rush into battle. T'Challa's name may refer to an actual historical king of Angola. *Zuri* is a Swahili word meaning "beautiful." Jabari, one of the fictional tribes, also comes from the Swahili language and means "brave" or "fearless." Despite the emphasis on Wakanda's superior technology, the filmmakers went to great lengths to reflect the importance of observing the nation's traditional dress and rituals throughout the film, not just giving life to the comic tradition, but dazzling audiences with a new world that has an old world feel.

Conclusion

The concept of the epic African warrior, even from afar in the Greek world, has long captured the imagination, not just for his martial prowess, but also his honor on and off the battlefield. It is a tradition that continues in the modern character of Black Panther. Memnon, however, is still a Western perception of the African warrior and not an indigenous African one. The creators of Black Panther, however, have carefully crafted a narrative that incorporates real African traditions, superimposing them on a fictional landscape. Both the uncertainty of Wakanda's location for us, and Ethiopia's geographic boundaries for the Greeks are quite similar. They represent distant horizons and ancestral lands, that have an almost other-worldly quality. This also speaks to the African American diaspora. For outsiders, Africa represents a nebulous and exotic place, for others it is the ancestral homeland preserved mainly in oral traditions. This same practice is demonstrated in the feasting scene with Priam when Memnon gives an account of his mother, the Dawn, and his homeland, where her sun steeds leap from the eastern waves, the boundaries of the earth, and the never-ending sea. Finally, the lack of continuity in visual culture is a sure sign of varying literary and artistic traditions, one that leaves Memnon's identity as the Other fluid and enigmatic.

VI

He Who Commands the Sea

Proteus, Scamander and Denizens of the Deep

Water. It is the ultimate source of all life on Earth. For millennia mankind has worshipped its awesome and nurturing power, nevertheless ever fearful of its fickle nature, for just as it giveth, it also taketh away. Tales of the great deluge—the destructive power of water and the sea—haunt the mythologies of many ancient cultures, particularly that of ancient Greece. Zeus, for example, unleashes a terrible flood to punish the Pelasgians for their *hubris*, leaving only Deucalion and Pyrrha as survivors. The theme also finds its way into Homer. In the wake of the Trojan War, for example, many a war weary hero such as Odysseus and Teucer are kept from their native lands, battling the wrath of Poseidon and the insurmountable power of the sea. Perhaps one of the strangest examples of this antagonism, however, occurs in Book 21 of the *Iliad*. Here, the hero Achilles, after defiling, taunting, and tossing the remains of his enemies into the River Scamander, confronts the watery deity himself. What results is a furious battle between the two, one which requires the aid of several Olympians including Athena, Poseidon, and Hephaestus to help turn the tide.

Scamander, Proteus, and Triton are fierce aquatic warriors with the power to summon the power of the sea. How do they necessarily fit into the heroic paradigm? It can often be hard to fathom. How do the Greeks anthropomorphize a part of the natural world they were surrounded by on three sides (at least), creating for the sea a literal life of its own? How do modern aquatic warriors such as Aquaman and Namor stack up to these ancient archetypes? How do they draw upon and alter the traditional concept of the sea-bred warrior? The purpose of this chapter is to explore the often-overlooked anthropomorphized power of the sea embodied in the aquatic warrior to understand how the ancient Greeks sought to understand their natural surroundings and imbued them with lives of their own.

Proteus

Powers and Mutability

For the ancient Greeks the sea was an awesome force. Bountiful, it provided a constant source of life and livelihood, but its fickle and ever-changing nature made it mysterious and thoroughly unpredictable. Rising up in an instant, it could claim the life of the ancient mariner, which is why most hugged the coasts rather than brave the open sea. At home beneath the waves dwell the aquatic heroes of legends past, living relics of a forgotten age, when mankind lived at the mercy of the sea. Creatures of incredible power, they could command the forces of nature and change their form at will. In Homer, for example, the prophetic god Proteus is a formidable shapeshifter, who confounds many a hero. When confronted by Menelaus, who wrestles him in order to secure his aid in finding his way home, the Old Man of the Sea transforms himself into a lion, a serpent, a leopard, and even flowing water.[1] As a lion, the king of beasts shows incredible strength. As a serpent, he is venomous and chthonic, while his powers of hydrokinesis display his control over the forces of nature, specifically the sea. Begrudgingly, Proteus reveals the fates of many of the heroes, including Odysseus who was shipwrecked on Ogygia, a prisoner of the nymph Calypso. The encounter reveals several relevant points: first is the idea that the sea is wild, monstrous, and entirely unpredictable. It can change its form at any time. For ancient Greek sailors, the sea could turn on them at any moment, from calm waters to fierce maelstroms in the blink of an eye. Second is the need for humankind to attempt to control the forces of nature, essentially to *tame* the sea.

Metamorphosis is not only emblematic of Proteus. Other sea-born divinities, such as the nymph Thetis, his daughter and the mother of Achilles, can also alter their forms. When Peleus seeks to woo her, her father Proteus warns him of her amazing powers.[2] When he encounters her, he must wrestle her as she transforms into flame, water, a lioness and a serpent.[3] The performance is almost exactly like that of her father wrestling Menelaus. In these examples, both Proteus and Thetis receive their powers from the sea. They, like an aquatic version of Antaeus who drew power from touching the earth, are vulnerable when away from their element too long.[4] They draw power from water, which is why Thetis undoubtedly attempts to immortalize her son Achilles by dipping him into the waters of the River Styx. Its waters make him invincible. Because Achilles is born of a sea nymph, it makes sense that he should likewise draw his power from the sea.

An Ancient Past

Origin stories are essential to both modern and ancient hero mythologies, and the aquatic warrior is no exception. Such beings typically share a deep connection to an ancient past, for they represent the vestiges of an earlier primordial world. The Apkallu (Ummanu), for example, sage-like creatures often described as part man and part fish, such as we find in reliefs from the temple of Ninurta at Nimrud, may be traced as far back as Sumerian and Akkadian mythic traditions. In the epic of Gilgamesh they are referred to as *muntalki*, "counselors."[5] The third century BCE Hellenistic writer Berossus in his *Babylonica*, for example, explains that Oannes, one

An example of a Near Eastern *apkallu,* this fish god was generally affiliated with the wisdom of the sages and usually served as semi-divine helpers of kings and heroes. This particular relief was near a palace entrance at Nimrud, emphasizing its apotropaic purpose. Image from *A Second Series of the Monuments of Nineveh* by Austen Henry Layard. London: Murray, 1853, pl. 6. Reproduced from https://isaw.nyu.edu/library/images/Dagon.jpg/view.

of the *apkallu*, had the body of a fish, and head of a man.[6] Figurines called fish-*apkallu* typically stood at thresholds and doorways—liminal spaces—to serve as guardians.[7]

Proteus shares a deep connection with the past. His name means *first born*. He is the offspring of Poseidon. Meanwhile, Nereus is the child of Gaia and Pontus, both primordial deities, and thus the heir to a much older generation.[8] Some scholars have suggested that a Near Eastern Poseidon may have supplanted earlier Aegean sea gods, such as Proteus and Nereus.[9] Curiously, Homer also mentions that the Old Man of the Sea, Proteus, is also father to the Nereids.[10] Hesiod claims that Nereus is called the Old Man for his gentle ways and just thoughts.[11] If we assume that Nereus and Proteus are indeed one in the same just with different names, then his origin story predates accounts from Homer's own time (ninth–eighth century BCE) or even earlier.

If Proteus' parents are ostensibly Pontus (the old sea god) and Gaia (Earth), this would make his siblings Thaumas, Phorcys, Ceto and Eurybia. Ceto and Phorcys' union produced a brood of some of Greek mythology's most fearsome creatures, including the Gorgons, the Graiae, and Echidna.[12] With such a lineage, it is easy to fear Proteus as a monster. It is in his blood. Anything primordial is unknown and terrifying, and, like the sea itself, shrouded in mystery. Waters often conceal monstrous dangers deep beneath their surface. As Seneca claims in his *Phaedra*:

> Come now savage beasts of the sea, now bereft of the sea
> Finally whatever Proteus hides within the deepest recess of the waters.[13]

Hybridity

Hybridity, or the combination of two separate races, is another mark of the aquatic warrior. Proteus, for example, is the result of the incestuous relationship not just between two different generations of beings, but also of two realms. He is thus amphibious, living between both the earth and the sea. As a result, he is always trying to strike a balance between the two. Yet he often chooses to live on the island of Pharos, a liminal zone, neither completely on land nor beneath the sea. He is an outcast, neither living with his own kind, other gods, nor within human society. Contrastingly, his brother Phorcys' hybridity manifests itself physically. The leviathan sports crab-like forelimbs and the upper torso of a man, lobster-like antennae, and a fish tail.[14]

Hybridity, however, is more than simply a genetic cocktail. It can often mean the mixing of worlds.[15] In this we observe that Proteus lives neither wholly in the sea, nor on land. He lives on the island of Pharos, but he sleeps on the beaches with the seals. Seals themselves live neither in the sea, nor on land, but both. The beach represents a liminal zone between worlds, between the land and the sea. Proteus can also see across time, recalling images from the past, present, and future. For example, he knows about what happened to all the heroes, where some like Odysseus still are, but he also can see into future events, such as when he predicts that Menelaus will wind up with Helen in the Land of Blessed, the ancient Greek equivalent to the Judeo-Christian heaven. His ability to see events through time as a continuum rather than a fixed point illustrates the fluidity of time for an immortal, but specifically the fluidity of the sea. Again, this demonstrates his liminal nature. He lives on the edge of time.

Ultimately, however, what Proteus provides us is a prototype of the ancient shepherd who preserves the wealth of the ocean. When we first catch sight of him in the *Odyssey*, he is counting the seals placed in his care by his father Poseidon. His daughter actually makes the comparison, likening him to a good shepherd of the seas. Despite his powers of prophecy and mutability, Proteus prefers to act as guardian of his realm rather than use his formidable powers to step beyond it. It may be, however, that he draws power from the sea, and thus cannot be far from it.

Scamander

> Achilles, emerging from the whirlpool in fear and desperation sprinted to get to the plain in the speed of his quick feet, but the great god would not let him be, but rose on him in a darkening edge of water, minded to stop the labor of brilliant Achilles and fend destruction away from the Trojans.[16]

As mentioned in Book 21 of Homer's *Iliad*, Scamander, whose name among the gods is Xanthos,[17] is the personification of the river at Troy. As a divinity, he is the ancestor of Trojan kings.[18] Because of this, it comes as no surprise that he should want to engage the Greeks. What actually draws him into the war, however, is Achilles' unconscionable behavior. He defiles the bodies of his enemies by tossing them into the river and denying heroic warriors their deserved funeral rights. First, in so doing, Achilles pollutes the river, not in modern terms, but in the ancient Greek sense of the word, i.e., *miasma*, or blood pollution. He complains to Achilles that the bodies of all the slain men are damming the river, στεινόμενος (*steinomenos*), and keeping his streams from reaching the sea.[19] Achilles' actions interfere with the natural order of Scamander's watery realm. They also hint at an economic burden. If the river cannot meet the sea, this also affects trade. Second, the fact Scamander tries to stop Achilles shows a different kind of consciousness, one that respects and preserves the code of the warrior. In this way, an anthropomorphized Scamander might be considered an epic hero.

As ridiculous as the contest between Achilles and Nature may seem, it serves the purpose of highlighting just that: the ridiculousness of a man driven mad by war, who, like our modern Don Quixote, attacks windmills, because he thinks they are giants to be slain. The river attacks less like a mortal and more like a terrible force of nature. His anger is equally matched with Achilles, whom Scamander rightly claims has acted savagely. All bets are off, and the river god summons the other streams to aid him.

Although never assuming human form, Scamander's powers are indeed awesome and dreadful. His strength is unmatched. He can run circles around Achilles and at several points overtakes him. His powers of hydrokinesis allow him to summon other water sources and form great waves and eddies, now filled with blood; he even uses the bodies of the dead, trees, and rocks against Achilles as well. There are many moments in the *Iliad* where one feels genuine dread for the best of the Achaeans, and this is certainly one of them. Scamander promises he will heap water and mud and stone upon Peleus' son, to make sure he, like the men he slaughtered, will not receive a proper burial. Again, here echoes the importance of performing the proper rituals and just how far astray from the path of the warrior Achilles has gone.

Homer claims that Scamander's wrath is so incredible it takes several Olympian gods to intervene. Beyond the personal battle between Achilles and Scamander, the reader is provided a snapshot into the politics of the gods as Hera, Athena, and Hephaestus, on the side of the Greeks, come to the hero's aid. The altercation represents an interesting political quagmire, as Scamander's loyalties lie with the land of Troy, rather than with a Greek whose mother is a nymph of the sea. At the end of the *Iliad*, Scamander is said to mourn the city's collapse, along with the nymphs.[20] One doubts Thetis was counted among these, especially since, if Troy has fallen and the Greeks were successful, it is because of Achilles.[21] This also means that he has his *kleos*; with this honor, however, will come swiftly his death. Thetis would mourn for that, certainly, rather than the tumbling of Trojan walls.

Scamander, however, is not the only example of a river god rising up against an army. Nonnus' *Dionysiaca*, for example, talks about Hydaspes attacking "Dionysus": [When the Indian River Hydaspes tried to drown the army of Dionysos:] Hephaistos (Hephaestus) took care of his sons the Kabeiroi (Cabeiri), and caught up both, like a flying "firebrand."[22] This seems to almost mirror Homer's epic encounter with Scamander, who is likewise thwarted by Hephaestus. Such traditions need not be resigned just to myth, nor only to Greece. The personification of the Danube River on the Column of Trajan, for example, shows the river god observing the Roman legions cross his realm. Likewise, on the Column of Marcus Aurelius, a god is shown delivering rain to the Roman legions during the campaign against the Macromani in 174 CE.

What all of this shows us is that rivers, at least in the ancient Mediterranean, can be personified, and more than that, can be heroes in their own right. And how exactly are they heroes? What parts of "the code" are they particularly fond of? For Scamander, it is the desecration of the warrior, Trojan warriors, and of the waters surrounding Troy, a lack of respect for the sacred balance. Scamander also represents a being that stands against power unchecked, against *hubris*. Like the great deluge unleashed by Zeus, the waters shall cleanse the land of human pollution and *miasma*. Rivers are also liminal. They travel and live between the worlds of land and water and have fluid boundaries, just like good and evil, hero and anti-hero.

The Telchines

Some creatures are so mysterious, they wander in and out of mythology like phantoms. Among these are the Telchines. Shrouded in mystery, these technologically advanced craftsmen were believed to be the children of the Sea and dwelled in watery grottos deep below the waves.[23] Bacchylides claims that they, along with the Furies and Aphrodite, were born from the gore of Ouranos' castration. Callimachus, the Hellenistic poet, attributed the forging of Poseidon's mighty three-pronged trident to them.[24] Strabo says that they came from Rhodes and that Rhea had charged them with raising the infant Zeus. One of the most detailed accounts comes from Diodorus, who claims the Telchines possessed the power of hydrokinesis. They could summon rain and hail at will, and like Proteus, they too could change their form.[25] In terms of form we know very little. Ovid in his *Metamorphoses* adds that they had eyes that could bring blight, while Eustathius claims they had fins for feet.[26]

What becomes of these creatures is equally enigmatic. Somehow, they had prior knowledge of the great flood and fled in mass exodus from their island home of Rhodes, whose history extends as far back as the Neolithic, and includes Minoan and Mycenaean occupation. The fifth century CE author Nonnus writes that the Telchines joined Dionysus in his campaign in India, driving Poseidon's chariot. What makes them fascinating is that they, with their power to change shape, control water, and maintain a liminal existence, are ambiguous. While their skills at making weapons, such as Poseidon's trident, might make them appear good and bearers of aid to the divine, they are ultimately seen as mephitic for that same talent, for developing a poison from the waters of the Styx that made fields infertile.[27]

Namor, the Sub-Mariner

Deep beneath the waves dwells Marvel's Prince Namor, a character in the vein of the aquatic hero. The leader of an ancient race of Atlanteans, the man called Submariner often appears, like his predecessors, a liminal character, caught between worlds, and enacting the role of both hero and anti-hero. Appearing in Marvel's *Mystery Comics* #1 (October of 1939), two years before DC's Aquaman, Namor is often touted as the "first" mutant, a nod perhaps to Proteus, who also appears as an antagonist in the series. Born of a human, Captain Leonard McKenzie, and an Atlantean princess, he stands as an example of a half-human hybrid. He is frequently shown with non-human pointed ears, but because of the pink color of his skin, Namor is treated as an outsider in the blue-skinned world of Atlantis. Considering the state of the world at the time, World War II, Namor represents a foil to the Nazi concept of the master race. He is also, like Proteus, the heir to a bygone era, a relic of a lost empire. His name Namor, spelled backwards is Roman, and his choice expletive—*imperius rex*—comes from Latin.

Namor's story really begins with his father, who, searching for the legendary Helmet of Power, leads an expedition to Antarctica. When his ship, the Oracle, becomes trapped in an ice flow, McKenzie sets charges that cause damage to the city of Atlantis below. The reigning Emperor Thakkor sends his daughter Fen, to investigate, but she is soon captured by the crew. In time, she and McKenzie fall in love. Afterwards, her father, thinking her a prisoner, attacks the Oracle, leading to the death of McKenzie and his crew. Returning to Altantis, Fen, now a single mother, is forced to raise her son Namor on the margin of both human and underwater realms.

Namor exhibits some extraordinary abilities. Like Superman, he has incredible strength. He, like Proteus of Greek myth, can live an unusually long-life.[28] He can breathe underwater, and his winged ankles like Hermes allow him to take flight. Yes, he can fly. Again, this makes him a marginal figure, able to navigate the sky, sea, and land. He can also speak to humans and Lemurians as well as his fellow Atlanteans. Like Proteus, he bridges the physical realms of land and ocean as well as the existential realms of humanity and his own race of sea people. His powers also

Interior panels from *Sub-Mariner* issue# 2 (1968–1974) showing the aquatic warrior Namor needing to return to the sea in order to replenish his power. It recalls the myth of the giant Antaeus who drew power from Gaea, and was invincible so long as his feet touched the earth. © 2017 Marvel Characters, Inc.

include hydrokinesis, which he uses to part the oceans. He has the ability to speak to various sea creatures and control them as well as to communicate telepathically with his fellow Atlanteans.[29] Finally, he wields the indestructible trident of Neptune (the Roman name for the Greek god Poseidon), which discharges bolts of energy and was entrusted to the people of Atlantis.

Namor is a dark, brooding, and complex character. His temperamental nature, bouts of detachment, self-righteousness, and anger frequently create waves with the surface world. Perhaps because of his hybrid nature, he is often divided between the sea and the surface world, which he claims is a constant threat. Sometimes the hero, sometimes the villain, like Proteus Namor is mutable, fluid, and as unpredictable as the sea. When he sides with villains, it is usually in order to protect Atlantis, but he also sides with the X-Men, Fantastic Four, and the Avengers for the greater good or when again it suits his interests. There's something about the mercurial hero that is almost paradigmatic in and of itself. It's like the club card of being a hero. Are you moody and dispossessed of any real loyalties other than to yourself? Yes? Great! Join the hero club! Namor is certainly a card-carrying member.

In issue #4 of *Fantastic Four*, we learn from Namor that Atlantis was destroyed by a nuclear detonation.[30] Afterwards, he becomes a king without a nation. After leading an attack on the surface world, which he holds accountable, Namor tries to unite his people. Eventually he finds them and plans to marry his cousin, Lady Dorma, while Lyyra of Lemuria, a rival kingdom, plots to unseat him from power.[31] Marrying a family member is taboo in modern Western society, but it is common in Greek myth, for example the union of Hera and Zeus. Again it lends an otherworldly quality. Namor also reconnects with his father, another heroic trope, but tragically loses him in a battle with a genetically altered hybrid Tiger Shark, who is part human, part shark, and part Atlantean.

Aquaman

With one foot in our world and the other firmly beneath the surface of the sea, DC's Aquaman, like Namor, tells the tale of an undersea hero imbued with near superhuman powers. Debuting in 1941, Aquaman, the creation of Paul Norris and Mort Weisinger, chronicles the tale of an undersea hero who originally lived on a sunken ship and fought Nazis and pirates—like one does. His powers include Atlantean strength, the ability to breathe underwater and communicate with various forms of sea life. During the Silver Age of comic book history, Aquaman's adventures continued in *Adventure Comics*.[32] At this time, we discover that Aquaman, Arthur Curry, is a hybrid: the son of a human lighthouse keeper and Atlanna, an exile from the lost world of Atlantis.

Atlantis. For many, the name instantly conjures up images of a utopian society powered by advanced technology forever lost in time. According to Plato, Atlantis existed 9000 years before his time and was a land larger than Libya beyond the pillars of Herakles. It consisted of a confederation of kings of great and marvelous power. Then in a single day and night of misfortune, the island was lost beneath the depths of the sea.[33] For Plato, it was the model of the ideal state, which was of course overcome by Athens. For us, it represents a distant and mysterious past, a time before time, and one that ties Aquaman to Greek myth.

In the Modern Age, Aquaman's origins are retold, emphasizing his hybrid nature and exposure on Mercy Reef for bearing the Mark of Cordax, i.e., his bold hair. Learning of his powers, he elects to serve as protector of Earth's oceans. We also learn that he has a half-brother Orm, who, weary of often being overshadowed by his brother, will become his rival, Ocean Master. This seems to echo the doublet of competing brothers that we find in the Loki-Thor modern mythology. We also learn of Aquaman's weakness. Unlike Namor, he cannot be out of water for more than an hour. The concept seems again to draw on old mythic cycles, like Antaeus who has to always be touching the earth in order to draw his strength. Aquaman's strength lies in the power of the ocean itself.

Eventually Aquaman becomes a founding member of the Justice

Opposite and above: The aquatic superhero Aquaman summons lanternfish, while Neptune uses hydrokinesis to attack a ship. _Aquaman_ #9, 1963. © DC Comics.

League of America. During the 1960s, he becomes king of Atlantis and meets Mera a regent from another dimension, whom he marries. As king, Aquaman wields the trident of Poseidon, granted to the Atlanteans by the sea god. More than simply an emblem of power, the trident can manipulate water as well as create storms and floods. It shoots bolts of energy, extends the wielder's powers of telepathy with sea animals, and can even transform into a sword. The 2018 film *Aquaman* has Jason Momoa play the role with dark hair, trident, and a gladiator-type suit that for many recalls those ancient depictions of Poseidon. One of the themes of the film is a battle with the surface world over harming the ocean, although the thrust of the story revolves around Aquaman claiming his heritage and trident, in order to become the rightful ruler of Atlantis.

There are some obvious similarities between Namor and Aquaman. Both were treated as outcasts and discriminated against based on their mixed race. Thus their mothers remove them from their natural habitats to raise them on their own, because ultimately, they do not fit in, extending their gestation periods, and only entering into their heroism a bit long in the tooth. Nevertheless, their mothers are highborn, and they both become regents with powers to control water and the animals within. They both wield tridents, symbols deeply rooted in Greek mythology. Namor takes personal issue with the surface dwellers for polluting the oceans. Aquaman's half-brother Orm is forming an alliance to fight the surface dwellers, who are polluting their kingdom. These all have ancient precedents. The idea of purity and the sea, however, extends back to Scamander who claims it interferes with the natural cycle of life. Proteus is an outcast and doesn't fit into either human or undersea kingdoms.

Conclusion

From the deepest ocean trenches to windswept shores of the wine dark sea, aquatic warriors often represent living relics of a distant past, a time when mankind lived at the mercy of the nature. Fierce in battle and highly adaptable, their powers and abilities reflect not only a fascination for, but also a deep fear of the sea, its chaotic nature, and its awesome power to transform. Moreover, its vast depths not only conceal boundless abundance, but also unseen dangers. At times, man and the sea lock horns in a contest for supremacy. In such contests, unless aided by the gods, the sea almost always wins.

Heroes such as Namor and Aquaman celebrate this tradition, often straddling the worlds of land and sea. What is different about modern adaptations is that man and sea are merged into one. While this hybridity creates stormy waves for them, it makes them seem more human, and allows us, the readers, to identify at least partially with their struggle. Instead of confronting and battling nature, like Achilles, these heroes have a deep respect for the sea and stick to a code to protect their realm, like epic warriors of old.

VII

Double Trouble

Divine Twins in the Epic Tradition

Twice the daring, twice the glory, double the trouble with twins in the story. With two faces and one mind—the concept of twin warriors is as old as myth itself. Appearing in almost every culture of the world, these formidable counterparts often pose a double threat to villains and heroes alike: Apollo and Artemis, the Dioscuri (Castor and Pollux), the Vedic Aśvins, the hero twins Hunahpu and Xbalanque, Romulus and Remus, Scarlet Witch and Quicksilver. Often, they represent binary forces: one divine, the other mortal, often united in cause, but they also represent a double-edged sword, as they are also doubly vulnerable. Scholars such as Douglas Frame and Gregory Nagy have taken the paradigm and effectively argued that the deeper connection between Achilles and Patroclus may be the result of twinning.[1] Even if they aren't born from the same parents, Patroclus, donning the armor of his dearest friend and appearing as Achilles, to the Greeks, supports the idea of the *therapon*, or ritual substitute, which in many cases we find twins to be.[2] Further, the same level of grief and temporary insanity as a result of losing one's twin is present in the case of Achilles and Patroclus.

There are, however, plenty of actual examples of twins in Greek mythology and other ancient mythologies as well. Besides the unique and surprising nature of multiple births in a society without ultrasound technology, why are twins so fascinating to them? Likewise, why do we find twins so interesting now? They seem to be imbued with some kind of magic, regardless of our temporal viewpoint. The focus of this chapter is to view some examples of twins in Homer's world as well as our own and grapple with the how the concept appears in terms of epic narrative and visual culture. What are the advantages and disadvantages of having a twin brother or sister in ancient texts and the comic book heroes of today? How does the paradigm of the hero work with twins, either in the Bronze Age or today?

Ancient Greece

Children of Leto

Without a doubt, the most famous myth regarding twin warriors is that of the god Apollo and his sister, the goddess Artemis, a formidable pair of archers who always have each other's back. Hesiod writes: *"And Leto was joined in love with Zeus who holds the aegis, and bare Apollon and Artemis delighting in arrows, children lovely above all the sons of Heaven."*[3] Hounded by Hera for sleeping with her husband, the Titan Leto wanders the world trying to find a land that will grant her safe harbor to bear her children. She finally comes to the island of Delos where she gives birth to Artemis, who straightaway acts as a midwife to her own twin brother, Apollo.[4] Homer, however, claims that Artemis is born on Ortygia and Apollo on Delos. Regardless, the two gods are seen as twins who share an indelible link not only to their mother, but also to each other.[5] Whenever one is near, the other is not far behind. Although technically not heroes, they do fight as warriors in Homer's epic, taking the battlefield on the side of the Trojans. This is unsurprising, as after their birth, Leto bathes her children in the waters of Xanthos, also known as the River Scamander.[6]

Ironically enough, despite being twins, never were two gods more unlike. We often hear tell of Apollo's lustful adventures, chasing nymphs through forests, though rarely catching them. Artemis, on the other hand, is the quintessential virgin, preferring the company of other virgin nymphs and the great outdoors. Apollo, handsome, with long hair and beardless, sporting perfumed robes, seems somewhat effeminate, preferring love and the lyre to war, while Artemis runs around in a tunic that stops at the knees, very unladylike, accompanied by wild dogs and shouldering a quiver full of arrows. To top it off, each are associated with the sun (Apollo) and moon (Artemis), opposites of the solar day.

Time and again, the dynamic duo swoop in on their chariots to defend their mother. The story of Tityus, for example, involves a rather nasty giant, who, in a fit of insane lust, attempts to abduct and rape Leto. The Titaness summons her children. Apollo and Artemis quickly dispatch the rather naughty villain to the Underworld, where he spends eternity in perpetual torment.[7] And who can forget the tale of Queen Niobe, the mother who boasted to be more blessed in motherhood than Leto? Enraged by this slight, Leto again sends Apollo to slay Niobe's sons with his silver bow, and Artemis likewise the queen's daughters.[8] In the *Iliad*, brother and sister join forces once more against the Greeks. At one point they even run their own ambulance service: Apollo rescues Aeneas, while Artemis cures him.[9]

Their bond was unique to say the least, perhaps even incestuous. This comes out in a second century retelling of the Orion myth. In most versions, Orion, a hunter and bosom companion of Artemis, boasts that he could and would kill every beast on earth. Gaia takes offense at this and sends a monstrous scorpion to finish him. Sadly, he succumbs to the creature's poison and is immortalized among the stars. In one version, however, Apollo hears that Artemis plans on marrying Orion.[10] Jealous, the sun god spies Orion swimming in a lake and dares his sister to strike the black shape swimming in the water. Never able to pass up a dare, especially where archery is concerned, she aims and fires, striking her lover in the head. Later he washes up on shore. Realizing the deception, Artemis weeps for him, eventually placing him amongst the stars. She also takes revenge against Apollo's lover Coronis in a deadly game of tit for tat.[11]

The concept of twin gods who are two halves of the same whole may have its roots deep in Greece's past. Dione, for example, the female equivalent of Zeus, appears as *di-wi-ja* in Linear B texts. The appearance of a female counterpart to Poseidon, *Po-s—da-e-ja*, also appears in Linear B texts from Pylos.[12] What is most surprising is that among divine twins, Apollo and Artemis are twins of opposite sex, while so many are male twins, e.g., Hypnos and Thanatos (Sleep and Death), Phobos and Deimos the sons of Ares and Aphrodite, Ploutous and Philomelos sons of Demeter. This epidemic, however, is not simply resigned to the gods. Hercules and Iphikles, Castor and Pollux, and Pelias and Neleus, the offspring of gods and mortals, are perfect examples. Less common, or perhaps less written about, are twin girls, such as Helen and Clytemnestra. Let us take a closer look at their unique interaction.

The Dioscuri (Castor and Pollux)

Proving two heads really are better than one are the much-celebrated Dioscuri, Castor and Pollux, or Polydeuces, twin brothers born of the mortal woman Leda, who had been seduced by the god Zeus in the form of a swan, an original if not bewildering choice in enticement, whose procreative acrobatics I shall leave to the reader's imagination.[13] Castor, fathered by Tyndareus the king of Sparta, was mortal, while his brother Pollux was born semi-divine. But Leda gave birth to two more twins, Helen and Clytemnestra. Helen, incidentally, turned out to be the most beautiful woman in the world, with the face that launched a thousand ships, while Clytemnestra seems to end up with the short end of the stick, marrying the brutish Agamemnon, then killing him, which led to her own death by the hands of her son. Helen's fate, however, is no better. She was kidnapped at least twice: once by the Attic hero Theseus while in her youth, and then again by Paris who was visiting the Dioscuri, who had in fact just rescued

Helen from Athens. It leads one to wonder if her marriage to Menelaus was not some sort of Greek version of the shotgun wedding. Wife stealing was quite in vogue at the time. The male twins, Castor and Pollux, go on to join Jason and his crew of Argonauts on their perilous quest for the Golden Fleece and have a major part to play in destroying the city of King Pelias for his wickedness.

Eventually, they are expected to marry, but they choose Phoebe and Hilaeira, the consorts of their twin cousins Idas and Lynceus. I already mentioned that wife stealing was in vogue, right? Humiliated, Idas and Lynceus in turn launch a cattle raid.[14] Enraged, and not to be outdone, the Dioscuri then launch their own cattle raid. Eventually, Idas wounds his cousin Castor, while Pollux in turn kills Lynceus.[15] As Castor lies dying, Pollux implores Zeus to save his brother by giving him half of his semi-divine nature, which means a quarter each, more or less. I will admit the math is a bit shady. Suffice it to say that the two become immortalized in the constellation known as Gemini and miss out on the Trojan War altogether, but they were there at the beginning, and perhaps make an appearance in visual culture from the time as two warriors behind a shield.[16] They show up later in ancient Rome, proclaiming prodigiously that the city will prevail at the battle of Lake Regillus, which earns them the lasting gratitude and veneration of the Romans.

Most notably, the Dioscuri are venerated as guardians of sailors. This we should not find surprising. During their tour of duty with Jason and his Argonauts, they encounter a terrible storm. Orpheus, who had been inducted into the cult of the Kabeiroi, offered prayers to the twin gods.[17] Subsequently, an epiphany of two stars appeared over the heads of the Dioscuri. Afterwards, they become the patron saints of sailors, as seen in the *Homeric Hymn to the Dioscuri*: "[The Dioskouroi (Dioscuri)] are deliverers of men on earth and of swift-going ships when stormy gales rage over the ruthless sea."[18] The twins are also associated with horses, particularly Castor: "O Castor and you, Polydeuces, tamers of horses, protectors of the homeless and guides of the guests."[19]

The two do not necessarily display overt superhuman powers *per se*. They aren't super strong, nor can they fly, but they do share the ability to calm the storms at sea, and, of course, they both garner a share of immortality. Castor was good with horses and Pollux a formidable boxer.[20] They are also like-minded. They both joined Jason, both stole their cousins' consorts, and both went on that infernal cattle raid. They are also psychically linked. In the *Argonautika*, when Polydeuces is being attacked, Castor swoops in to strike.

In terms of duality, the brothers have been equated with various opposing forces, for example: mortality and immortality, dusk and dawn, the morning and evening stars, bringers of light, much like the twin gods Apollo and Artemis or even the Aśvins of the Indic Vedas.[21] In so doing, they represent a beginning and an end to a cycle, like many of the savior gods associated with mystery cults. Mystery cults are exactly how they sound: a mystery. We do not know specifically what took place during worship, because members, such as those associated with the Eleusinian mysteries, were sworn to secrecy under pain of death—a bit like ancient Fight Club. Typically, however, these cults provide insight into what happens to the soul after death and use figures like Osiris or Dionysus as dying and rising gods to demonstrate the process. Dionysus, for example, was ripped from his mother's burning womb by Zeus and sewn into his leg, only to be reborn again. Osiris, the Egyptian god, was hacked to pieces by his brother and reassembled by his sister/wife Isis to become god of the dead. Talk about family dysfunction. Often such gods are associated with cycles and seasons, such as Demeter or Cybele and Attis.[22]

In art, Castor and Pollux are pictured more or less identically. An Athenian red-figure kylix attributed to the Penthesilea painter and dating to the fifth century BCE, for example, shows the two marching off to rescue their sister Helen.[23] One carries spears in both hands, while the other is mounted on a pair of horses. They both appear almost pre-pubescent, i.e., clean-shaven with long ringlets of hair and stylish fillets, forever young in their endless lives as immortals.

The Kabeiroi

The Kabeiroi were a pair of divine twin craftsmen descended from Hephaestus, who assisted him at the forge.[24] They were believed to have had their own mystery cult and possibly even oversaw the mysteries held in honor of Demeter at Samothrace. Diodorus Siculus equated them with the Trojan *dactyloi*, a race of immortal beings associated with the mother goddess figure, possibly located on or near Mt. Ida.[25] Herodotus claims that they are sometimes depicted as dwarves.[26] They appear in the *Argonautika* welcoming Jason and his crew and may have been conflated with the Dioscuri, divine twins and expert horsemen, who sometimes come to the aid of sailors.[27]

In his *Dionysiaca*, Nonnus refers to them as Eurymedon and Alcon and claims they fought on the side of Dionysus during the Indian War. He describes them as having fiery eyes like their father Hephaestus and being blacksmiths; they are always well armed. Eurymedon wields a Lemnian spear forged by Hephaestus and a flashy fiery sword. Meanwhile, his brother brandishes a fire-bolt in one hand and a festal torch of Hecate in the other.[28] The torch then links Alcon with the underworld, death, and the second life, or as a psychopomp guiding souls through it, a light in the darkness. Hecate helped Demeter by providing a torch when she was looking for her daughter Persephone. In this sense one brother might represent the darkness and death, while his brother symbolizes rebirth and the light.

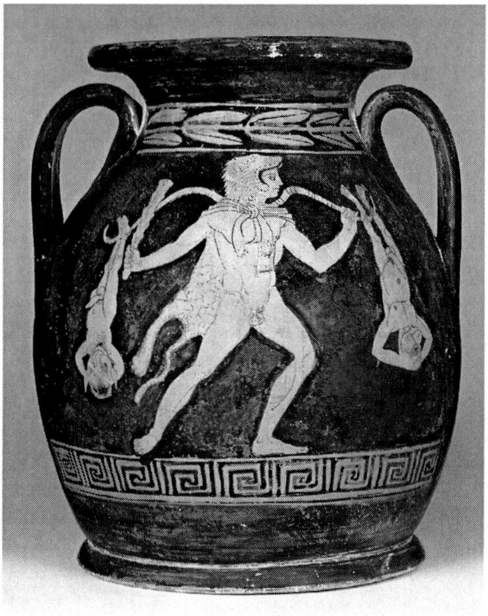

A Lucanian pelike dated to 380 BCE highlights the Greek hero Hercules, dressed in a lion skin, holding the Kaberoi at bay as they attempt to attack. 28.5 × 23.2 cm (11¼ × 9⅛ in.), 81.AE.189. The J. Paul Getty Museum, Villa Collection, Malibu, California, Gift of Milton Gottlieb.

In the epic, the two brothers act as one. When Eurymedon is struck down by the Indian chief Morrheus, Alcon instantly comes to his defense, covering him with his shield and brandishing his spear. Eurymedon then calls upon Hephaestus, his father, to intervene, and does he ever. As you can see, there are some similarities between the Kabeiroi and the Dioscuri. For example, when one is mortally wounded, the other is there to offer support; each knows when the other is in danger and calls upon his divine father for aid.

Herakles and Iphikles

Speaking of twins, probably lesser known is the story of Herakles, son of Alcmene and Zeus, and his brother Iphikles, son of Alcmene and mortal Amphitryon. Confused? So were Alcmene and Amphitryon. It all began one cold Theban night. Amphitryon, great grandson of Perseus, had gone off to fight the Taphians and Teleboans, and Zeus being Zeus saw his opportunity to sire yet again another hero, one that would protect the gods. Disguised as Amphitryon, he burst into Alcmene's bedroom, declaring his victory in war. The two lay with one another, during which time Herakles—originally named Alcaeus, or Alcides—was conceived. That same night the real Amphitryon returned to announce his victory, with much the same result, thus Iphikles was conceived.[29] As time passed, Zeus rather haughtily announced to his fellow Olympians the birth of a descendant of Perseus, his son.[30] Hera, being a suspicious woman—and can you blame her?—senses something foul afoot and sends Eileithyia, the goddess of childbirth, to prevent the arrival of the child. Crossing her fingers, toes, legs and everything she could think of, Eileithyia tried her best to jinx the birth.[31] Nevertheless, a maid-servant by the name of Galanthis, recognizing Eileithyia through her disguise devised a plan to distract the goddess. She shouted that Alcmene had given birth to a son. The ruse worked. Utterly vexed and distracted, Eileithyia shot up, uncrossing herself. Moments later, Herakles was born, a day later followed by his brother Iphikles. This is an example of what is commonly referred to as *heteropaternal superfecundation*, or twin babies created by two different fathers.

Growing up was not easy either. Fearing Hera's wrath, Alcmene later abandons Herakles by the side of the road. He would have died if not for Athena, who convinces Hera to accompany her on a walk. When they discover the whimpering child, Athena coaxes Hera to tend to it, unaware of its true identity. The goddess nurses the infant, but when he bites down hard, Hera rips him from her breast, sending a stream of milk into the night sky thus creating the Milky Way. Hera's anger, however, does not end there. While still infants, the twins face a pair of deadly serpents, sent by Hera to murder them.[32] Imagine the shock when hearing the cries in the middle of the night, Alcmene and Amphitryon rush into the nursery to discover Herakles, playing with the strangled serpents like a pair of rattles, with Iphikles cowering in the cradle.[33] Thus he earned the name Herakles, the "kleos" or glory of Hera. And so begins the tale of Herakles and his incredible strength, his prestigious career in pest control, and of course his famous Twelve Labors.

What happens to Iphikles? Well, mythology tends to overlook mere mortals, but if mere mortals are your thing, rest assured, he appears again. Later, he joins Herakles on his journeys. He is at the first war with Troy, which precedes Homer's tale by at least a generation. Captured by Laomedon, Iphikles learns of the king's evil plan to wrangle Herakles into battling a sea monster, incidentally leaked to him by Laomedon's own son Priam. After mounting an escape, Iphikles relays the nefarious plot to Herakles. Herakles agrees to kill the sea monster but will accept only the payment of Laomedon's majestic horses (horses, mind you, given to the king by Zeus himself in recompense for the king's son Ganymedes). When Laomedon refuses to part with the horses, Herakles kills the king. Later Iphikles joins his brother against Hippocoön of Sparta but dies in the encounter. Herakles is overcome with grief, unable to imagine his life without his twin.[34]

Apollodorus tells the story that prior to the encounter with Hippocoön, Herakles established an Arcadian army and marched against Augeas, who had appointed the Elean generals and twins Eurytus and Cteatus.[35] The story goes that, like the Dioscuri, their mother Mollione was impregnated by a god, here Poseidon, who, like Zeus, had taken the form of a bird. They are born from a silver egg rather than a golden one and are conjoined rather than separated.[36] Though at the heart of an ongoing debate, a mysterious two headed-figure on a chariot carrying a shield, thought to be Eurytus and Cteatus, appears on the Agora Oinochoe.[37] Some claim that the figure, based of the incompleteness of the vase, should not be seen as twins but rather the joining of two moments in time. This interpretation, however, does not bear scholarly scrutiny, for rarely does the charioteer also carry a shield as he grips the reins. Examples showing this dual formation of charioteer and soldier include a lekythos from Delos depicting Achilles dragging the body of Hector to the tomb of Patroclus and dismounting from a chariot, with a chariot driver still at the reins.[38] Homeric warriors often worked in teams of two, with an armed warrior and a charioteer. One can hardly imagine a charioteer racing, then stopping to pick up a shield, and continuing on, as suggested by two moments in time. Instead, what seems more likely is that the image is of two figures, either joined or standing fairly close together.

A study of Mycenaean vase paintings, however, clearly shows that artists took great pains to make a distinction. A Late Helladic IIIA (1375–1350 BCE) chariot krater at the Metropolitan Museum of Art, for example, shows a charioteer and a passenger side by side. Fragmentary pottery from Tiryns dating to Late Helladic IIIC depicts chariot drivers standing in front of and apart from their spear-bearing passengers. The point here is to show the chariot driver separate from the passenger, as a chauffeur to the warrior because is a sign of wealth and prestige. Interestingly, later vase paintings, such as an Attic Black-figure amphora, picture Herakles confronting the giant Geyron, who is shown with three heads and three shields but a single pair of legs between them.[39] Such an example shows how artists rendered conjoined triplets; this particular piece is reminiscent of the Agora Oinochoe, which I believe shows the twins, Eurytus and Cteatus.

In the end, after Herakles falls ill, the battle between the Molliones and Herakles is postponed.[40] Eventually, they meet again at Cleonae, where he slays them. It is a strange encounter to say the least, and seems to suggest that the death or separation of one set of twins may be a precursor to the death of another. Thus, with the death of Iphikles and the Molliones, the demise of Herakles is not far behind.

In the preceding three cases—the Dioscuri, the Kabeiroi, and Herakles and Iphikles—the fear of losing one's brother is often debilitating, and I would argue akin to losing one's self. In the cases of the Dioscuri and Herakles, it has been shown that in many cases twins are matched against twins, again preserving a type of binary opposition.[41] These binaries are not only common in Greek story-telling; they appear to be a cross-cultural, cross-linguistic phenomenon that also appears in Indic myth as well as New World mythologies, especially that of the Maya.

India

Aśvins

In the *Rig Veda*, the Aśvins are divine twins born of the sun god Surya and the goddess Saranyu. The two brothers share a single name, referred to in the dual as *aśvina,* or *aśvinau,* meaning "those having to do with horses."[42] By referring to them in the dual, they are two parts of a single whole; they have no identity apart from one another, so they never appear that way. Like the Dioscuri, they are bearers of light.[43] Classical scholar M.L. West notes they are "bright with fire," *didiyagni*, "much gleaming, resplendent" *pursuścandra*, and a bright light to men.[44] They are also referred to as the "darkness slayers" (*tamohánā*, 3.39.3), and often symbolize the light of sunrise, and the other sunset.

An Etruscan (Caerean) hydria, dated to 520 BCE and attributed to the Eagle painter, shows Hercules armed with a club and Aeolus with a sickle, tackling the nine-headed hydra. A raging fire appears below the figure of Aeolos, to help cauterize the heads. 44.6 × 38 × 33.4 cm ($17\frac{9}{16}$ × $14\frac{15}{16}$ × $13\frac{1}{8}$ in.), 83.AE.346. The J. Paul Getty Museum Collection, Malibu, CA.

Like the Dioscuri, they bring good fortune, good health, and even rescue mortals from death.[45] In the *Rig Veda*, they heal

The Ashvins were twins that first appear in the *Rig Veda*, the hymns of ancient India. Often described similarly to the Greek twins, Castor and Pollux/Polydeuces, they also have a bit in common with the divine twins Apollo and Artemis, especially with their connection with the celestial light of both day and night. In this depiction, the Ashvins are dark and light, representing the sun and the moon. Wikipedia.

Reblia who was "hidden in a cave and well near death."[46] They also rescue sailors from imminent danger, like Bhujyu, son of King Tugra, who, after being sent on a naval expedition, finds himself shipwrecked in a storm.[47] They ride around in a chariot, like the Kabeiroi. In the *Mahabharata* and the *Puranas*, the twins were royal physicians to the Devas.[48] In the *Rig Veda* the Aśvins are always seeking soma, which is akin to ambrosia, the elixir of immortality for the Greek gods.[49] When they finally learn how to perform the rites to obtain it from Dadhyanc, they become immortal. The twins may also be related to the Nasatya of the Hittites dating as far back to the second millennium BCE.[50]

The New World

Like our classical Greek and even Indic examples, the Hero Twins of the Quiché Mayan mythology Hunahpu ("One blowgunner") and

Xbalanque ("Jaguar Sun"), the "War Twins," represent both complimentary and opposing forces: youth, rebirth, but also the light-giving sun and moon. Ironically, Hunahpu is associated with the sun, while his brother Jaguar Sun is associated with the moon.[51] Their mother, Xquic, is descended from one of the lords of Xibalba, the Mayan underworld. Their birth, like so many, is supernatural. Their father, One Hunahpu, also a twin, had been killed by the Lords of Death. Subsequently, and unceremoniously, his head was hung in the crook of a tree. When their mother Xquic passed by the head, it spat into her hand thus giving rise to the twins.

After the twins are born, they are raised by their grandmother along with two older brothers, One Howler Monkey and One Artisan. The older brothers often mistreat them, forcing the twins to find clever ways of tricking them as siblings are apt to do. For example, in one encounter, they tell their elder brothers that all the birds they acquired from their hunt were caught in a tree. When One Howler Monkey and One Artisan climb the tree, it magically grows taller. Whether the work of the gods or the twins is uncertain, but there is something definitely magical about the pair. They can perform agricultural tasks with great efficiency, for example clearing an entire field with a single swing of an axe.

The brothers were also ballplayers, whose raucous matches inadvertently grab the attention of the less than enthusiastic underworld lords. Like their fathers before them, they are summoned to Xiabalba and forced to participate in a series of tests, trials, and tortures with such repugnant titles as Dark House, the Razor House, and the Bat House. Eventually, they play ball with the Lords of Death and win. In the end, however, they allow themselves to be killed by being burned alive in a fiery oven knowing full well that they would be reborn when their ashes were sprinkled into a nearby river. Reborn they are, first as fish before taking human form, but now appearing as beggars. They could also do amazing magic tricks, including bringing each other back to life. When the Lords of Death learned of this, they commanded them to sacrifice one another, which they did to great applause. They then asked to be sacrificed themselves. This leads to the twins' victory, for after they are sacrificed, the twins elect not to bring them back to life. After this, they find the head of their father, Hun Hunahpu and restore him. With their quest completed, they take their place in the heavens as the sun and the moon.[52]

The similarities are striking between the Mayan Hero Twins and the Dioscuri. The two are the result of a magical birth. One is associated with war, while the other is not. One dies so that the other may live. Eventually, both are immortalized and become binary sources of light, the sun and moon. Regardless of Old World or New, twins seem associated with the sun and moon (or some kind of celestial light), light and darkness. Is this a binary that all cultures struggle to understand and therefore use to explain their world, like so many etiological myths?

Modern Wonder Twins

Few cartoon characters give rise to comic book traditions. Usually, it is the other way around. The extraterrestrial superhero twins Zan and Jayna are one of those exceptions. Making their debut on the *All-New Super Friends Hour*, this brother and sister team from the planet Exxor had the ability of transformation whenever they made physical contact, the world's first fist bump, and exclaimed, "Wonder Twin power activate!" Zan could transform himself into any state of water and appear as anything from a whirlpool to a sheet of frozen ice. Jayna, on the other hand, could transform herself into any number of animals, limited only by her knowledge. Here it seems the emphasis of their power is on physicality—touching. Each twin draws strength from the other. This recalls for many the tale of the despotic wrestler Antaeus, who drew his strength not from a twin, but from his mother, the Earth.[53]

Because the twins are extraterrestrial, they seem to act even more divine than their ancient models. None of the twins we have mentioned usually transform, such as the Dioscuri, although Apollo and Artemis have been associated with the transformation of others, for example Artemis turns the unwitting hunter Actaeon into a deer, or Apollo's desire, Daphne, whom her father transformed into a laurel tree to help her escape her would-be rapist. For the Wonder Twins, they can change their own form, making them appear like the primordial being Proteus, who can change his form into both animal and water. In addition, the two exiles shared a telepathic link highlighted in the episode "The Village of Lost Souls." What the pair Zan and Jayna show us is that the power twins usually have can only be activated when combined—thus they are two parts of a greater whole.

The same might be said for Wanda and Pietro Maximoff, known respectively as Scarlet Witch and Quicksilver. Debuting in *X-Men* #4 in March of 1964, they have attached themselves to the Brotherhood of Evil Mutants, under the direction of the super-villain and long-time rival of Professor Xavier, Magneto. In a strange twist, Magneto, as it turns out, is their father, by a woman named Magda, who leaves him when she is pregnant for the country of Transia. You won't find this one in Fodor's Guide. After their mother dies, the twins are cared for by foster parents, but after a fire forces them to flee, they wind up wandering Europe, homeless, and by and large relying on each other. Eventually, they join the ranks of the

Wonder Twins #1 shows the exiled aliens Zan & Jayna activating their unique transformative powers using touch. © 2019 DC Comics.

Avengers.[54] At one point, Wanda is shot, leaving her brother to rescue her and rejoin Magneto.

From the very start, Pietro and Wanda are as close as any brother and sister could be … sometimes, too close. While not explicit in the MCU, their relationship went beyond sibling love, as writers chose to make them lovers as well. In the *Ultimate Marvel* series, the twins share an incestuous relationship. Traditionally Quicksilver had never approved of his sister's paramours—Hawkeye and the android known as Vision—and now we know why. It recalls the same type of relationship between Apollo and Artemis, even including the love triangle with Orion. In the MCU, *Age of Ultron*, Quicksilver dies trying to save Hawkeye and a young boy from Ultron. Scarlet Witch senses the death of her brother. She radiates a blast of hex energy that destroys the sentinels. She eventually hunts down Ultron. The robot warns her to flee the city or else she will die. Her reply is that she just did, referring to the death of Pietro. "Do you know what it felt like?" she asks. "It felt like that…" she cries, ripping the core processor from Ultron's chest. The scene demonstrates the inseparable connection between her and her brother, like wearing one's heart outside of one's own body. A twin is an *alter ego*, another "self." Closer than a friend or even another sibling, twins have a special bond that non-twins can hardly fathom, much less experience.

Two-in-One: Two-Face, the Janus of Crime

Heads or tails? Fans of the Dark Knight are all too familiar with the coin-flipping prince of crime known as Two-Face. Once Gotham City's young and aspiring District Attorney, Harvey Dent, the character was disfigured after infamous crime boss Sal Maroni douses him with acid. The sight of his own reflection—half his former persona and half a disfigured monster—drives Dent insane. Obsessed with the concept of duality, Two-Face represents a different kind of twin, conjoined, like Eurytus and Cteatus, but they are two halves of the same whole, and like the Hulk and Bruce Banner, each personality struggles for dominance.

In DC's Post-Crisis comic series, it is revealed that Harvey has a dark past, an abusive father, who flips a coin to decide whether or not he will brutalize his son. He also begins to show early signs of bipolar disorder. In *Batman: Jekyll & Hyde* we learn that Harvey once had an older brother named Murray, who died in a fire, because Harvey was too sacred to save him. It is further explained that Murray is Harvey's second personality, his *therapon*, which surfaces after his break with reality. In the two-issue mini-series *Batman: Two-Face Strikes Twice!*, Two-Face plans to abduct the twins of his former wife and her new husband Janus, only to learn later he is the father.

Throughout his history, Harvey and Two-Face see each other as separate entities, with Two-Face calling Harvey spineless, but we are never really sure who is in the driver's seat. Is Two-Face really a different persona, Harvey's perception of Murray, or his true self? At several points, when Harvey is healed from his accident, Two-Face returns. This raises the question: was the disfigurement merely the awakening of Harvey's twin personality, which was there the whole time either as a form of guilt or inadequacy in the demise of his brother? The emergence of his dark side could also represent a latent trauma response to his father's abuse.

Conclusion

In the ancient world, at a time when infant mortality was relatively high, twins represented a miracle of nature. Beyond this, they carry an additional mystique in that each represents a living, breathing mirror of the other. In many instances, twins share a special bond. They are at many times inseparable, work together with the same mind, and in some instances can sense the thoughts and feelings of their other half. When one dies, the other feels the pain. In this we may surmise that while providing the closest and most intimate of companions, an inseparable wingman, twins selves also leave the hero open to extreme vulnerability, for the loss is not necessarily the loss of a sibling, but the loss also of the self, of an identity formed on a binary model.

VIII

Defending the Epic City

Gotham and Troy

Soaring towers, impenetrable battlements, shimmering halls—the city of Troy, forever immortalized in the words of Homer, has played host to some of epic's most enduring heroes: Hector, Paris, and Aeneas to name just a few. Nevertheless, this magnificent city, whose mighty walls were believed to have been built by the gods themselves, has typically been viewed as merely the backdrop to the heroes who fought there. Often we fail to recognize the city itself as a major character with a life and death all its own. Cities such as Troy, for example, are often accompanied by themes of wealth, decadence, and moral decline. One could ostensibly argue that ancient citadels like Troy were the Gotham cities of their day. The city's auspicious placement along the Bosporus had garnered it enormous wealth and power, so much so that its kings, such as Laomedon, were emboldened to threaten even the gods with slavery.[1]

Throughout the *Iliad*, Homer's illustrious city teeters on the razor's edge of moral decline, its mighty warrior class reduced to preferring ransoms to combat, and its royal family providing repeated examples of poor *xenia*. Nevertheless, for the Trojans, the city acts as though an enduring and protective force, as if a mother to her brood. What more can Homer's tale reveal about Troy? In this chapter, we shall explore the character of the epic city and its relationship with its heroes, looking specifically at the anthropomorphism of its architectural features, its towers, gates, and walls. How does Homer take urban landscape and breathe life into it? How do those who dwell there view it? We will then compare Troy to the modern fictional setting of Gotham City, the sprawling metropolis that gave birth to one of the comic book world's most enduring heroes, the Dark Knight. Finally, we shall compare the enigmatic Batman with Hector, as both prince and defender of their respective home towns.

Homer's Troy

The modern site of Hisarlik, along Turkey's north west coast, sits atop a rocky, windswept plateau at the mouth of the Dardanelles, overlooking the deep blue waters of the Aegean. Homer's Troy, however, is not necessarily Hisarlik, or even a real-life Bronze Age citadel, *per se*. Nevertheless, Homer's city does stitch together many traits that were common to Bronze Age sites by taking into account the remains of ancient sites still visible to them, oral tradition that contains only partial information about the actual site, and using a fertile imagination. Ostensibly, Troy, the city we have come to recognize as the epitome of the Bronze Age town, only ever lived in Homer's words.[2] That being said, what Homer manages to do is to create, perhaps like Plato's Atlantis, a model for what ancient Greeks saw as the ideal place to live, a beacon of light at the edge of an impending dark age looming in the distance, a place of grand beauty with wide streets, shining halls, imposing gates, and soaring towers.[3]

Among Homer's many wonders were several sacred sites such as the Temple of Apollo, Athena, and Aphrodite, and the tomb of Ilus, the original settlement's founder, beyond the walls of the city. It also had fixed *loci*, places that hosted major life events that embodied the collective consciousness of its people, such as the old oak at the Scaean Gate.[4] Around these we must imagine the sites created by war: a ramshackle Greek fort with walls and battlements, and ships that served as homes. Homer not only creates a believable world that continues to capture the imagination, but he gave it life as well by providing it a biography, focusing on both its foundation and its development. Like its main characters, Troy and its surrounding plain are in a constant state of change. For the purposes of this chapter, we will explore some of these features and how they lend character to the city.

Well-Built Walls

Walls are a vital feature of any ancient or medieval city. Not only do they provide a source of defense and security, they help delineate "us" from "them," and instill in the residents a sense of identity. Walls create liminal zones, which allow the Trojan old men and wives to watch their sons and husbands from a distance, literally serving as a theater of war. So it is in Homer's tale. Many of the heroes come from great walled cities, which speaks to their ability to defend themselves.[5] When Homer describes Troy, he mentions its "great walls," τείχεα μακρὰ (*teichea makra*), or even "well-walled" emphasizing their strength and construction of stone rather than simply mud brick.[6] The gods themselves built this city's walls. In Book 21,

Poseidon recalls his and Apollo's labor in constructing the city's walls for king Laomedon. This in and of itself highlights their importance: they are not merely for protection from outside forces, but they also have the interior protection of the gods who built them.

In addition to providing refuge, the walls of the city often lend strength and support to her people. In the opening of Book 3, Iris leads Helen to the walls to observe the fight. Priam and his advisers are there, Antenor and Ucalegon, whom Homer describes as bloodless. In their old age and frailty, the walls are supportive of the old wise men, whose fighting days are done. In ancient Greece, the role of supporting old men typically fell to women, usually a daughter, wife or even a mother.[7] The supportive role for aging male heroes may be feminine, but the walls of the city itself are often without gender. The actual Greek word for walls is neuter in gender, but interestingly enough, when used in the context of Troy, they become feminine. In Book 21, for example, Homer refers to the great walls of Troy, Ἰλιόφι κλυτὰ τείχεα (*Iliophi kluta teichea*).[8] Here, the noun Ἰλιόφι (*Iliophi*), an epic genitive, is feminine, thus lending a feminine quality to the city. Thus, many modern translators of Homer's text have long upheld this tradition, translating them as "her walls," though no such pronoun "her" exists in the actual Greek. Thus when we find Achilles chasing Hector around the walls of Troy, it is as if he is chasing him around the *peplos* of the mother city. Although Homer never expressly states it, Troy does provide the comfort and protection of a mother figure, which can be gathered in analyzing its features. For a medieval counterpart, we may look to the walls of Cologne, which were similarly protected by the patroness of the city, St. Ursula, as well as her 11,000 virgins as noted in a plaque commemorating the successful defense of the city during the siege of 1268.[9]

Gates and Towers

Of all of Troy's features, its gates are its most defining. They stand as a symbol for strength, power, and resolve. They are often the focus of war, for the ultimate goal is to have access to the open gates of the city. At various points in Homer's epic, the heroes find themselves before the gates, πύλας (*pulas*), of the city.[10] Πύλας is a feminine word, lending at least grammatical gender to the city of Troy. We might perceive these gates as the face of the city, witnessing the encounters of the heroes.

Most of the major conflicts happen in front of Troy's Scaean gate.[11] It is where Hector eventually confronts Achilles.[12] It is also where Hector says Achilles will meet his end at the hands of Paris.[13] The location is marked by an old oak, which has a recurring place in the epic. Mentioned at least 17 times, it is where returning heroes gather, e.g., Sarpedon is carried there when wounded, where Apollo and Athena meet as carrion birds, and where families come to hear the latest news about their sons, brothers, and husbands.[14] Associated with the gate and protection, the oak also stands for strength, endurance, and of course, is associated with the king of the Olympian gods, Zeus himself.[15] Though not named specifically in Homer's text, the second gate would have been the Dardanian. Curiously, it is marked by a fig tree, standing as a bookend to the oak, perhaps as a sign of fecundity and youth. It is one of the features of Troy that Homer shows us, almost marking the scenery and pulling our attention away from the main action, which at this point is Achilles pursuing Hector around the walls of the city.

Towers are another important feature of Troy. Without them, according to Homer, cities stand no chance.[16] Often described as lofty, like walls, they broadcast a message of power. More importantly, they provide the city with its intelligence, granting views of the surrounding plain, and thus part of a network of visual communication and strategy. At one point, in Book 16, Achilles relates his secret desire to have himself and Patroclus alone bring down Troy's mighty crown of towers. The term he uses is κρήδεμνον (*krēdemnon*), a neuter noun, which refers metaphorically to the battlements, but more specifically to a woman's headband, replete with veil.[17] The allusion is not lost on the reader, and once again makes Troy appear lady-like.

Luxury and Decadence

Homer casts Troy as a city of lavish pleasures. Overlooking the Hellespont, the city is the gateway between the Black Sea and the Aegean. It also sits at the confluence of two rivers, the Simoes (*Iliad* 5.773–4) and the Scamander, making her plains wet and fertile, again imposing a feminine persona upon the city. It is thus an apt metaphor for the "Orientalizing" city, one at the center of trade and lavished in decadence.

Elsewhere may be found more explicit signs of decadence. In Book 6, Homer describes the palace of Priam as having been adorned with "polished colonnades" and containing "fifty roofed chambers of polished stone."[18] In terms of Bronze Age standards, it is a fantastic display of wealth and power. While many Bronze Age homes were made of mud brick on a stone socle, Priam's palace is made completely of stone, which is expensive to quarry, cut, fashion, and transport, much less polish.[19] More work means more costs and thus, more money. Bernard Knox in his introduction to Fagles' translation of the *Iliad* has noted that at any given time, the

Trojans resort to wealth to buy their way out of a problem, offering bribes and paying ransoms to get what they want.[20] While the city's wealth may have brought it economic prosperity, its related attitudes of warrior behavior set the city on a path for decline, with heroes such as Paris resorting to stealing other men's wives, thinking he can get away with it, because his father can buy his way out. Paris' gamble clearly does not pay off.

Luxury, *habrosyne*, had long been seen as Eastern and effeminate to the Greeks, but according to Leslie Kurke, this really only becomes obvious after the Persian Wars.[21] It seems, however, that there is already fear of foreign lavishness in Homer. While Troy's resources have made its people wealthy, it has also made them weak. They rely on ransom rather than fear of their military forces, and their wealth like a magnet drew many a greedy eye. In Book 6, for example, the Trojan warrior Adrestus is defeated in battle and begs Menelaus for his life, promising him a priceless ransom from his father, if he would just let him live. Menelaus is about to spare him, until his brother Agamemnon arrives and chastises him for being soft.[22] The deeper irony is, that while Menelaus came to Troy for Helen, Achaeans like Agamemnon came to its gates for plunder, like a swarm of locusts stripping the land of its bounty.

The City as Mother Protector

Homer engenders Troy with feminine qualities, especially those of a mother. For example, in Book 2 Odysseus recalls the tale of the prophet Kalchas who presaged the fall of Troy, when recalling the omen at Aulis of the snake devouring a mother sparrow and her brood.[23] Throughout the epic, we find Troy's walls likewise offering refuge and protection to her people. We might liken this to the modern view of ships, often named for women, perhaps because they care for the sailors in their charge by seeing them safely home. So, too, should we see Troy as though a protective and nourishing mother, providing strength and an identity to her children. Though not in Homer, the modern film *Troy* shows Hector rallying the troops, entreating them to fight for Troy, the mother of us all.[24] The terrain even rises up against the Achaeans, as when Achilles fends off an attack by the nearby river god, Scamander. Why is this important? Because if we understand Troy to be like a mother figure, then it deepens our appreciation for Hector as a dutiful son, not just to Queen Hecuba, but to the city of Troy herself. In return, the city will mourn his loss and allow him to sleep in her fertile plains.

At times, Troy's heroes seem to draw strength from her. As Andromache notes in Book 22, she fears her husband Hector has been cut off from the city.[25] When she reaches the battlements and spies the corpse of Hector, she casts off her marriage crown. This simple act has profound bearing on our interpretation of the city. Not only does it foretell the city's fall, with the falling of its battlements like the falling of Andromache's crown, but it also creates a parallel between the city and a wife and mother. Cybele, the goddess of the city, is frequently shown wearing the mural crown, that is a crown of walls. In fact, Tyche takes on the attributes of Cybele during Hellenistic times to become the goddess of the city.[26] In this way, we may interpret the siege of the city as a form of reciprocal bride stealing for the abduction of Helen, but ultimately an act of violation, this time perpetrated by the Greeks.

Seated figure of the goddess Cybele with the portrait head of a priestess, dated to about AD 50, replete with her crenelated crown that represents the city. Marble, 162 × 70 × 64.5 cm (63¾ × 27⁹⁄₁₆ × 25⅜ in.), 57.AA.19. The J. Paul Getty Museum, Villa Collection, Malibu, CA.

The theme of rape is not at all far-fetched. If you consider the text, the constant theme is bringing down the city's walls, the city's protective armor, if you will, despoiling her just as a soldier would any fallen foe on the battlefield. Ultimately, Troy succumbs because she is lured to bed with the gift of a horse, a virile, overtly masculine creature. Once inside, hundreds of Greek soldiers are released, setting fire to the city. Even at the very base level, the sexual innuendo cannot be missed: the Greek soldiers, inside the virile horse, spill as if seeds into the opened gates of Troy. Therefore, I would argue that the siege is seen as a retaliatory action for the abduction and rape of Helen.

Hector, Protector of Troy

One of the most fascinating, if not tragic, characters in the *Iliad* is Hector. In terms of Homeric heroes, he has no special powers. Unlike Achilles, he is not semi-divine, and yet he is one of the strongest characters by virtue of his heroism, but also his humanity. He is a just leader, a good son, and a loyal husband who, for the most part, extols the warrior code. He does not approve of his brother's abduction of Helen and even chastises him for running away from Menelaus and not acting like a man. He is a dutiful son and tender father. His interaction with his son Astynax is one of the most memorable and heart-breaking in all of epic. It also shows us a character who, unlike so many around him, is not fighting for glory but for his family and his home. Homer explicitly calls Hector the defender or "guardian" of Troy, ἐπίσκοπος (*episkopos*).[27] Time and again he comes to its rescue. He is its stark defender. In Book 7, for example, he challenges the Achaeans, demanding to battle their best warrior.[28] Many times Hector routes the Achaeans, driving them back to their ships. Only after he strips Patroclus of his (Achilles') armor do we begin to see his *hubris*. Throughout the epic, he has acted honorably, even more so than Achilles, who walks away from battle. It only takes one act, however, to remind us that Hector is, after all, human, and that human pride may be punished by the gods.

The intrinsic link between Hector and the city can be felt in Book 22 when his father and mother, Priam and Hecuba, beg him to return to the protection of the walls. Whenever Hector returns from battle, he consults his mother, Hecuba, whose own walls—her uterus, her arms when he was a baby—protected him. In this again we find the city of Troy linked metaphorically with motherly protection. The link between Andromache's crown and the battlements of the city places Hector at the center of a unique sort of bigamy: with Andromache on the one hand, his wife, and Troy, the city to whom he is wedded on the other. In this sense, Hector's loyalties seem to always be divided between duty to the city and duty as a spouse. In the end, his loyalty to the city takes him away from life with his wife and infant son. He ultimately sleeps forever in the cold embrace of Mother Troy.

The Dark Knight, Defender of Gotham

Gotham City, likewise, acts as mother figure, giving birth to a modern breed of epic hero and villain. Dark and gritty with soaring skyscrapers, decadent neoclassical sculpture, and airships circling like birds of prey beneath a sky of grey haze, the atmosphere of Gotham is almost otherworldly. And yet certain elements resonate with modern audiences. It could be any major metropolitan city in America today but on steroids. In comics, as in film, Gotham City provides a battleground for the hero and the villain alike with dens uniquely suited for their purposes, whether an abandoned factory, amusement park, or forgotten subway station. Like Troy, it is a city besieged—not by Achaeans, but by home-grown criminal forces eager to dominate her. And like Troy, Gotham has its defender, Batman, known also by his epithet: the Dark Knight.

Cape billowing in the wind, the masked defender scours the shadow-drenched streets of the city with tireless eyes. Having witnessed the murder of his parents first hand and haunted by their memory, billionaire Bruce Wayne dons the armor to become the ultimate modern superhero. Dressed like a bat, he wages an endless battle, striking fear in the hearts of the city's most complex criminal masterminds and common street thugs alike. Similarly, like Hector, he does so without the aid of super powers or divine lineage or aid. He earns the respect of his fellow heroes, including Superman, who gives him the highest praise: "I have powers. I had to do this. All he has are his wits and his will. And he chooses to do this. Everyone wants to be him. He's just a better man than I am."[29]

Batman's story is entrenched in the city that took his parents from him. For most of his life, Bruce had led a sheltered life far from the corruption and crime that was slowly taking root in Gotham, until that fateful night when in an alley behind the old movie house known as Park Row, a petty crook named Joe Chill changed their lives forever. After the traumatic events of that night, Bruce vowed a war on crime and spent years traveling the globe outside of Gotham's protective walls, honing his skills in martial arts, criminal detection, and technology. Armed with an array of sophisticated weapons and with his fortune behind him, Batman took on both street level crime and major threats to the whole city, taking refuge behind the walls of Wayne Manor and the Batcave, a lair buried deep beneath the streets of the city.

Like Troy, Gotham is a major economic center with a commercial seaport. The cityscape itself borrows from various urban landscapes such as New York and Chicago, but brief glimpses of the city's unique and mysterious origins can be seen. In *Batman: The Cult*, we learn that the site used to host the Miagani, an ancient tribe led by a shaman named Blackfire, who continues to haunt the city.[30] We also learn of Judge Solomon Wayne, who, with the aid of architect Cyrus Pinkney, designed a city with thick walls to protect the virtuous, and instead he realized only too late that "I wished to lock evil out of men's neighborhoods and hearts. I fear that instead I have given it the means to be locked in."[31] From this we gather that Gotham was once a walled city but has since fallen into urban decay.

In the crossover Batman, "No Man's Land," after a cataclysmic quake, the city descends into a massive turf war, with various criminals carving up the city and taking control. As a result, the government deems Gotham unredeemable and cuts it off from the mainland by blowing the bridges.[32] Likewise, Troy has descended into a type of urban decay. Not a turf war per se, but its citizens have succumbed to its wealth at the expense of the heroic ideal; for example, we tend to find Trojans offering ransoms rather than fighting to regain their loved ones. The same recurring theme of corruption appears in the Fox Television series *Gotham*. Civil servants, such as Commissioner Loeb, are just as much a threat to the city and its well-being as the Joker.

As gritty as Gotham is, the city, like Troy, is cast as feminine and motherly, with the womblike Batcave providing a safe haven for the caped crusader. So, too, do criminals have their dens, each uniquely suited to their personal needs—the Iceberg Lounge, for example, for Penguin, Amusement Mile for the Joker. One of the landmarks is the Statue of Justice, also known as Lady Gotham, a statue much like our own Statue of Liberty, except blindfolded, holding a sword in one hand and scales in the other. Gotham offers both hero and villain alike equal shelter to thrive.

Gotham's maternal persona not only shelters, but also gives new life to both heroes and villains within her realm. As we have seen, Bruce Wayne is reborn as Batman after emerging from the bat cave, an act that is repeated night after night. His arch nemesis, after plummeting into a vat of chemicals, is reborn as the clown prince of crime known as the Joker. Mr. Freeze, Two-Face, Cat-Woman—time and time again, everyday people are transformed by the city into the monstrous villains we know and love. In *Batman: The Animated Series*, Victor Fries is transformed into a super villain after a skirmish at Gothcorp where he is doused with chemicals that leave him able to thrive only in sub-zero temperatures. In the film *Batman Returns*, Selina Kyle is transformed by the city after being pushed out of a window. In the comics, she has various origin stories, but during her formative years, it is revealed that life on the streets has forced her to turn to theft, again transforming her into the villain we come to recognize. The theme of a corrupt city giving birth to villains is played consistently throughout the entire five year run of the television show *Gotham*, so much so that one of its recurring characters, Harvey Bullock, remarks on one villain's death, "He's dead, remember? Not that that matters much in this town anymore."[33] Characters like Poison Ivy, Solomon Grundy, and Fish Mooney, after being brought to the edge of death, are transformed by the urban fabric of the city itself.

Conclusion

Ultimately Batman shares many of the same traits as Hector. Like Hector, Bruce Wayne descends from a long line of ruling founder figures. Both Batman and Hector, despite being merely human, nevertheless strike terror in their foes. Both are intrinsically tied to the cities of their birth, and both tend to show a deep compassion for humanity, despite their hardships, and both are willing to risk their own lives for their city and home. Cities such as Troy and Gotham not only provide a backdrop for their epic battles but are also imbued with traits that make them into characters with lives of their own. These urban environments both stand on the edge of collapse, relying on their defender to constantly pull them back from the brink. The city for both Batman and Hector also acts as a protective mother. Whether ensconced in a cave or behind its walls, the symbolism of being nurtured in the womb is ever-present and gives both characters their *raison d'etre.*

IX

Swift and True

Tales of the Epic Archer

With an arrow straight and true, the role of the archer has long held a special place in the epic tradition. Herakles, Odysseus, and Teucer were fearsome and formidable arbalists sending many of their enemies screaming into the arms of Hades with a well-knocked arrow. Lest we forget, even the mightiest of Greek warriors, Achilles, fell beneath the bowman's arrow. And yet, an ineffable tension has always existed between the archer and the front-line soldier. Often viewed as a second-string hero, these ancient equivalents of the modern sniper nevertheless provide a vital balance to the protagonist and the narrative itself.

The aim of this chapter is to elucidate the role of the archer, whose skills with a bow often turn the tide of battle, but whose role is sometimes seen as questionable, dishonorable, or lesser than those who fight hand-to-hand. In this we will look to both the occasional bowman and the professional archer, at Paris, Teucer and his brother Ajax, Odysseus, and Philoctetes. We will then compare these marksmen of Greek myth with the modern archers of the comic book universe: Avenger's Hawkeye and DC's Green Arrow, in order to find a common thread among attitudes toward archers and how they often are relegated to the role of side-kick.

The Epic Archer in Homer

Paris

There are many archers in Homer: Odysseus, Teucer, Meriones, Epeus and Philoctetes.[1] There is of course the far-shooter, the god Apollo, whose arrows hum through the air, like an angry swarm, delivering plague unto the soldiers of the Greek camp.[2] But perhaps the most famous archer of all is the Trojan prince, Paris. The quintessential middle child of Priam's brood, he is seen as a perpetual trouble-maker, foretold by his own sister to be the firebrand of Troy. Furthermore, Paris fails to observe proper *xenia*, going so far as to steal the wife of his host, Menelaus. Although wife-stealing was for the Greeks akin to what we might consider pinching the college mascot, cow-tipping, or other such forms of boorish fraternity humor, Menelaus didn't find it very funny. Paris' patron god is actually a matron, for it is Aphrodite who is always at hand to save him from fortune's fickle hand. In short, Paris is hardly the stuff from which heroes are made.

In the beginning of Book 3, both his own brother Hector and Helen chastise him for his cowardice.[3] Hector calls him a beguiler, mad for women, with no strength in his heart, more likely to pick up the lyre than the spear.[4] That's sibling rivalry for you. But Paris can't help it. He's a lover, not a fighter. Interestingly, his choice weapon is the bow, again highlighting his non-conformity to the code of the hero. In Book 11, he manages to wound Diomedes in the foot with an arrow as the Greek is stripping off the armor of Agastrophus, and taunts him. Nailed to the spot, his foot gushing with blood and throbbing with pain, Diomedes rends the air with foul curses, and shouts:

> Bowman, slanderer, master of the shining bow, seducer of maidens. If you had tried to stop me man-to-man in armor, then your bow and thick flying arrows would have helped you not. For now, having grazed the flat of my foot, you boast in vain.[5]

Continuing his tempestuous slander, he calls the young prince a coward, comparing his attack with arrows like that of a witless child or a woman, and if he had used a sharp spear instead of an arrow, he actually might have dispatched his enemy.

Diomedes is clearly hurt and vexed by the prospect of being sidelined, but that should not nullify his attack on Paris. His views are a warrior's views on the use of archery on the battlefield. His belief seems to be that enemies should be dispatched quickly and face-to-face. Those about to die should know their killer. Fighting a warrior beneath one's warrior status also fails to earn one honor on the battlefield. Therefore, to fall to an archer, rather than from a fellow infantryman must come as a terrible blow to one's valor. Perhaps it is just Paris that gives the character of the archer a bad name, rather than being a bowman *per se*. It is ironic then that Paris should take down the greatest warrior Achilles from afar,[6] and yet not hold his own in battle against Menelaus. Equally ironic is Paris' fate: being taken down by another bowman.

An arrow is ultimately a quick way to die. In epic, the heroic duel is not about mowing down one's enemies quickly, but meeting them face-to-face. We know, for instance, that Diomedes and Glaucus actually stop fighting, because their grandfathers were friends, and for the sake of *xenia*, they rekindle those old ties of friendship. This is quintessentially the warrior code. If Paris shoots from afar, he never gets a chance to ask or interact with his mark. Then again, we already know also just how Paris feels about ties of *xenia*....

Pandarus

The bow can also reveal the moral character of a hero. On the verge of reclaiming his wife Helen, Menelaus is struck by an arrow shot by the bowman Pandarus.[7] Pandarus, companion to Aeneas, is the son of Lycaon, a "godlike" hero renowned for his skills with a bow. When we find him, the Achaeans and Trojans have formed a truce. It appears that the war is finally over. Athena, however, eager to begin the conflagration once more, has other plans. Disguised as a spearman and speaking winged words, she convinces him that he would win eternal glory if he breaks the truce and takes down Menelaus with his arrow.

> Listen to me now, skilled son of Lycaon.
> Have you the courage to discharge a swift arrow
> Against Menelaus and gain the favor and glory for all the Trojans
> And most of all King Alexander?
> And from him you would bear foremost of all splendid gifts
> Should he see Menelaus the warlike son of Atreus,
> Laid low by an arrow and laid upon the grievous pyre.[8]

Pandarus stands with the shield bearers, who provide him cover so that he may draw his bow. The bow itself has a story, being constructed from the horns and sinew of a wild ibex, which he had taken down in a hunt. After propitiating himself to Apollo, lord of the bow, he fires an arrow, which would have found its mark, if Athena had not foiled the shot. It strikes Menelaus but does not go deep enough to kill him.

What is the takeaway to this encounter aside from the gods are always interfering in the lives of mortals? First, Pandarus is willing to use subterfuge to earn personal glory. This seems to fly in the face of the warrior code, but then so do many of the actions taken by those we call heroes. Odysseus, for example, is willing to stab Diomedes in the back at one point—and they're on the same side! War turns men into animals, regardless of race, religion, or here, weapon of choice. Second, Pandarus is not at the front line but hiding behind the shield bearers. The implication is subtle but still there: plotting behind a shield is un-heroic. Is it necessarily his fault though? Athena interfered, and archers are by nature ineffective on the front line. Later in the epic, when Pandarus encounters Diomedes, he is useless up close.

For the epic warrior, being able to handle oneself on the battlefield is the mark of a true soldier. Fighting from far away is not. Hence claiming the bow especially as a weapon reveals a hero's moral character. Then again, why does there seem to be a distinction between the spearman and the archer, since both are projectiles? Perhaps because even though one throws a spear, in Hoplite warfare, the spear and shield are used to protect the ranks of the front line.[9] Finally, deceptive or not, Pandarus the bowman has the power to turn the tide of battle. His single arrow can take out Menelaus, whose death would have changed the outcome of the war.

Teucer

The son of King Telamon and Hesione,[10] Teucer fought behind the shield of his half-brother, Ajax the Greater. Claiming the lives of many a Trojan hero including Hector's charioteer Archeptolemus, Teucer's arrows always find their mark. So adept in fact is he that Apollo has to frequently step in to even the score and to make things interesting by diverting arrows meant for Hector, whose fate was meant for Achilles. At one point, Zeus confounds the hero, destroying his bow and sending it smashing to the ground.[11] Ajax advises him at that point to pick up a spear and shield to join the fight. After his half-brother's suicide, he spars with Agamemnon and Menelaus over dispensing with a proper burial.[12]

Teucer is an interesting character, mostly because he appears as a reservist and second-string hero, literally living in his half-brother's shadow. He is also always challenging Hector, whose destiny it is to face Achilles in battle. Although his grandfather has semi-divine status, Teucer does not. He lacks divine favor and thus must rely on his wits. Thus, he never really gets his chance to shine, because the gods are always playing favorites. Unlike Paris or Pandarus, he is not necessarily seen negatively because he is an archer. This is chiefly because he can, if need be, pick up a spear and do the same job as a front-line soldier. He also defends his companions and is an otherwise avid protector of the warrior code; for example, he guards Ajax's body after his suicide and demands that the proper burial customs be observed. The chaotic nature of Homeric warfare would seem to suggest that archers such as Teucer would choose and attack opponents at random without their knowing, like when Teucer tries to fell Hector. Only through Zeus' interference—breaking Teucer's bow—is Hector saved. Perhaps we should understand this event as Zeus saving Hector to ensure he meets his destiny with Achilles in battle. Alternatively, Zeus could be stepping in to make sure the match is fair. In the Homeric mindset, dealing death from afar rather than up close and personal is an un-heroic attribute.

Philoctetes

Perhaps the greatest archer of all is, ironically, the one we hear practically nothing about in Homer's text. Abandoned by his fellow Greeks on a distant island, the character known as Philoctetes is one that does not receive a lot of attention, but he should, for he is the epic warrior whose arrows never miss their mark.[13] He owns the famed bow of Herakles and is the one who puts Paris down for good, effectively ending the decade-long war.

A glimpse of the famous archer Philoctetes after he has been abandoned on the island of Lemnos by the rest of his crewmates on a 5th c. BCE Attic lekythos. His bow, gifted to him by the hero Herakles, rests on a rock at his feet. The Metropolitan Museum of Art, NY; Fletcher Fund, 1956 56.171.58.

The son of King Poeas, it is said he inherited the bow from Herakles in gratitude for helping the hero ignite his own funeral pyre.[14] Once a contender for the hand of Helen, he thus is duty bound to honor the Oath of Tyndareus, an oath made by all Helen's suitors to come to the aid of her chosen spouse, should she ever be abducted. There are various stories of what happened next. According to Homer, after receiving the bite of a water snake, often howling aloud in great pain, and likely suffering from a gangrenous infection which made the wound smell exceptionally foul, Philoctetes is left behind on the island of Lemnos by the Achaeans on their way to Troy.[15] After learning from a Trojan seer that to win the war, the Greeks need the bow of Herakles, they mount an expedition to retrieve him. In the eponymous Sophoclean play, we find Odysseus trying to trick Philoctetes into giving up the bow. In the end, Neoptolemus feels it is wrong to come away with the bow and not the archer, and so he tries to convince Philoctetes to come with them, finally, to the theater of war. Only after an appearance by Herakles, now deified, who claims that Philoctetes is destined to kill Paris, does he relent. The themes presented in Sophocles' play include both the guilt at abandoning a wounded warrior and the need for one's story to be told to be remembered.

Eventually Philoctetes is healed and continues on to Troy where he confronts Paris in a duel of the fates.[16] After Paris aims and misses Philoctetes by a hair, Philoctetes, incensed, returns with two shots. The first strikes Paris in the wrist. The other finds its mark between the flank and groin. The last we see of him, he is retreating from the battle, eventually dying from his wounds. Smyrnaeus calls Philoctetes a lion, rushed at by a dog, Paris. Again, we have two archers with two vastly divergent characters treated differently—not because of their weapon, but because of their adherence to the warrior code. It seems a strange sort or irony that he kills Paris, as both are archers, or perhaps it is an issue of classism, where both are also princes rather than kings. A deeper irony lies in the fact that Philoctetes was an original suitor of Helen, though he lost out to Menelaus; it seems only fitting that *he* should emerge triumphant over Helen's abductor.

If it had been Menelaus, Agamemnon, or Achilles who had been struck by a serpent, the question would hardly have been to leave the hero behind. Philoctetes is seen as a minor character, a side-kick, which is why he is left behind. Only after the Achaeans learn that they need his bow does he become important. Even then, as Sophocles seems to suggest, it may only be because of his bow rather than the man himself.

The Weapon of the Hunter

One of the oldest weapons, the bow has been wielded by many an epic hero in battle, but the weapon has always been the mark of the hunter rather than the soldier. Orion, the Theban hero Actaeon, Hippolytus, Herakles, and Odysseus all used the bow to hunt. The bow, then, is often associated with the royal hunt, or the sport of kings in ancient Mediterranean traditions. Orion is the son of Poseidon and Euryale, daughter of King Minos.[17] Actaeon was part of the royal house of Cadmus, and Hippolytus was the son of Theseus, Athens' king. Odysseus was king of Ithaka, and Herakles the son of Zeus and Alcmene, daughter of Electryon, king of Tiryns, and Amphitryon, Herakles' earthly father, was the son of Alcaeus, the king of Tiryns in the Argolid.

The hunt is also especially prominent in royal symbolism of the Near East. The now famous stone panel from Room B at the North-West Palace

Relief panel of Ashurnasirpal II (Neo-Assyrian, 883–859 BCE). Armed with bows and arrows, the king hunts lions from his chariot, accompanied by a charioteer and entourage, from the North-West Palace (Room B, Panel 19) at Nimrud (British Museum registration number 1847, 0623.11). © The Trustees of the British Museum/Art Resource, NY.

of Nimrud, now ensconced in the British Museum, shows the ruler Ashurnasirpal II armed with bows and arrows, hunting lions from his chariot, accompanied by a charioteer and entourage. Here the king of men slays the king of beasts, a metaphor perhaps for non–Assyrian kings. Like Ashurnasirpal, the Greek heroes armed with the bow might be viewed as a distinctive social class. The idea of connecting the royal hunt with heroism stands out in Greek lore with such stories as the Calydonian boar hunt.

To slay a human foe like an animal, however, is something else entirely, as we have seen with such cases as Pandarus, Paris, and Teucer. First, it demonstrates a difference in social status, with the bowman as predator and his rival as prey. Trying to fit this into the mold of Homeric epic is challenging, especially when you have two opposing and disparate forms of warfare—that of the Hoplite phalanx and that of hand-to-hand combat. Clearly, in Homer's epic, hand-to-hand combat is the preferred method of the epic warrior. The archer, however, almost seems an archaism, more aligned with Greek myth. To pit a mythological archer, at least in Homer's mind, against a warrior in modern warfare, is almost like placing the Titans among the Olympian Gods. Archers are echoes of a former age, one ruled by kings rather than a burgeoning *demos,* such as we find during the 6th/early 5th c. BCE recension of the epic.

The bow is also typically associated with Near Eastern and Asiatic forces rather than Greeks and warriors of the West. The Scythians and Parthians are good examples of "Other" people being bow-bearers rather than sword-wielders. Herodotus clearly states that the army of Xerxes was comprised of highly trained archers who carried long bows.[18] To these he adds also the Bactrians, Carians, Indians, and Arians. The materials of the bows range from reed to palm-wood. None, curiously, are made of animal horns, as is the bow of Herakles. Rarely, if ever, do we find Greek soldiers wielding the bow on vase paintings. While some may indicate that this is a direct result of the Persian War, I argue that the bow is never used as the primary weapon in battle, but again more as a personal weapon reserved for hunting or contests. What we do find is Eastern forces, such as the Trojans, Paris being a key example, and Persians employing the bow.[19] The influence of the Persian War would have had a profound effect on the prevailing attitudes toward archers in general.

Green Arrow

Attitudes towards archers and archery are different today. Despite its simplicity, the bow continues to be a popular weapon. Throughout the Middle Ages, the bow becomes a popular weapon especially at encounters such as the Battle of Crécy where French crossbowmen were pitted against the traditional English and Welsh longbowmen. Surprisingly, the English win out over the more sophisticated cross bow, validating both its effectiveness as a long-distance weapon, and of course highlighting the adeptness of the traditional English archer. Moreover, for many modern audiences, the classic image of the archer is the English Robin Hood, with Errol Flynn or Kevin Costner as the famous face representing the lawless renegade who stole from the rich and gave to the poor.

Elements of Robin Hood appear in DC's Green Arrow. The title character of Oliver Queen dresses in green, wears a Robin-like hat, or bycocket, and barbed beard. In one issue, writers even poke fun of this fact by having him stand next to a poster of the swashbuckling adventurer. Like Bruce Wayne or Tony Stark, however, Queen is an eccentric billionaire playboy. His life of privilege is sent into a whirl when during a sailing trip, Queen is double-crossed by his assistant, stranding him on a deserted island. Once there, Queen has to learn to survive. One of the skills he masters is that of the bow. If the story sounds familiar, it should. It is essentially the tale of Philoctetes, who, like Queen, is of noble blood, yet left to survive on the isle of Lemnos by his fellow Achaeans with only a bow to both defend and feed himself. While on the island, Queen discovers he is actually not alone. There is a local tribe being enslaved. Queen fights for their freedom and makes his way back to civilization where he comes to recognize that he has changed. No longer self-obsessed, Oliver Queen turns his attention to fighting crime and defending the meek. With his new skills of tracking and archery, he fights for the little guy he used to trample over.

Like Philoctetes, it is only after his return to society that Green Arrow

In a prime example of what Marvin Carlson calls "ghosting," Green Arrow sees his very own echo in the poster of Robin Hood. *Green Arrow: The Wonder Year* #2 (1993). © DC Comics.

discovers his fated purpose. Debuting in 1943, while Green Arrow is featured on the cover of *More Fun Comics*, he doesn't get his own comic until the 1980s. He more often appears alongside other heroes such as Green Lantern, Superboy, and members of the Justice League. On cover art, Green Arrow often appears with his trademark bow and arrow, a traditional weapon, as he takes on villains and thugs armed with guns. When compared to heroes that can fly, repel bullets, or move super fast, however, Green Arrow seems green with envy, relying on his skills as a marksman, rather than superhuman abilities.

Hawkeye

The hero known as Hawkeye, Clint Barton, has remained a loyal member of the Avengers, but he is hardly what one might call a heavy hitter.[20] Hawkeye's history, while tragic, is not overtly heroic. After losing his parents in a car accident, Clint and his brother Barney run away to join the Carson Carnival of Traveling Wonders. There, Clint falls under the tutelage of the villainous Swordsman and an archer named Trick Shot. After uncovering an embezzlement scheme initiated by Swordsman, Clint is beaten within an inch of his life. In the wake of this attack, Clint trains himself to become the world's greatest marksman. At heart, Clint is everyman. Inspired by Iron Man, he longs to become a superhero. Soon, however, he suffers a strange twist of fate, and is accused of a robbery he was trying to thwart. Offered sanctuary, he becomes involved with the Russian superagent known as Black Widow, who has her eye on Stark and his technology. Eventually, the situation is sorted out, and Hawkeye is given a second chance by Stark. Eventually he joins the Avengers, but his independent and often self-absorbed nature clashes most vehemently with Captain America. His amorous feelings toward Scarlet Witch also cause friction between him and her brother Quicksilver and eventually Vision. When things finally settle down, Hawkeye becomes a regular fixture of the team. He winds up marrying the S.H.I.E.L.D. agent known as Mockingbird.

In the Marvel Cinematic Universe, we see a different Hawkeye. For example, while at times appearing the loner, he is later depicted as a family man, married to a non-hero Laura and having a family. After the battle with Thanos, like so many, he loses everything. In the final moments, after training and watching his daughter hit her first bull's-eye, he retrieves the arrow, and turns around to find everyone vanished, victims of the Snap. He then strikes out on his own under the alias Ronin, fighting gangs and criminal syndicates. Ronin is a Japanese term used to refer to a masterless warrior who often fights alone. In the film *Avengers: Endgame*, it is revealed

ALTHOUGH I POSSESS NO SUPER-POWERS OTHER THAN MY UNFAILING ACCURACY AT TARGET SHOOTING, I CAN DO WHATEVER OTHERS CAN DO BY MEANS OF MY ARROWS!
FOR INSTANCE, IF I SHOULD WANT TO "FLY" TO THAT ROOF-TOP...

Interior panel showing the superior marksman Hawkeye taking aim.

that Ronin massacred a cartel in Mexico. Rhodes remarks that the Federales found a room full of bodies, who never even got a chance to draw their weapons, echoing the encounter Odysseus has when confronting Penelope's suitors. Ultimately it is up to Hawkeye to rescue the Soul Stone after Black Widow sacrifices herself. His role is to live on and to keep the memory of his fallen comrades alive.

In addition to archery, Hawkeye dazzles us with other amazing abilities. He is a master swordsman and acrobat. He has been trained by Captain America in hand-to-hand combat and employs a number of trick arrows against his foes. These have included acid, bolas, boomerangs, cables, grappling hooks, EMPs, explosives, Greek Fire (my personal favorite), Kryptonite, and Net arrows, to name just a few. His foldaway bow is unique, and taking a page from Odysseus' book, can only be drawn by him.[21]

Like the epic archer, Hawkeye always takes the high ground, assessing the situation from a distance. Despite his talents, however, Hawkeye is never the leader of the Avengers. He frequently plays second tier to Captain America, Iron Man, but also to Vision and Quicksilver. One wonders, is it because of his challenge to traditional authority, his non-super abilities, or because he began in a supportive role? In terms of the superhero, while Hawkeye has no super powers *per se*, it is his human abilities the team needs most, keeping them grounded.

Conclusion

With the twang of the string and shrill cry of an arrow, the epic archer appears an ambiguous figure, sometimes honorable, sometimes not, but always in a supportive role. In the exchange between Diomedes and Paris, it seems the use of a bow, akin to a sniper's bullet, is an ineffective and un-heroic method of dispatching one's foe and certainly not preferred to hand-to-hand combat. It seems to suggest an unfair advantage. To draw a bow takes incredible strength and skill to use, but those who wield it, when firing at close range, stand at an extreme disadvantage. Moreover, while the bow has had a longstanding and honored tradition in Greek culture, it has primarily been used in hunting, rather than as a fixture of battle. Only opposing forces use the bow as part of their infantry. The preferred weapons for the Greeks are the sword and spear. Thus the bow qualifies its master as "Other" or outside the usual ranks. There may also be a socio-economic class distinction between the archer and the front-line soldier. The archer may be a hunter, a member of a royal hunt, or he may be a soldier in the ranks of Homer's epic. Inasmuch as the soldier may also be royalty, he need not be to fight valiantly alongside kings.

Many of these values have been transferred to the modern heroic archer. When it comes to a team, such as the case with Hawkeye or Green Lantern, they are outsiders. With Hawkeye there is always some friction in terms of accepting authority. Similarly, if we recall, Pandarus also does not follow orders. He chooses personal glory over the glory of his people and breaks the truce with the Achaeans. In the case of Green Arrow, he is a billionaire who chooses to champion the weak. Both, however, lack superhuman abilities, and are thus treated as outsiders among their superhero clans. In some cases, such as Hawkeye or even Teucer, they occasionally fight on the front lines, but usually they resort to stealth to gain the upper hand rather than brute strength. Nevertheless, while the archer is not a superhero *per se*, he remains a vital part of the team and often serves to keep the memory and glory of their fallen comrades alive.

X

Gods Among Us

Hero as Man and Superman

Faster than a speeding bullet! More powerful than a locomotive! Able to leap tall buildings in a single bound. He is the most recognizable superhero of all time. Fleeing his doomed world of Krypton aboard a rocket ship, Kal-El arrives on Earth a helpless child and a stranger. His powers place him among the gods, and yet he is vulnerable to kryptonite and to the same human emotion that affects us all: love. Known for his unrelenting virtue and incredible strength, he is a source of inspiration and a symbol for peace and justice, the best humans could ever hope to be, and yet he is not even from this world. I speak of course of Superman, that all-American hero from his adopted town of Smallville. His tale draws heavily from several mythic archetypes. A combination of Herakles and Achilles, he acts as an intergalactic intercessor, protector, and ultimately, the *pharmakos*, or savior figure for all mankind.

This chapter delves into the semi-divine hero, born of celestial parents, who, by some strange twist of fate, is forced to live among mortals and his journey of self-discovery. Beginning with the modern comic heroes of Superman and Thor, we will explore the topic of exile and exposure, how secret identities allow heroes to bridge between human and divine realms, and the heroes' purpose as savior figures. Why do so many of us feel a connection with the Man of Steel? Do we identify more with the god-like hero, Superman, or Clark Kent, his *alter ego*? How does Superman's story echo the paradigm of the savior figure, the oldest of Indo-European traditions of the rising and falling god? What views, if any, does this paradigm help to express in terms of modern religion?

Superman

Taking to the skies in 1938, the hero known as Superman has long captured the hearts and imaginations of readers and film-goers alike. Part hero myth, part coming of age story, the Man of Steel's journey begins among the stars. Escaping his doomed planet of Krypton as an infant, Superman, Kal-El, arrives on Earth with a bang, literally, as his ship crash lands in the town of Smallville. Despite his already present superhuman abilities, he is still a very small child, and he is essentially adopted by local farmers, Jonathan and Martha Kent. Naming him Clark, they treat him as their own son, guiding the young man, instilling in him morals and values as he develops and learns to control his super-powers. With his trademark red cape and costume created by his mother, Clark heads off to take on the world, battling villainy wherever it rears its ugly head.

Equipped with super-human strength, the ability to fly, x-ray vision, and a secret identity, the Man of Steel instantly thrilled contemporary audiences. Some would also say that Superman's appeal comes from his small

Interior panel from *The Man of Steel* #6. Superman receives a vision from his father. Story and Pencils: John Byrne. Inks: Dick Giordano. Cover: John Byrne. © 1996 DC Comics.

Superman coming to terms with his Kryptonian heritage in *The Man of Steel* #6. Story & Pencils: John Byrne. Inks: Dick Giordano. Cover: John Byrne. © 1986 DC Comics.

town upbringing, conservative values, his inherent ability to see right from wrong, and a firmly rooted sense of justice, but there is a deeper level of symbolism that often goes unnoticed, beyond the red cape.

The Heroic Paradigm

The character of Superman resonates with Western audiences on a number of different levels. He represents in many ways a heroic chimaera, that is, a combination of different mythic archetypes inherited from Greek legend and folklore. For example, his super human strength appears a lot like the Greek hero Herakles. His ability to fly recalls the gorgon slayer, Perseus.

Of all the Greek heroes, however, Superman inarguably most resembles Achilles. Both are strong, god-like, and even have mothers who supply them with their telltale armor.[1] Like the iron-hearted heroes of epic, the Man of Steel is the symbol of strength and honor in our time. Both also share vulnerabilities. In order to vouchsafe Achilles, Thetis dips her infant son into the waters of the underworld River Styx, granting him almost godlike powers; the waters make him immortal, so his recognition of the mortal struggle is, shall we say, skewed. Alas, the point at which she holds him, his heel, leaves him vulnerable, as this is the only part of his body that remains fully mortal and susceptible to harm.[2] It adds a constant sense of drama to the epic as listeners are always wondering if and when Achilles will fall.

Likewise, Superman is vulnerable but only to Kryptonite, an ore from his home world, which leaves him weak.[3] This is his Achilles' heel. Time and again, villains such as Lex Luthor exploit this weakness hoping to either manipulate the Man of Steel or to cause his general destruction. Moreover, it is this vulnerability that not only garners sympathy or even empathy, since we all know too well what it means to be mortal, but also creates a heightened sense of drama. The fear that the audience feels in these dramatic moments draws people in and connects them with the character at a very human level. In short, without his weakness, the Superman story would lack the emotional intensity needed to capture its audience.

Noble Birth and Exile

Kal-El represents an extraordinary child of noble birth. Jor-El and Lara, his biological parents, are a noble family on their home world of Krypton. Kal-El is sent to Earth at a time of great turmoil: the eve of his world's destruction. He is then hidden until the appointed age, raised by traditional but non-royal parents until he comes into his own to claim his legacy. This is a recurring archetype in myth and mythic history. Achilles, for example, is hidden away by his mother Thetis on the island of Scyros, dressed like a maiden to blend in with the daughters of the local king, while also secretly being educated by the very-down-to-earth centaur, Chiron. When his time comes, it is Odysseus who reveals Achilles' true identity, at which time he lays claim to his own fate, namely, to die young but gloriously.

Another mythical example of a young man of noble birth reclaiming his birthright at the appropriate time would be when Acrisius, King of Argos, learned of a prophecy that claimed he would be killed by the son of his daughter, he imprisoned his daughter. Later, after being visited by Zeus who showers her in fertile gold raindrops, Danae became pregnant with the hero Perseus.[4] The Hellenistic writer Apollodorus claims that once Acrisius learns of this, he quickly sealed both mother and child in an ark and cast them into the sea. Curiously, the term he uses is *larnakes*, a word meaning both ark and casket. Those who study funerary customs know that the *larnax* could be used for many purposes. Here we should see the *larnax* as both an ark *and* a coffin, for the hero, in addition to surviving in the box as if it were a boat-like ark, he is also, like the god Dionysus, twice born.[5] Only through divine intervention do mother and child survive, arriving on the shores of the distant land of Seriphos. Caught by a local fisherman, they are freed from their caskets, and Perseus, like many mythological figures, is reborn.[6] When his mother lifts him out of the box, it is like she is once again giving him birth. Coming of age, he embarks on a quest for the head of the gorgon Medusa, a creature so hideous that a mere glance at her will turn one's flesh to stone. Along the way, he receives aid from the gods Athena and Hermes in the form of divine gifts—armor, if you will.

Exposure of prodigious children should also resonate with Judeo-Christian audiences. In the Old Testament, for example, to escape death at the hands of the Pharaoh's men, the prophet Moses was hidden in a basket by his mother and floated down the Nile. Eventually, most auspiciously, and because Fate is about as funny as a wooden leg, Moses winds up washing ashore near the palace, where he is raised as part of the royal court. Essentially, the hero is sent away in order to survive. Later he returns to lead his people.

Herodotus relates a similar tale of Cyrus the Great, whose grandfather Astyages has a dream that a fruit-bearing vine would sprout from his daughter, which quite inauspiciously was interpreted to mean her child would supplant him. Thus, quicker than a whip, he orders the death of his own grandchild. The ghastly duty falls to Mithridates, one of the king's shepherds. Alas, the king's man finds himself unable to perform the task and instead passes a stillborn child off as Cyrus. He then raises the real Cyrus as his own child.

Other examples of this heroic paradigm in the Mediterranean world may be found in ancient Rome. Romulus and Remus are an excellent example. Sired by Mars, god of war, and Rhea Silva, a reluctant Vestal Virgin, these semi-divine twins were similarly tossed down a river to be later discovered and adopted by a shepherd. Romulus and Remus later lay claim to their birthright of kingship, when they return to the city of their birth.

The most recognizable analogue for Superman for Christian audiences is of course the figure of Christ. Also seen as a prophet, he experiences an extraordinary divine birth. Mary, his mother, learns from angels during the Annunciation that she is to give birth to the son of God. Christians call this the Immaculate Conception, that is, birth free from the stain of sin. Mary, still pregnant with the Christ child, flees during the massacre of the innocents under Herod. This divine child will be raised by non-noble parents Joseph and Mary, a simple carpenter and his wife. Joseph and Mary serve as surrogate parents to the Christ child, who is the son of God. Jonathan and Martha, with the same first initials as their Biblical counterparts, act similarly as surrogates to Kal-El, an equally unearthly child. Martha has also never had children, which leaves her, like Mary, untouched by the stain of original sin.

Human Disguise

Hardly Heideggerian angst, whether the world is simply unready to embrace them, or too ready to utilize their powers, or to protect their loved ones, superheroes often have to hide their God-given talents behind a mortal mask. Donning the persona of Clark Kent, reporter for the *Daily Planet*, he can maneuver the mortal world with greater ease. Wonder Woman likewise assumes the identity of Diana Prince. When he is not busy thwarting Dr. Octopus and the Green Goblin, Spider-Man also hides behind the guise of Peter Parker, an average teenager and reporter for the *Daily Bugle*, while the Dark Knight, Batman, can hide behind the facade of billionaire boy scout Bruce Wayne.

The trope of disguise is one familiar to students of Greek myth. All throughout the *Iliad*, gods assume mortal guise in order to interact with humans. Athena, for example, secures the aid of Pandarus disguised as a spearman, or as Mentor, guiding Telemachus on his journey into manhood. Apollo and Poseidon, when building the walls of Troy, passed themselves off as human laborers. In the case of the Homeric gods, it seems that their human disguises are meant to protect humankind rather than necessarily hoodwink them.

What happens when a mortal looks upon the true form of the divine and experiences *darśan* or epiphany? When Metaneira discovers the goddess Demeter, disguised as an old nursemaid, trying to immortalize her child Demophöon, the goddess suddenly turns on her. She chastises the queen for not trusting her and literally grows huge in her anger.[7] The halls are filled with the light of her radiance and the scent of perfume. In the case of Semele, she is vaporized by a fiery lightning bolt for daring to look upon the true nature of her lover, Zeus. Tiresias was blinded for gazing upon Athena while she bathed. In similar fashion, the hunter Actaeon was metamorphosed into a deer and dismembered by his own hunting dogs for spying on Diana.[8] Mortals who gaze upon the gods are ill equipped to handle the reality of something they don't quite understand.[9] In this way, while the superhero acts as a champion for mortals, in many cases their semi-divine nature also introduces a threat to quotidian existence. In order to protect themselves (and the people they try to serve), the (semi-)divine or extraterrestrial hero does better to disguise him- or herself as human.

In terms of mortal heroes in epic traveling in disguise, we already have mentioned Achilles disguised as a girl in the coterie of King Lycomedes' daughters at Scyros, in order to escape the attention of the Achaeans. Odysseus, who is also disguised as a peddler of clothes, thwarts this effort. Hiding manly weapons—a spear and shield among the clothes—he soon outs the hero. Odysseus is a master of disguise, second only to his divine partner-in-crime, Athena, who often enhances his efforts. In the *Odyssey*, Athena sees that Odysseus has his game on when he reaches the shores of Phaeacia. He then travels as a beggar when he reaches the shores of his homeland Ithaka in order to go unnoticed and determine the loyalties of his house.

What we find in addition to protecting their identities is that the disguise often allows heroes to learn truths that might otherwise remain hidden, sometimes to be caught and taken in, like a proverbial Trojan horse. For the semi-divine, it also provides a brief glimpse into everyday mortal existence. For Superman, it means that despite being a hero and from another world, he is at heart, human. He is one of us: he can be disappointed, hate, fall in love with Lois Lane. One must wonder after a time which is the real disguise—Superman or Clark Kent—and what happens when one, either the human disguise or superhuman persona, begins to take over? In the film *Superman II* for example, Kal-El's love for Lois Lane led him to abandon his super-powers, leaving him vulnerable to General Zod. In the end, it was his human persona that allowed him to turn the tables and to steal the powers of Zod and his renegade soldiers.

Interestingly enough, the figure of Christ also wrestles with his human and divine sides. In the book of Matthew, for example (15:21–28), a Canaanite woman approaches Christ, and she begs him to heal her daughter. Initially he turns her aside, claiming he only attends to the lost sheep of Israel, but eventually Christ relents because she addresses him as Lord. Some have seen this episode as Christ showing human discrimination. Of course, the famous overturning of the tables also shows a very human Christ, who is susceptible to anger, rage, and frustration—very human qualities indeed. In many cases, the semi-divine hero must constantly question his identity, as he is often keenly aware of both his shortcomings as a mortal and his unusual strengths as an immortal.

The Hidden Threat

To us, the hero's mask or cape also hides an underlying threat. One of the unnerving aspects of the hero Achilles, for example, is his stormy unpredictability. He is hot-headed and susceptible to frequent outbursts of violence. Agamemnon claims that of all his heroes, Achilles is the most wretched, a blighter of the first order. After all, Achilles almost comes to blows with Agamemnon over his war prize, the girl Briseis. The underlying issue, however, is accepting Agamemnon's absolute authority in taking and redistributing whatever he wishes to his men. Restrained by the goddess Athena, Achilles walks off the job and retires to his tent to sulk. Only the death of his companion Patroclus rouses him from his tantrum. Descending into madness, he becomes a terrible force, seeking revenge, dishonoring the heroic code by despoiling bodies after death and even taunting them. In this way, Achilles, though the greatest warrior among the Achaeans, is also their greatest threat.

Recent films like *Man of Steel*, *Batman vs. Superman: Dawn of Justice*, and *Justice League* have highlighted Superman's alien nature and the inherent danger to humankind his superhuman abilities pose. The fear goes back to our inability to understand the nature of the godlike hero, the limits and source of his or her power. Compounding the issue is, of course, the protective disguise, which causes general distrust, even if meant to protect the hero. Ultimately, we want to put our trust in the hero, but we cannot bring ourselves to do so because of our suspicious nature, because hiding one's true identity ultimately invites suspicion (just why *does* he need to hide who he really is anyway?).

Some would argue that Christ was crucified not because he overtly challenged authority, but because they didn't understand his message. In Matthew 26, when the high priest Caiaphas interrogates him, asking him if he is the son of God, he merely states that it is as you say, but that he and the other elders will see the son of man sitting at the right hand of the Power, advancing on the clouds of heaven. Immediately he is condemned for blasphemy and is subsequently delivered to Pontius Pilate, who, despite claiming to be a just man, washes his hands of the affair. In both cases, the semi-divine hero is persecuted for being semi-divine, mostly also because we, as mere mortals, often cannot fully understand their actions, much less their intentions.

For Superman, it is more than that. Add to this his alien nature and name Kal-El, and we begin to identify a recurring undercurrent of xenophobia in modern society. For us, Superman is the epitome of the superhero, but his race is something Other. We don't understand Krypton or Superman's powers, and few earthlings are aware of his origin story. He is thus a mystery and a threat, just as Christ was to the ancient Romans. For those who have not been inducted into Christian teachings, the symbolism of drinking blood and consuming the body of Christ, famously highlighted in Matthew 26, must have seemed barbaric, as it bespeaks of cannibalism. Even the mystery cults of ancient Rome or the cult of Cybele had no equivalent ceremonies. Thus, ignorance bred suspicion. In the DC Comics tradition, those descendants of Kal-El, the original Superman, such as Superman Secundus are often referred to as "blood of his blood."[10] The reference is to the Superman dynasty that arises after the original Kal-El sets off to wander the universe. What is most striking about the reference is that Superman survives not only by blood, but also by mission. His offspring, or disciples, are left in charge of saving humanity and carrying on the faith. Eventually, the Superman of the future merges with the sun, to become the son of the sun, an overt reference again to a celestial Christ-like figure.[11]

Savior of Us All

Why do we need heroes like Superman? In many ways, characters like Superman hold up a mirror to our own fears and insecurities. Despite being superhuman, there are moments Kal-El is vulnerable, alone, and very human. He has lost his world but cannot quite fit in ours. His journey is one ultimately of self-discovery. He acts as an intercessor on behalf of our world, conquering outside threats, but he also plays the role of the dutiful son. In *Man of Steel*, Kal-El, traveling under multiple disguises, reactivates a Kryptonian scout ship in the arctic and learns from the projection of his father Jor-El that he had been sent to Earth to guide its people. An unearthly father providing wisdom to his son, defining his mission to lead humanity—one cannot help but recognize the messianic and overtly Christian symbolism behind Superman's call to adventure.

Of course, all good things must eventually come to an end. Savior figures, by definition, must perish in order to save the greater good. The death and resurrection of Superman is a theme played again and again. For example, in *Man of Steel*, when General Zod demands Earth hand over its savior, they reluctantly do so. At one point, Superman descends to the bottom of the world to stop Zod's terraforming machines, only to rise once again to stop Zod. In *Batman v. Superman*, Superman is lured into a trap set by Lex Luthor, who has kidnapped Lois Lane and Martha Kent. In the altercation, Luthor unveils his ultimate weapon, a genetically engineered beast, created from his own DNA spliced with the genetic material from the now deceased General Zod. The creature is referred to as Superman's "Doomsday." Although Superman overcomes the beast using a kryptonite spear, he himself tragically succumbs after prolonged exposure to the poisonous ore.

In the comic tradition Superman also encounters Doomsday, a creature likewise resulting from genetic experiments intended to produce the perfect killing machine. Known as The Ultimate, Doomsday was subjected to countless deaths in order to improve its survival abilities, making him hate all life. Eventually, The Ultimate frees himself from his scientist master, Bertron, and travels the universe spreading chaos. Arriving on earth, he easily subdues the rest of the Justice League, leaving only the caped hero to defend the Earth. In the final battle, both lay crushing blows resulting in their mutual demise. The *Death of Superman* comic cover features the Man of Steel's ripped and tattered cape, standing as a military trophy over a rubble grave.

Superman's death shocks the world. In both film and comic book versions, Superman is buried, but his body mysteriously goes missing. In the comic, Eradicator steals his body and places it in a regenerative matrix within the Fortress of Solitude. In the film version, Bruce Wayne comes up with a plan to resurrect Superman by using the genesis chamber on board the Kryptonian scout ship and a device known as the Mother Box, in an effort to provide humanity with hope. With the help of the Flash, the project is a success, and Superman is resurrected, although he is stripped of his memories. Eventually, with the aid of Lois Lane, he returns to battle Steppenwolf and saves the world.

Obviously similar themes are found in the Christian belief that Christ, who was crucified and buried, went through an incubation period of three days before finally being reborn into the heavens to sit with his Father, in order to save the human race. Ironic, if one considers that Nietzsche's Übermensch, translated as "Superman, Hyperhuman," was originally perceived as a foil to the otherworldliness of Christianity, and as a figure that focused

Superman stops the world-destroying creature known as Doomsday from laying waste to the Earth in *Superman: The Death of Superman*. In one of the final scenes, Lois Lane holds the lifeless body of the title character after the epic battle. Written by: Dan Jurgens, Jerry Ordway, Louise Simonson, & Roger Stern. Art by Jon Bogdanove, Brett Breeding, Tom Grummett, Jackson Guice, & Dan Jurgens. © 2016 DC Comics.

instead on the terrestrial realm rather than the divine.[12] Then again, one needs to ask, if Nietzsche was right, and God really is dead, why do people still seek guidance in religion or look to superheroes rather than reading Nietzsche? Try to wrap your head around that one.

Yet Christianity isn't the only religion that venerates a savior figure. In terms of epic figures, two stand out: one Greek, the other Roman. Achilles, seen as best of the Achaeans, stands as a savior figure. To win the war, the Achaeans need Achilles, but the war will never be over until the prophecy has been carried out, and Paris kills Achilles. Achilles must die to bring the war to an end. In the very beginning of Homer's tale, Achilles readily admits that he was destined for a short life, but if he goes to Troy, he will at least earn lasting glory.[13] Knowing this has perhaps granted Achilles with a very real death wish.

Aeneas, the semi-divine son of Aphrodite, is also for the Romans a savior figure, and one that surprisingly demonstrates many parallels with Superman. Both board ships to escape their dying worlds, both act as guardians of their separate cultures, and both find refuge on an alien world. Both also have mortal arch-enemies. Superman has Lex Luthor, a homegrown Metropolis business magnate thoroughly driven by a desire for power. His hatred stems from jealousy over Superman's popularity. Aeneas, likewise, has Turnus, king of the Rutilians, who is supremely bitter and equally jealous when he is supplanted by Aeneas as consort to Lavinia, to whom he previously had been betrothed. Both Lex and Turnus are self-made men, lacking superhuman abilities. They are thoroughly preoccupied with their own fortune rather than the plight of their people, making them the perfect foil to the savior, who places others above himself.

Temptation

Temptation is another marker of the savior figure. In Matthew 4, Christ is said to have been led into the desert and tempted by Satan. First, the devil demands he turn stones into bread, to which Christ replies, "Man shall not live by bread alone…."[14] The demon then transports them to the top of a temple, where he demands Christ demonstrate his divine nature by throwing himself off. To this Christ replies, "You shall not tempt the Lord your God."[15] Finally, Satan takes them to a mountaintop to show him the kingdoms of the world. He promises to make them his, if he bows down and worships him, to which Christ responds, "Away with you, Satan! You shall worship the Lord Your God. Only him shall you serve."[16] The temptation of Christ represents not only a moral crucible for the savior figure but for all mankind. Do we accept our fate as humans under God's law or not?

Superman endures a similar ordeal, as others have observed. Blogger Ian Dawe, for example, writes about the deeper connections between Superman and the Christ figure.[17] His focus is the Superman story from the comic book "For the Man Who Has Everything," by writers Alan Moore and Dave Gibbon.[18] In it, Superman is overtaken by the "black mercy," a mysterious alien plant that attaches itself to its victims and feeds them hallucinogenic dreams that cater to their heart's desire. Superman dreams of a normal life on Krypton. Dawe compares this with Nikos Kazantzakis' controversial 1955 novel, *The Last Temptation of Christ*. In the book, Christ likewise is offered a normal life, should he step down from the cross. In both instances, the savior figure resolves that to do so goes against the very nature of who he is. This theme also occurs in films such as *Superman II*, where our token Kryptonian is tempted to sacrifice his powers to lead a normal life with Lois Lane. At the end of the film, with General Zod victorious and no one left to stop him, it is apparent to Kal-El that there will always be a Zod, that the world needs Superman more than he needs to be human. He is bound to his destiny, like Christ and the epic heroes of old, especially Achilles. What makes both Christ and Superman tragic figures more than anything is that they can never lay down their mantle. They are by nature epic heroes and they must live … and die … for the greater good.

Throughout the Superman saga, the Man of Steel is frequently plagued by his arch nemesis, Lex Luthor, and is constantly having to right his wrongs. The temptation to act human, to kill his opponent and be rid of him for good, particularly one who has caused him such personal pain, is ever-present. His ability to resist these natural human urges once again demonstrates his moral strength, which counters Luthor's intellectual strength. This is why at the end of *Man of Steel*, Superman snapping Zod's neck seems to go against his nature, and why Batman is undoubtedly attracted to the idea of stopping him. At various points, Luthor tempts Superman with power, like Satan tempting Christ. Ultimately, the son of Jor-El adheres to the code of the savior hero. He survives temptation, undergoes transformation through death, and is resurrected with a new wisdom about the world.

The God of Thunder

Across the Rainbow Bridge of Åsgard, where the booming heavens roar, comes the greatest of all the Marvel superheroes: the god of thunder, mighty Thor. With all his incredible strength and endurance, Thor certainly seems like a celestial deity. Like Superman, he, too, is sent to Earth by his father, though for reasons other than the destruction of his world. Stripped of his powers, Thor comes to Earth as an exile; Odin sends his son away to learn humility and to actually earn the right to wield the hammer, Mjölnir. Starting off as a bad boy, Thor soon learns that his actions have major ramifications, and he takes up the mantle of hero to protect the innocent against threats such as his brother, Loki, and the Destroyer. He also finds himself falling in love with a mortal woman, Jane Foster. In the comic series, Odin sends Thor to Earth but erases his memory. His *alter ego*, disabled med student Donald Blake, has no idea he is an Åsgardian prince. Here, too, he falls in love with Jane, who is a nurse. Throughout the comic saga, Thor develops an affinity for Earth and its people, becoming its defender.

In the Icelandic epic tradition, Thor emerges as a savior figure. In the 13th century *Prose Edda*, Odin exiles his children, Fenrir the wolf, Hel, and

Jörmungandr (also known as the Midgard Serpent), whom he tosses into the sea. Eventually, Jörmungandr grows so big it winds up encircling the world, hence its epithet World Serpent, or serpent biting its own tail. In the Eddic poems *Hymiskviða* and *Völuspá*, we learn of Thor's perilous encounters with Jörmungandr: once during a fishing expedition, and a second time eventually culminating in a final encounter, Ragnarök, the end of times. It is foretold that Fenrir, once freed, will set the world on fire, while Jörmungandr rises up from the deep, letting go its tail to spew poison into the air. Although Thor defeats the serpent, nevertheless it manages to deliver one final death blow, poisoning the god. The Lord of Thunder takes nine steps before stumbling and falling into death's embrace. Nevertheless, he saves the world.[19] This theme is honored in the Marvel comic tradition as well, when Ice Giants seek the Midgard Serpent to engage the god of thunder in one final battle.[20]

In the Marvel Cinematic Universe, Thor does not have to hide behind a secret identity. He is sent to Earth by Odin to learn humility, and he engages with his half-brother Loki as well as Thanos. Thor is not a god on Earth; he has been stripped of many of his powers. Like Superman, however, Thor is still another alien with powers beyond our own human ones, so he seems godlike to us. Yet it is his humanity, ultimately, that resonates with the modern audience … and who knows? Maybe it worked the same way for Homeric listeners as well who found Achilles not only palatable but compelling enough, despite the fact that he is partially divine (not of our world). It may be what makes Hector even more compelling is that he really is wholly human. So perhaps it's not that surprising that even the super-est of superheroes, because the writers that create them still utilize many of the same paradigms, are as compelling to us as Achilles was to Alexander the Great.

Conclusion

Superheroes such as Superman or Thor resonate with modern audiences because so much of their story has been drawn from mythic paradigms that are embedded in our own modern psyches. Such characters provide us brief but refreshing glimpses into our own humanity, perhaps calling to us to reach ever forward to become our best selves. For example, like many of us, Superman and Thor are outsiders who struggle to understand what it means to be human; they have the added challenge of trying to understand what it means to be divine as well as human. Their secret identities, however, allow them to navigate the complicated human world, while their superhuman abilities allow them to accomplish great deeds,

Two raging gods locked in immortal combat; mighty *Thor* saves the Earth in the epic battle. *Thor* #126 (1966), p. 10.

and we as avid readers live vicariously through their exploits. Our inability to recognize and accept them and their abilities speaks to our inability to accept and understand the incomprehensible plan and intent of the divine. Like epic heroes of the past, each one stands as the savior and nonpareil of their culture. Unlike epic heroes of the past, the emphasis is less on personal glory and more on the glory and security of humankind.

XI

Wind Walkers and Winged Warriors

Hawkman, Falcon and the Sons of Boreas

Swift as the wind with the power to soar above the clouds, few heroes stand out like the winged warriors of Greek myth: Daedalus, for example, the tragic inventor who built a set of wings to aid him and his son Icarus escape their prison on Crete; Phaethon, the hapless youth who commandeered his father Helios' flying chariot; then there are the Boreads, Zetes and Calais, warriors born with the innate gift of flight.[1] This chapter focuses on the aeronauts, those unique liminal warriors who tread the air, between the lands of the earth and sky. What makes them special, and how do they figure into our story of the epic hero? What does the power of flight represent for ancient audiences, and what does it represent for us?

Our story begins in the Near East, with some of the earliest depictions of winged heroes in the most unlikely of places. Cylinder seals, such as the Morgan Seal 747, depict winged heroes. This one in particular is armed with a scimitar and is shown lifting a bull while fending off a ferocious lion. Likewise, many gods such as Enlil, Marduk, and Astarte are also shown with wings. An Akkadian seal dating much earlier (to 2350–2150 BCE) does in fact show the goddess with wings and horns trampling a lion. Reliefs from the palace of Ashurnasirpal II at Nineveh likewise show genies, i.e., ancestor spirits, with elaborately carved wings. It is, therefore, hard to discern whether or not what is suggested as a hero is not in fact a god. For some, perhaps it did not matter, as heroes such as Gilgamesh were semi-divine and were often fully deified after their death.[2]

The strong artistic bias of winged figures being divine doesn't stop with the Near East, however. Birds and winged creatures of all kinds are quite prevalent in Greek lore as well. We shall start here with Homer in a

A Neo-Babylonian cylinder seal intricately depicts a winged hero subduing a bull and while facing an attacking lion. While the lion rearing on its back legs bears its razor sharp claws, the hero, appearing stoic, wields a scimitar. The Morgan Library and Museum in New York, accession number: Morgan Seal 747.

discussion that I trust won't go to (just) the birds. By investigating the common occurrence of wings and flight in Homer, I hope to link flight with divinity and show how the same motif is still suggested in the modern-day comic universes of DC and Marvel.

This Akkadian seal of Inanna with lions dating to c. 2200 BCE and now housed at the Oriental Institute of Chicago (accession number: OIM A27903) shows the winged goddess with a worshipper nearby (https://oi-idb.uchicago.edu/id/a2e9a82c-3da6-4a32-b97c-d1a0d5816adc).

Birds in Homer

The *Iliad* abounds with avian similes. In Book 2, the Greek army is compared to a flock of birds on the plain, while in Book 15 Hector is described specifically as a bird of prey:

> just as a shining eagle descends upon a flock of winged birds who are feeding by the river, geese or cranes or long-necked swans, so did Hector rush at the ship.[3]

The same analogy is applied to Odysseus and Telemachus when they swoop down on the frightened suitors:

> as vultures with crooked talons and hooked beaks coming from the mountains rush on small birds....[4]

While Hector is likened to an eagle and Odysseus a vulture, both are, nevertheless, raptors, birds of prey. In these cases, distinctions are not made between Greek and Trojan, but rather between predatory warrior and their prey. Is it any wonder bird iconography is so prevalent in Archaic pottery?

At other times, birds seem to represent something else entirely, for example, freedom. In Greek tragedy, women wish to become birds in order to be free. In the *Odyssey*, Homer likens Penelope to a nightingale that, perched among the foliage, wails for her child.[5] Additionally, Athena, when she takes her leave of Telemachus, assumes the form of a bird:

> Thus spoke the goddess gray-eyed Athena,
> And she left flying heavenward like a bird.[6]

After this, Odysseus' son is filled with hope. We may then take Athena's bird-like form as a sign of her divinity, not merely her ability to change form, but also the power to escape the mortal realm and to sail high above the clouds. Whether birds of prey, or birds that *are* prey, such similes should be considered when analyzing winged warriors in epic and mythology.

In art, many gods, of course, are actually represented as winged—Eros, for example, the god of love, and Iris, "golden-winged" Eos, the Dawn, the goddess Nike, the harbinger of victory, as well as Thanatos, Death, and his brother Hypnos, Sleep, the Anemoi, gusts of wind, Zephyrus, Boreas, Notus, Euryus, and a host of minor winds. Gracing the relief panels of the great Altar of Pergamon is also a host of winged Titans, the race that predated the Olympian pantheon of gods. One might infer that winged men and women then are seen as heaven sent, belonging to the sky, and having a deep connection with a primordial past. In the mythologies of the Near East, winged genies usually appear as older bearded men with wings, and act as protective spirits to the hero-king.

The Boreads

Joining Jason and his crew of audacious Argonauts are the Boreads, Zetes and Calais. Like their Near Eastern counterparts, they are the erstwhile defenders of kings. In fact, when they arrive at the kingdom of Thrace, they became the protectors of the woeful King Phineas. In the *Argonautika* of Apollonius we discover that in his *hubris*, Phineas had revealed the secrets of the gods and was subsequently punished for this transgression and blinded. Adding to his woes he is continuously tormented by the Harpies, winged hags with a thoroughly disagreeable disposition, who, shrieking, would swoop down and rip away his food or befoul the meat.

Soaring into action, Zetes and Calais chase down the Harpies until the goddess Iris halts their dogged pursuit at the Strophades Islands.[7] The Strophades are as far West as you can go and still be in Greece. As with many of the winged gods—Hermes, Iris, Eos—the Boreads are quintessentially liminal figures. They travel between worlds, treading between different areas of safety … and danger. At the end of the Greek world, at the threshold of the far West and lands unknown, the Boreads finally quit their chase of the horrible Harpies.

What becomes of these flighty brothers? Pausanias claims that they died in their encounter with the Harpies.[8] Apollonius, on the other hand, says that Herakles later kills them for persuading Jason to abandon him while he searched for their lost companion, Hylas.[9] Other ancient writers claim that they survive the voyage, return home, and even take wives. What is certain is that they serve as protectors in the epic. They are quick, can go anywhere, see anything, detect unforeseen dangers, and cross the terrestrial and aerial realms with ease, and in a fair fight, are an even match for the horrific Harpies. Interestingly, Apollonius describes the Harpies as the winged hounds of Zeus. Likewise, as the Boreads strike at the Harpies, they are likened to hounds on the hunt, snapping their jaws. Thus, like the Garuda of Hindu, Buddhist, or even Jain tradition, they combine various aspects of animal and divine qualities and are seen as protectors to the rightful king, in this case, Jason.

Jason is a different kind of hero for a different age … neither remarkably strong, nor incredibly cunning, neither semi-divine, nor overtly courageous. He's the kind of hero you call when all others are on holiday, who really needs all the help he can get. I mean, he walks around with only one sandal, loses some of his best men, and willingly enters into an affair with a witch. Those aren't necessarily things to write home about. He does, however, have three things going for him: the favor of the goddess Hera, whom we don't really hear much about in the story, a magical ship, and of course his crew of loyal mates: Herakles, armed with boundless strength, a seasoned warrior and slayer of monsters, the musician Orpheus who can charm both man and beast with song, and the swift winged twins, Zetes and Calais.

What is truly fascinating is the perception of the brothers. Pindar, for instance, claims that the Boreads had fluttering, purple wings on their backs.[10] Meanwhile, Apollonius places the wings at their ankles and says that they gleamed with golden scales.[11] Pseudo-Hyginus describes them with dark blue hair and places wings both on their heads and feet, like Hermes.[12] Ovid, the Roman poet, further elaborates that they were not born winged, but that the wings grew in when they reached manhood.[13] Visual representation of these aerial acrobats is equally ambiguous. Of great visual delight is the 5th c. BCE. krater from Altamura by the Leningrad Painter recounting the story of Phineas. It clearly shows one of the brothers with wings protruding from his back. Similarly, a Hellenistic red figure vase from Apulia, dated to 360 BCE at the National Archaeological Museum at Jatta shows wings attached along his dorsal side. By contrast, consider a Laconian cup showing the Boreads pursuing Harpies dating to the mid–6th century BCE, now in Rome, at the Museo Nazionale di Villa Giulia. Here

Interior of a Kylix cup dating to the 6th c. BCE from Cerveteri showing a Boread pursuing Harpies with the Sphinx looking on from below. Currently housed at the Museo Nazionale di Villa Giulia in Rome. Universal Images Group/Art Resource, N.Y.

the artist has chosen to place the wings about the ankles. Regardless of the location, the Boreads are always depicted with wings, and those wings are always being put to good use; these are creatures of action.

Perseus

One of the most celebrated figures in all of Greek myth, Perseus defines what it means to be a hero. Courageous and cunning, he manipulates the Graiae, slays the hideous gorgon Medusa, and on his return journey defeats a hideous sea monster, and marries a princess to boot. You also have to love his origin story. He is the grandson of a tyrant king, Akrisios, who, fearful of losing his kingdom to his progeny, has his daughter Danae locked up in a cell. Zeus, of course, likes a challenge and visits the young maiden as a shower of gold.[14] When Akrisios discovers she has given birth to a child, he locks both mother and child into a chest and tosses them into the sea. Arriving on the shores of Seriphos, they are rescued by a fisherman. This makes Perseus an example of the twice born hero—born in a cell with his mother, buried in a casket, and reborn on Seriphos when the floating ark is opened again. He is also every bit the Mama's boy, spending much of his infancy in close quarters with his mother. Is it any wonder that his coming of age ritual involves subduing the mother-figure, the gorgon Medusa, who, upon her own death, gives birth to both Pegasus and Chrysaor?

A local king by the name of Polydektes falls in love with Perseus' mother. Naturally, he tries to rid himself of the youth by sending him on a fool's errand—to fetch the head of the dread gorgon Medusa—hoping he will perish in the attempt. Now, the Gorgon is the kind of creature you might meet on your very worst day. A winged demon with a crown of writhing, hissing snakes and a hideous, hag-like face so horrible that those who gaze upon it are instantly turned to stone—the ultimate foe for the nubile hero looking to cut his teeth. Never fear, Zeus sends his very best—his loyal children Hermes and Athena—to aid the young boy on his quest. When they find him, they inform him that his father is Zeus and present him with the gift of a sword and a radiant shield. One could easily imagine Perseus standing before them, vacant expression, mouth gaping, utterly gobsmacked. Gods showering him with gifts, discovering you father is the king of the gods—it must have seemed to the fledgling hero as though he had won the ancient equivalent of the lottery. Then, they advise the young hero to seek the Graiae: Enyo, Pephredo, and Deino. These three wizened and weird sisters reveal the location of the Nymphs who hold three key items needed to complete his quest—winged sandals (*talaria*) to transport him, a sack (or *kibisis*) to safely contain the poisonous head of the gorgon, and finally the cap of Hades, which renders the wearer invisible.[15]

Slipping on the sandals, Perseus sets off on the perilous journey across the sea with the greatest alacrity. Cushioned by pillars of wind, he eventually touches down on the desolate shores of an island shrouded in mist. Through the veil appears a forest of what appear to be statues carved from stone. Drawing nearer, however, he is shocked to discover the hideous expressions cast on their faces. No mere statues are these, but what manner of creature could turn hot-blooded men in their prime into icy stone? The sharp hiss of serpents breaks the silence. One word bubbles up from the depths of his fear: the Gorgon. Creeping up upon the sound, he finds Medusa sleeping aside her sisters. Remembering the legend, he dares not look upon her, but instead, using his shield as a mirror, he strikes at the creature, severing her head from her body. Screaming in agony, the gorgon awakens her two sisters, who chase after the hero. Alas, the magical sandals spirit Perseus away to escape the fury of Stheno and Euryale. This spectacular scene is captured in a red-figure hydria dated to 460 BCE. It shows Perseus, adorned in a winged helmet and sandals, fleeing with Medusa's head. The decapitated and bloody body of the gorgon inanely clutches at the ground. But this is not the end of Perseus' story.

A red-figure hydria attributed to the Pan Painter shows the young hero Perseus fleeing the gorgons, the head of Medusa in his bag, and Athena running behind him. The hero appears with winged shoes and winged hat and carries a sickle. A trickle of purple blood flows from the decapitated body of winged Medusa, who seems to be searching for her head. From Capua, Italy, 460 BCE; British Museum inventory number: 1873,0820.352; h. 34.29 © The Trustees of the British Museum/Art Resource, N.Y.

The sandals carry Perseus to the distant shores of Ethiopia, where he chances upon Andromeda, a local princess in need of rescuing from the scaly clutches of a terrible sea-monster. Defeating the creature, he marries her but soon realizes

Attic Black figure kyathos (ladle) attributed to the Theseus Painter, and dating to 510 BCE, shows the famed son of Zeus, Perseus, with winged sandals and hat and bearded, chasing after winged Medusa, with his sword drawn. The gorgon, with a look that can turn one to stone, turns to face the viewer (14.7 × 7.9 × 11 cm [5 13/16 × 3 1/8 × 4 5/16 in.]), 86.AE.146. The J. Paul Getty Museum, Villa Collection, Malibu, California.

that married life puts a serious kink in his heroic journey and sets off again to complete his quest. Along the way, he stops at the mysterious land of the Hyperboreans and encounters Atlas, whom he turns into a mountain after exposing him to the gorgon's stare. Finally setting foot again on Seriphos, Perseus uses the gorgon's head to turn Polydektes likewise to stone. Quest fulfilled, he returns the sandals, for they were fashioned for the gods rather than mortals. Such humility and wisdom in a young hero is unique. Since he is semi-divine he's not supposed to have technology built for the gods. They are only on loan. But this isn't to say that technology is not forged for semi-divine heroes, e.g., the shield of Achilles, but that such items are personalized for the mortal wearer.

Bellerophon

Famous for taming the winged horse Pegasus and defeating the dreaded fire-breathing chimaera, Bellerophon is one of the most popular, if not most hubristic, heroes of Greek myth, offering a sharp contrast to Perseus. The offspring of the sea god Poseidon and the mortal Queen Eurymede, he was originally banished from his home of Corinth after accidentally killing his brother. Arriving in Argos, he sought purification for his past sin from Proetus the King, but instead accidentally aroused the lust of the queen. He does not return her affections. Spurned, she accuses him of trying to violate her, and he is exiled to Lycia and the kingdom of King Iobates.[16]

Before leaving, Proetus sends him with a letter of introduction which requests Bellerophon be instantly put to death upon his arrival. Iobates instead assigns the youth an impossible task: to slay the fire-breathing creature—part lion, part goat, part serpent—known as the chimaera. Mounting the winged horse Pegasus, with the aid of Athena, Bellerophon kills the chimaera by skewering it with a lead tipped spear.[17] Afterwards, the king demands he slay the Amazons and the Solymoi tribe. Time and again, like Herakles, he completes the assigned tasks, unscathed. Emboldened by his successes, Bellerophon attempts to fly to Mount Olympus and join the court of the gods. Zeus, astounded by the mortal youth's *hubris*, sends a gadfly to sting his mount, Pegasus. When bitten, the horse bucks its rider, and Bellerophon tumbles to the earth.[18]

On this terra-cotta bail-amphora dated to the Hellenistic period (c. 330–310 BCE), Bellerophon, mounted on Pegasus, his winged steed, flies over and wounds the chimaera. Attributed to the Ixion Painter, this Campanian (South Italian) vase highlights the impossibility of the task *without* his wings, even if they don't belong to him (H. 24 ¾ in. [62.9 cm]). The Metropolitan Museum of Art in New York; Rogers Fund, 1906; Accession Number: 06.1021.240.

A Laconian black-figure kylix by the Boreads Painter, dating to 570–565 BCE, shows the hero Bellerophon piercing the belly of the fire-breathing chimaera, with the aid of the winged horse Pegasus (12.5 × 18.4 cm ($4\frac{15}{16} \times 7\frac{1}{4}$ in.), 85.AE.121. The J. Paul Getty Collection, Malibu, CA.

Though he survives, he becomes a broken and bitter man. Here our hero uses magical charms to mount a winged beast, which can still be controlled by the gods. The moral of the tale is of course the greater one aspires, the farther one falls. For Bellerophon, the power of flight was a gift of the gods, not an innate ability, and thus can be taken away, especially if one misuses the gift to claim ascendancy beyond one's social status. When the power of flight is misused, the mortal must be brought down to earth, in essence, clipping his wings. Ultimately, like Daedalus, the same gift that allowed Bellerophon to ascend to great heights, metaphorically, is the same gift that brings about his downfall.

Daedalus

> He urged him to follow, and showed him the pernicious art of flying, moving his own wings and looking back at his son. Meanwhile, a fisherman hunting with a quivering rod, a shepherd leaning on his crook, a ploughman resting on the plough handles, saw

them, perhaps, and stood there amazed, believing them to be gods being able to seize the sky.[19]

Innovative and cunning, the character of Daedalus likewise soars to new heights on a pair of waxen wings. Trapped on Crete with his son Icarus, the fugitive inventor is forced to create a mechanical cow suit to placate the bestial desires of Minos' queen Pasiphae. After the birth of the Minotaur, Daedalus is tasked with creating a vast maze to contain the creature, but he likewise unwittingly provides Ariadne, smitten with Theseus, with the secret of escaping it. Once the Minotaur is defeated, it is only a matter of time before Minos discovers Daedalus' deception.

Fearing the punishment of the king, Daedalus must find a way to escape the island with his son. Always clever, the famed inventor therefore fashions wings from feathers and wax and trains his son Icarus in the ways of flight—not too high for fear of the sun, and not too low for fear of the sea—both potentially spoiling the wings. Alas, Daedalus, despite his genius, cannot account for human weakness. After launching themselves from the cliffs of Crete, Icarus wanders from the path his father set. Flying too high, his wings begin to melt, and he plummets into the sea that bears his name, leaving his father, broken and bitter, to bury him. The tale, as with Bellerophon, suggests that those not endowed with wings naturally are teetering on the edge of hubristic disaster by using them.

Angels and Nephilim

Of course, no discussion of winged saviors would be complete without considering the angels of Biblical lore. Clearly an example of the divine, the angel is an anthropomorphic being that protects both humans and God, the king of heaven, from the forces of Satan. The greatest of these warriors were referred to as archangels: Michael, Gabriel, Raphael, Uriel. Most are shown winged, and some such as Michael are shown battle-ready with armor and spear in hand attacking the devil. In Hermes-like fashion, the *malach,* Hebrew for messenger, often carry messages from Heaven to the earth, and so have to straddle both realms. For example, Jacob wrestles an angel in Genesis, and as a result receives a blessing. Of course, in the New Testament, Mary is visited by an angel who delivers the Annunciation.

We have a few other descriptors as well. The book of Isaiah (6:2) mentions *seraphim* with six wings: Two cover the face, two the feet, and the other pair are used to fly. These seem akin to the *genii* we find in Near

Eastern art. In Genesis, the *nephilim* are described as the sons of God, "in the earth in those days, and also after that, when the sons of God came in unto the daughters of men, and they bore children to them; the same were the mighty men that were of old, the men of renown."[20] These sound a bit like the Boreads, especially when one consults the Qumran texts and learns that some *nephilim* are believed to fly.[21] One in particular, Mahawai, flies like an eagle with hands as that of bird. In a Uygur manuscript, Mahawai was warned by Enoch, like Icarus, not to stray too close to the sun lest his wings catch fire.[22] Of course, the Book of Giants is considered good old apocryphal fun, not the kind of thing one would hear about in Sunday school. Nevertheless, it does show that at the time of their writing, in the last few centuries BCE, the perception of the sons of God and mortal women as having wings like the Boreads did exist in ancient imagination.

Hawkman

Modern society has its own brand of unique winged warriors. Infused with a mysterious otherworldly element known as Nth metal, the superhero Hawkman is given powers beyond mere mortals, including strength, living armor, and the ability to fly. Created by Gardner Fox and Dennis Neville for Flash Comics in 1940, the character of Hawkman began life as Carter Hall, an archaeologist.[23] When Hall discovers a mysterious crystal blade, he falls into a coma, recalling his life as an ancient Egyptian prince named Khufu. Khufu and his wife Shiera had been sacrificed by Hath-Set, a priest of the god Anubis. Before dying he swears to take revenge on Hath-Set. Fast-forward to modern times. Hall awakens and encounters a woman who is the reincarnation of Shiera, and who is having similar dreams. After she is captured by Anton Hastor, the reincarnation of Hath-Set, Hall uses Nth metal to create an anti-gravity harness and wings to help him fly. He frequently uses artifacts from the museum he curates to fight crime. He also becomes one of the founding members of the Justice League.

During the Silver Age of comics, Hawkman undergoes a major makeover, and is re-introduced as Katar Hol, an intergalactic peace officer from the distant world of Thanagar. This is quite a change and worthy of thought. Initially, Hawkman's powers are not divinely given, but like Daedalus achieved by terrestrial, mechanical means. His later incarnation, an alien from another world, places Hawkman within the realm of the divine. The Nth metal also gives him and Hawkgirl, his companion, the ability to speak to birds. He still relies on the mysterious Nth metal, but in this reboot, it can only be found on Thanagar, much like kryptonite can only be found on the planet Krypton.

Archaeologist and winged crime-fighter Carter Hall confronts the Shadow Master in *Hawkman* # 16. ©2018 DC Comics.

Although a protector of the earth, this time around writers made him short-tempered, rebellious, and savage—he uses a mace. Often he follows his own sense of justice rather than the word of the law, unlike our Boreads. This type of character seems more like a bird of prey, like those distant epic heroes Homer describes. Likewise, Hawkman seems at odds with himself, trying to find the balance between his role as protector of the law and his role as a warrior. Hawkman seems to be a character in search of a paradigm to call home; at one time human and at another otherworldly and nearly divine like Superman, Hawkman is endowed with the gift of flight in both realms.

Falcon

Another high-speed hero with the gift of flight is the Avenger known as Falcon. Born Samuel Wilson to parents Darleen and Paul Wilson, a local minister in the heart of Harlem, as a young boy, Sam had a fascination with birds and raised pigeons. Following the death of his parents due to crime, Sam became a social worker. On a trip to Rio, his plane crashes in the jungle. There he is discovered by Red Skull, who, using the Cosmic Cube, gifts Sam with the ability to communicate with birds telepathically, with the intention of having him battle Captain America. Debuting in *Captain America* 117 (November 1968), Cap is able to free Falcon from the mind control of Red Skull. As a result, he and Sam defeat the villain. Returning to America, Falcon works hard to change his community and aids Cap. Eventually, Captain America asks Wakanda's crown Prince T'Challa to reward him with a set of jet-powered wings that allowed him to fly.[24]

The wings and harness, like those of Daedalus, are detachable, made from lightweight materials and solar cells that convert sunlight into energy for sudden blasts of speed. Later, Black Panther provides Sam with a new suit with a vibranium weave, just like Cap's shield. Vibranium, as we have seen before, is an otherworldly material, much like Hawkman's Nth metal, serving to elevate both of these characters from the every day. What is interesting about this exchange is the wings are given by T'Challa, an African king, but also a character who himself is liminal, received divine aid, and walks between the spirit realm and reality. He is also a bit like Hephaestus, providing arms and armor for various heroes.

The wings prove transformative to Sam, allowing him to soar to new heights. With his new abilities, Sam joins the ranks of S.H.I.E.L.D. as Falcon. In the era of the Civil War, Falcon sides with Steve Rogers, until Rogers is assassinated. Afterwards, Falcon and Bucky Barnes team up, until Bucky is killed. Eventually, Sam takes up the shield and costume of Rogers, to become the New Captain America and leader of the Avengers.

In the film *Captain America: Civil War*, Sam, a former para-rescue airman, who retired after his wing-man Riley died in the line of battle, helps other veterans suffering from PTSD. Sam runs into Steve Rogers while jogging through the park, who later recruits him after learning of a Hydra plot to infiltrate S.H.I.E.L.D. Sam uses a prototype winged jetpack mounted on his back, the EXO-7, to fly and a drone named Redwing to gather reconnaissance. His wings are bullet proof and can launch missiles. Eventually, as in the comics, Sam will take up the shield of Captain America after being resurrected from the Snap.

What makes Falcon so interesting is even without supernatural powers he possesses a natural talent for flight and understanding of birds. In the film version, his experience in the Air Force allows him to master the EXO-7 flying harness. The telepathy in the comics is replaced by the technological drone named Redwing. Falcon also gets his wings clipped in the MCU after siding with Captain America during the events of the Civil War, when he is imprisoned on the Raft. Like mythological heroes of old, he suffers a fall from grace for reaching too high.

Conclusion

In Homer's time, certain birds held special meaning. Birds of prey were mighty hunters and smaller birds were their victims. Predatory birds on vase paintings may have indicated for later Greeks a connection to those Bronze Age warriors. The bird could also represent visitation from the divine, whether Athena, Aphrodite, or Zeus. It is safe to assume that some of these metaphors persisted as epic tropes well into the Hellenistic tradition.

Powered by their own wings, warriors such as the Boreads proclaim the message that they can go anywhere and do anything, and by extension that Jason and his crew of Greeks can do likewise. This sets them apart from the average epic warrior. Endowed with flight from birth, these heroes are exempt from the *hubris* of mere humans. Mortals who strive to new heights on borrowed wings do so only under the discretion of the gods. For those mortals to whom the gods give wings, that gift can become both a blessing and a curse. For Perseus the gift was returned before fate could intervene. For Bellerophon the gift proved to be the making of his own downfall.

The same holds true for the modern comic book. Those who wield the power of flight by mechanical means often do so at the whim of natural forces, whereas mutants such as Archangel or other worldly creatures such as Superman are not. Falcon is human yet given his wings by Black Panther—wings made from extraterrestrial vibranium. Hawkman starts off human, but then he becomes essentially divinized by re-writing his origin story as an extraterrestrial alien instead of a human.

How do we grapple with winged heroes? Are we influenced enough by Judeo Christian tradition that we only think of winged superheroes as angels? Does this same tradition color our perception of human versus the divine, natural versus mechanical means of flight, and the dichotomy of natural wings as good and constructed wings as bad? Still those who are otherworldly, such as Superman or Archangel, are also exploited for their abilities. One thing is for certain: winged heroes transcend our ordinary daily lives and allow our imaginations to take flight. They act as intercessors between human society and the divine, which is expressed by their hybrid nature of man and bird. Such beings, like birds, are not bound by the confines of human existence *per se* and can escape danger through flight. Taking to the sky, in short, brings the winged one closer to the divine.

XII

Dangerous Beauty

Helen of Troy and the Femme Fatale

"Beauty, terrible beauty, a deathless goddess—so she strikes the eyes."—Homer, *Iliad*[1]

She is the most beautiful woman in the world, semi-divine, whose enchantments started the war that brought an end to the Bronze Age: Helen of Troy … or is it Helen of Sparta? Her ambiguity is one of the most interesting aspects of her character. Did she go willingly with Paris to Troy? Was she kidnapped? Why is she in a book about epic heroes? For many, Helen represents the quintessential *femme fatale*, a woman who uses her natural assets to disarm friend and foe alike to get exactly what she wants. But that is the real question … did she? At one point in the *Iliad*, we see Helen refuse the goddess Aphrodite in order to do what she feels is right. For modern audiences, to do what we feel is right—to do what is ethical—is heroic. The question we shall examine is, was doing what is right necessarily part of the heroic paradigm for those ancient Greeks? This chapter looks at Helen as the mold from which we cast the modern *femme fatale*, and how many comic book heroines both resemble and diverge from the epic heroine.

Helen of Troy

To modern audiences she is the face that launched a thousand ships, but to ancient audiences Helen represented something of an enigma. She was the product of an unnatural birth. Her mother, Leda, despite being married to Tyndareus, was seduced by the god Zeus who appeared to her as a swan. Thus, she was born from one of a pair of eggs, each with a double yolk. The first egg brought her and Clytemnestra into the world, while the other carried the twins Castor and Pollux. When she came of age, she was kidnapped by the hero Theseus, though she was safely returned. Following this, she and her sister are married off to Menelaus and Agamemnon. The two brothers had arrived at the court of Tyndareus as fugitives, after their father Atreus had been murdered, and were welcomed with open arms. Had they but known that Tyndareus had forgotten to make the proper sacrifices to Aphrodite, they may have paused to reconsider. Ah yes, Aphrodite, goddess of love, desire, and beauty, often invoked as "laughter loving." One might think her to be the more amenable of gods, but there you would be wrong, for her power, the burning power of love is probably one of the most formidable of the Olympians. Bitter because of Tyndareus' oversight and jealous of his beautiful daughters, Aphrodite curses them, making them deserters of their husbands.[2] Is it any wonder that every man lusts after Helen then? It hardly seems fair to cast her as loose, given her recent abduction by Theseus and Aphrodite's grudge. Tyndareus, thusly, makes all the suitors vow an oath to come to the aid of the winner of the marriage match, here Menelaus, should there be further Helen-snatching.

On top of this, we must remember the judgment of Paris. You know, the beauty contest involving the goddesses Aphrodite, Athena, and Hera? The story goes that at the wedding of Thetis and Peleus, Eris, goddess of strife, brooding over being left off the guest list, decides to prank the trio by tossing a golden apple among them onto which was etched the phrase, "καλλίστῃι (*kallistei*), To/for the fairest." Unable to discern the "fairest," and after a lot of hair pulling and name-calling, the goddesses call upon Zeus to settle the dispute. Zeus being Zeus, and in a moment of infinite wisdom, declines the invitation to certain doom amongst his wife, his daughter, and the goddess of sex, and instead nominates the mortal Alexander, also known as Paris, to judge the match. Each of the goddesses promises something different if she is to be chosen the winner of the contest: Athena offers strategy in battle, Hera, all the kingdoms of the world, and Aphrodite the most beautiful woman in the world. Being a lover and not a fighter, as we have previously discussed in Chapter IX, Paris automatically, and in one of mythology's most pivotal moments, sides with Aphrodite, sparking the fire that will bring down his hometown of Troy. No wonder he is called the "firebrand." Likewise, to say Helen is the victim of cruel fate would be a gross understatement.

Now you may be wondering, what is Helen of Troy doing in a book about heroes?[3] If we consider, however, the principal characteristics of the epic hero, we find that she does fulfill many of the descriptions. She comes from a noble birth, the daughter of Queen Leda. Unusual birth? If you consider being born from an egg unusual, then yes. Reputed to be the son of a god? Close enough. She is the daughter of Zeus. Is she spirited away? In a manner of speaking, if you consider her abduction by Theseus as such, but no attempt is made to expose her as a child. Later, she is returned to her original kingdom (Sparta) by her brothers Castor and Pollux. Furthermore, she also embarks upon a quest to a far-off place. Whether willingly or not, she sails from Sparta to the other side of the Greek world with Paris.

Does Helen receive divine aid or have any superhuman abilities? Well, sort of. She surpasses the beauty of every mortal woman in the world. Men fall helplessly in love with her, and even Aphrodite seems to envy her. To begin with, Helen's fate is both a blessing and a curse. While she may appear unfaithful to her husband, technically she has received the gift of supreme beauty from Aphrodite. While she may have been beautiful before, her curse of twice and thrice married makes it clear every man wants her and would risk everything to obtain her as a prize. When Paris asks for the most beautiful woman in the world, Aphrodite choses Helen, again setting her up as the most beautiful. Furthermore, when Troy finally falls and Menelaus is about to take his revenge on Helen, she exposes her breasts in front of the Temple of Aphrodite, proving once more her ability to use beauty to beguile.[4] She returns to Sparta with Menelaus where they live a relatively normal life, at least according to the *Odyssey*. Like many epic heroes, she

An Attic red-figure bell krater attributed to the Persephone Painter (c. 440–430 BCE), showing Helen fleeing from her husband Menelaus. As she flees, she looks back, and when she catches Menelaus' eye, he drops his sword. The Toledo Museum of Art; Object Number 1967.154; H: 12 13/16 in. (32.5 cm); Diam (lip): 14 25/32 in. (37.5 cm); Diam (foot): 7 3/32 in. (18 cm); purchased with funds from the Libbey Endowment, Gift of Edward Drummond Libbey.

earns a better afterlife merely because of her heredity. Helen, despite her infidelity, is said to have gone on to the Isle of the Blessed along with her husband, Menelaus.[5]

Obviously, Helen does not fit every single aspect of Raglan's heroic paradigm. Then again, neither do many such characters we consider epic heroes. One of the most distinguishing characteristics of Helen, however, is her acumen. She stands up for what is right, the heroic code, as it applies to women. Throughout the *Iliad*, Helen bears the mark of shame. She has, it appears, run out on her husband and child. Curiously, when Paris fails to duel Menelaus, a breach in the heroic code, she outright refuses the gods. Strikingly, in Book 3, when disguised as an old woman, Aphrodite visits Helen, encouraging her to make love with Paris. Helen initially refuses the goddess, because her own code of conduct repudiates her lover's cowardice. Thus she declares: "It would be treason to share his bed; the Trojan woman would hold me liable."[6] Aphrodite, unaccustomed to being told what to do, especially by mortals, lashes out:

> Provoke me not vile bitch, lest enraged I forsake you
> So that I would hate you as much as I now fiercely love you,
> And I devise miserable hatred between both
> Trojans and Greeks and you die a miserable fate.[7]

Wow! Who knew the goddess of love could be so beastly? It's probably a good thing she doesn't have a mother, because I doubt very much she would kiss her with such a raffish mouth. Helen's reaction is nevertheless telling, for it reveals she is not necessarily just a prize to be won but an equally compelling character with her own thoughts and emotions.

Eventually Helen relents rather than face the wrath or guided misfortune of the gods.

The problem for a modern audience is reconciling Helen's subservience. Why does she cave? As we have seen, to go against the will of the gods and not accept one's fate is dually seen as non-heroic. In this way, therefore, Helen again proves she defends the code, even if she does not agree with it. Helen maintains her own heroic virtue by doing what must be done, even if it is unpalatable. As a result, instead of suffering a tragic downturn, she is rescued by her virtue, which we as a modern audience see, ironically, as non-virtuous. What Helen then provides us is a moral mirror for male dominated Greek society; she ultimately does what is expected of women, what is expected of the hero.

Helen's story, however, does not end there. What if the beautiful queen of Sparta never went to Troy? What if she were hidden in Egypt by the gods and a double sent to Troy in her place? That is the premise of Euripides' play *Helen*. In it, the titular character, having been stolen away by the gods before Paris' abduction and placed in Egypt under the stewardship of King Proteus, now has to contend with his son, Theoclymenos, who is smitten with her and intends on making her his wife. She might very well have considered it, too, after being abandoned by her husband and the gods for over ten years, but on the eve of her nuptials, she learns that a stranger has landed in Egypt; she holds out hope that the stranger is in fact her long lost husband, Menelaus. When Menelaus discovers the real Helen (the one he took from the flaming walls of Troy was a copy, an *eidolon*), he refuses to believe it is really his wife, as he has just hidden away her ghostly double in a nearby cave. Only after a sailor reports that the *eidolon* has evaporated does Menelaus come to his senses. Newly reunited, the couple must still figure out how to dupe the local king and escape from Egypt with their lives. Helen hatches a plot. Since everyone believes Menelaus dead, she convinces Theoclymenos that she must perform the proper rites for his funeral—a funeral at sea. Unwittingly, the king agrees and provides her with a boat that she and Menelaus use to escape.

Although Euripides affords us a faithful Helen and an unfaithful illusion, which makes for an interesting plot twist (thank you very much, Herodotus), we nevertheless still have the problem of Helen's enchantments. Throughout the play, Helen's comeliness continues to beguile, whether she wants it to or not. Theoclymenos wants to marry the most beautiful woman in the world. While Euripides casts Menelaus as the seducer rather than Helen,[8] it is still Helen who ultimately comes up with a way to deceive the king (Eur. *Helen* 1049–1090): "My husband, if you can believe that even a woman can give sound advice, then listen: Would you allow it to be known that you are dead, even though you are alive?"[9] One wonders whether Euripides is really defending Helen or condemning her. Yet it is she who heroically saves the day, and their lives, by using not just her sex, but also her brains. Interestingly, in the *Troades*, Euripides returns to the original concept of Helen as a beguiler of men. In one scene, when Menelaus is considering what to do with his wife, Hecuba encourages him to have her killed in order to keep other cities and men safe: "I thank you Menelaus, if you will slay that wife of yours. Her eyes! Her eyes enslave the eyes of all men, enslave their cities and set their houses on fire. Thus are her enchantments."[10]

Enchantment and tragedy seem to run in the family, especially considering Helen's twin sister, the equally cursed Clytemnestra. If we compare the two, we find many similarities, but also many differences. First, she marries Agamemnon, Menelaus' brother, and while he is away at war, she takes a lover, Aegisthus, who had originally murdered Agamemnon's father Atreus.[11] The two plot to kill her husband after his return. This may seem shady, placing her in a bad light, but if we consider that she, too, is the victim of fate, we start to see her more as a tragic figure than a villain.

According to Euripides in his *Iphigenia at Aulis*, Clytemnestra had been married previously to Tantalus the king of Pisa, but was abducted by Agamemnon who had killed her husband and first-born son. Next, as the Greek armada is about to set off for Troy, the winds turn unfavorably and Agamemnon, to placate Artemis, sacrifices their daughter Iphigenia for the goddess' favor. In some variations Artemis rescues Iphigenia, but for the most part Clytemnestra thinks her daughter dead. A husband and child murdered, a second child sacrificed, and ten years away from home at war? Is there any wonder Clytemnestra took a lover and perhaps gained a few neuroses? Finally, when Agamemnon returns home, he has taken a concubine, the Trojan princess Cassandra, who can see into the future. There are many versions of what happens next, but all of them involve the death of the king either by Clytemnestra's hand or Aegisthus.' In Aeschylus' *Agamemnon*, Clytemnestra waits for her husband to bathe, and, catching him as though a minnow in a cloth net, plunges her blade. Afterwards she and Aegisthus rule, until Orestes kills his mother in retribution for the evil deed.

Is Orestes' act of matricide evil, though, or is it revenge? This is the theme of Aeschylus' theatrical trilogy the *Orestia*, in which Orestes is put on trial. While Orestes is guilty of a revenge murder, so, too, is Clytemnestra. In terms of Greek standards, Clytemnestra is morally responsible for the death of her husband. She is seen as unfaithful and treacherous, and attracts many lovers, making her appear every bit the *femme fatale*, but fate, circumstance, rape, the murder of her children, and absence of her husband all seem to tip the scale in her favor. Moreover, I would argue that her actions are all based on a trauma response. A victim of Stockholm Syndrome, Clytemnestra for years goes along with her erstwhile kidnapper, Agamemnon, who had murdered her previous husband and child before her very eyes. Then he kills their daughter, Iphigeneia, in order to obtain favorable winds from the goddess Artemis. Clytemnestra just plain snaps. She actually *returns* to reality, albeit a twisted one, breaking the already tenuous link between herself and Agamemnon. On the surface, however, we simply see Helen and Clytemnestra as two yolks in one bad egg.

The sea nymph Calypso and the witch Circe represent more obvious examples of the *femme fatale*. Despite saving Odysseus from the sea, for example, Calypso nevertheless keeps him from leaving, dominating the life of our hero. Wanting to transform him into her immortal consort, the hero begins to forget himself and his quest to return home. He is imprisoned in a womb-like cave, waiting to be reborn. In his chapter on "Woman as Temptress" in *The Hero with a Thousand Faces*, Joseph Campbell adeptly notes:

"The seeker of life beyond life must press beyond her, surpass the temptations of her call and soar to the immaculate ether beyond."[12] Circe, after bedding Odysseus, eventually has to let him go to complete his ill-fated journey. Ironically, she warns him of the sirens and their songs that overtly draw men off course.

Silver Swan

Such examples prove the model for the modern *femme fatale,* who reflects male fear of powerful women, fear of being dominated, and fear of the unknown. Black Widow, Cat Woman, Mystique, Electra—all these identities inspire fear and suggest mystery, magic, and poison. Of all these, however, the closest match to a modern-day Helen is of course DC's villainess Silver Swan.[13] The adversary of Wonder Woman, Silver Swan began life, ironically enough, as Helen Alexandros, a ballet star, who, tired of being ridiculed and passed over, makes a deal with Mars for unsurpassable beauty. Mars reveals that she is a descendant of Helen of Troy, transforms her from an ugly duckling into a beautiful swan, and grants her the power of flight, superhuman strength, and the swan's song, a sonic scream that could cause massive destruction. The catch? Helen is only able to transform into Silver Swan for an hour at a time. Only after the death of Wonder Woman will Mars allow her to keep her beauty long term.

When Wonder Woman stumbles upon a gang of bank robbers, Silver Swan appears to lend a helping hand. In reality she uses the chaos to abscond with a briefcase containing top-secret documents. Later, as Helen, she takes up lodging with Diana and stashes the briefcase in their apartment. When Wonder Woman tries to return the briefcase, Silver Swan defeats the heroine in battle, but rather than killing her, blames the theft on her. Eventually, she and Steve Trevor, who is under the control of Doctor Psycho, fall in love and team up. They plot to take out Wonder Woman and also assassinate the current president by crashing Wonder Woman's invisible jet into the White House. Eventually, Wonder Woman overcomes Silver Swan and foils the wicked plans, and Mars retracts Helen's powers.

Silver Swan, in this incarnation at least, mirrors Homer's epic heroine in a number of ways. She has power and beauty, but it is under the control of the gods. Here, however, it is Mars rather than Aphrodite who is calling the shots. Like Helen, Silver Swan is a man stealer. Her beauty beguiles Steve, Wonder Woman's long-time main squeeze. Ultimately, she is a tragic character, who elicits sympathy despite her flaws. As an audience we understand why she takes the deal, for modern society shuns women who appear ugly, especially in the cutthroat world of professional ballet. This is also why she is a great foil to Wonder Woman, who appears flawless, for despite being a voice for women's rights, Diana's beauty also sets her apart as the ideal rather than the real.

Black Widow

Beautiful, beguiling, and bold, Marvel's Black Widow, as her alias suggests, proves to be the deadlier of the species. Born Natalia Alianova Romanoff in Stalingrad, Russia, this orphan was part of the clandestine "Red Room" program where she was brainwashed, biologically altered, and trained in espionage to become a super spy. A top KGB agent, Romanoff later joins the ranks of S.H.I.E.L.D. as an operative and becomes a vital part of the Avengers team, using her beauty to disarm her opponents before moving in for the kill. In the film *Avengers*, she pretends to be captured by Georgi Lucknov, a weapons dealer. During the interrogation, agent Coulson from S.H.I.E.L.D. orders her to come in, that her friend Clint Barton has been compromised. Romanoff terminates the interrogation, frees herself and takes out Lucknov, displaying without a doubt that she always had the upper hand.

Romanoff and Barton have a unique relationship in the film. Barton, confesses Romanoff to Loki, had once been sent to kill her, but that he had made a "different call." We are not quite sure why Hawkeye made this call. Perhaps it was her skills, which he thought could be used. Perhaps it was her beauty. In later films, such as the *Age of Ultron* we find Romanoff playing the Beauty to Bruce Banner's Beast, i.e., the Hulk. She seems to be the only one who sees him, and he her. There are several tender moments, when Romanoff is able to touch the Hulk and quiet his anger.

The comic book tradition sees her in a slightly different light. First appearing in *Tales of Suspense* #52 (April 1964) she plays a Russian spy sent by Khrushchev to kill Tony Stark. She introduces herself as Madame Natasha, explaining that she and her brother Boris have travelled to see Stark's technology. Stark is instantly smitten by her beauty and takes her to dinner. During dinner Stark learns of an explosion at his plant; he leaves to investigate only to be captured by Boris, who has donned the Crimson Dynamo armor. Eventually, Stark defeats Boris, and Natasha escapes, but her cover is blown. Later, in issue 57, we meet Hawkeye, and Black Widow returns, rescuing the beleaguered marksman after a foiled bank robbery in which he has been implicated.[14] Taking him to her underground lair, her cave of sorts, she beguiles him with her beauty, and convinces him to use his unique marksman abilities to take down Iron Man. Like Helen or Calypso,

Panel introducing the marksman Hawkeye who has been seduced by the charms of Black Widow, a Russian spy. *Tales of Suspense* (1959–1968) #57. ©1964 Marvel Characters Inc.

Romanoff is a woman who uses her power to manipulate men into carrying out her will, although hardly ever playing the role of victim.

Poison Ivy

Some would call her a villain and others a hero, but Pamela Isley, one of the most prominent adversaries in Gotham's rogue gallery, is undoubtedly a *femme fatale* ... or is she? Preferring plants to people, this botanist turned super villain uses her beauty and pheromones derived from plants to control men. She first appears in the late 1960s in the Batman comics and quickly rockets to stardom.[15] Her origin story, like so many, is complicated. Initially, Poison Ivy appears as Lillian Rose, a botanist, who is manipulated into stealing an artifact that contains ancient herbs. Her accomplice, Marc LeGrande, afraid she will double-cross him, then tries to poison her, but the plan backfires, and she survives with a resistance to plant toxins.

After the Post-Crisis re-launch, Ivy is recast as Pamela Isley, a brilliant botanist who is manipulated and experimented on by Dr. Jason Woodrue, aka the Plant Master. Once again, her character is a victim of male aggression. Poisoned, she dies, and comes back as the poison itself to take revenge on the male-dominated society that had cast her aside. Her body produces powerful pheromones that control the minds of men. She also employs plants and poisons, traditionally passive tools, which she manages

The quintessential femme fatale, Poison Ivy delivers a toxic kiss in *Batman: Poison Ivy* #1. ©1997 DC Comics.

to weaponize. With her toxic lipstick, for example, she can kill her enemies with a single and seductive kiss.

In many ways, Ivy represents a vengeful mother earth, the goddess to whom we all return in the end, but like so many *femme fatales* of Greek tragedy, she also walks a thin line between good and evil. She can use her wicked enchantments, like Calypso, to make men forget everything and fall blindly in love with her—emasculation to be sure, but also death to the male ego. But she can also play the hero. In the "Ends of the Earth" arc of *All-Star Batman*, for example, Ivy devotes herself to finding a cure to combat a deadly bacteria unleashed by Mr. Freeze. Ultimately, characters such as Ivy, or even the gorgon Medusa, are female monsters created by men trying to take advantage of them. Villains, therefore, like heroes, have a propensity for both good and evil with Fate often deciding who carries which moniker.

Conclusion

In summary, while we typically see Helen of Troy as the ultimate *femme fatale*, she is ultimately as much a victim of fate and fortune as any other epic hero. More than that, she represents a moral mirror for a phallocentric society, how not to act, as opposed to Penelope, who is the model wife. Characters like Helen and Clytemnestra, however, were not always villains. They made choices, perhaps bad ones, but these were in response to some sort of trauma—the murder of a child, abduction, and rape. In modern comics, writers tend to use a Helen-like model for women who use beauty and feminine sexuality to obtain their goals.

These women, though not always under the control of the gods, are subject to fortune. We see them as bad eggs, again because of their choices, but it's a little unfair if one considers that again many are reacting to some sort of trauma. Poison Ivy herself is poisoned before becoming a poisoner, Silver Swan is tormented for her ugliness, and Black Widow, trained to be a killer, uses every means possible just to survive. These *femme fatales* are for us a reverse moral mirror, showing us not how women should behave but conversely how society treats them. Instead of showing the weakness of women, they represent the indomitable strength of women, who survive given the often exceptionally poor hands Fate has dealt them. This is why we find the *femme fatale* so interesting, because despite their checkered pasts, they are warriors keen in the art of survival.

XIII

The Hand of Fate

The Infinity Gauntlet and the Moirai

For Homer's heroes, fate and free will are driving forces and function in tandem with the warrior's code, something we have explored quite extensively throughout this book. One's fate, or *aisa*, was largely determined by three mystical goddesses known as the Moirai. There was Clotho, the Spinner who wove the thread of one's life, Lachesis, the Allotter who measured out the thread, and finally Atropos, the eldest, whose burdensome and dreadful task was to cut the thread. These three sisters controlled not only the lives of mortals, but also the gods.[1] The nature of fate versus free will in ancient Greece, however, is complicated.

According to the great lawgiver Solon, the fates bore both good and ill to mortals, gifts that were inescapable.[2] Homer even says that once the gods have allotted a person's fate, s/he is left with no choice but to bear what comes.[3] One's destiny then was preordained, however, this is not to say there was not some degree of flexibility. There were certain loopholes—knots, if you will, in the thread—that could be undone perhaps extending one's destiny, but this depended largely on one's social status. Achilles, for example, claims he has a choice in the unfolding of his own fate:

> For my mother, silver footed goddess Thetis, says that double fates carry me on to the day of death. If I remain here and besiege the city of Troy, my return home is lost, but my glory will be everlasting. And if I return to my beloved home in the fatherland, my pride and glory will die. The life given me will be long and the fulfillment of death will not come on me swiftly.[4]

For Achilles, the choice of eternal glory or an ordinary life was a no-brainer. What Homer's narrative demonstrates is that fate is flexible. One might alter destiny by earning distinction on the battlefield and by keeping to the heroic code. Achilles refutes this, saying that death comes both to the idle man and to those who work, that both the coward and the courageous man are bound by the same honor.[5]

Despite what Achilles says, he clearly has at least some power over his own destiny. He is presented with two paths, two diverging strands in his life thread, and he choses the one that shall bring him glory. The choice, however, is based on his inner character or *thymos*.[6] He is, after all, a warrior. Odysseus knew this to be true, which is why he wagered Achilles would be lured from hiding at Scyros if presented with arms. He is also brave, which frequently earns him the aid of Athena. His courage, then, does make a difference to his destiny. Also recall that his mother, Thetis, hid him away to prevent his departure to Troy, attempting to change his fate.

Finally, consider the final confrontation between Achilles and Hector in Book 22. When Hector is on the run, Zeus holds a balance and weighs two portions of woeful death.[7] Hector's side of the scale sinks downward to Hades, indicating his death.[8] The Greek term for this rite is called *kerostasia,* and it absolutely throws a wrench into the works. For if a hero's death was already predetermined by fate(s), why would Zeus need to measure out death? Equally troubling is the value system employed. What is it that causes Hector's fate to sink? Is it his defilement of Patroclus? Does a single act of *hubris* erase a life of adhering to the heroic code? What about Achilles? Are his pride and equivalent acts of defilement not also damning? Readers are left in the dark. One possible explanation, suggested by J.V. Morrison, is that Zeus is simply removing any further interruptions in destiny, forbidding the possibility of divine intervention, essentially untying those knots in fate's thread.[9] Nevertheless, there are still inconsistencies.

Some heroes, who are blinded by their *thymos* and try to circumvent fate, are clearly kept in check. When Patroclus, for example, tries to scale the walls of Troy, he is met by Apollo who pushes him back three times, then delivers a stern warning: "Stand down Zeus born Patroclus. It is not your destiny, I say, that the city of Troy should be laid to waste by your spear."[10] Only on the fourth time and with Apollo shouting terribly does Patroclus finally relent. Nevertheless, he still ignores Achilles' initial command simply to protect the ships. Instead, emboldened by the armor, he chases a greater prize.

His initial *hubris*, however, greatly stirs the wrath of Apollo, who convinces Hector to hunt him down. In the final moments of the battle, Apollo himself weakens the armor, making Patroclus vulnerable to Hector's attack. Hector buries his spear into the belly of Patroclus, who sputters these words. "Boast while you can Hector; it was Zeus and Apollo that have given you an easy victory … it was fate and Leto's son (Apollo) who killed me."[11] It is the combination of Zeus, who weighs divine intervention, Apollo, and fate that ultimately caused his downfall. Ironically, Patroclus never takes responsibility for his own choice to take the walls of Troy. Blinded by glory, he rushes to his fate. Before dying, however, he himself delivers a prophecy to Hector, that the Trojan prince will fall beneath the stroke of Achilles. At this Hector merely laughs, spurning destiny, and demonstrating his own *hubris*, a fault the gods always punish heartily.

Diomedes is also a firm believer in fate. When Agamemnon plans to depart Troy, convinced Zeus has turned against them, it is Diomedes who offers to stay and fight, reminding them of the prophecy that Troy indeed will fall. Afterwards Agamemnon sends a delegation to offer recompense to Achilles, to lure him back into the fight. Nevertheless, overtaken by his pride, Achilles threatens to sail home and counsels others to do the same—suggesting once more that he has a choice in his own fate and even that of others. At the end of Book 9, however, after Odysseus reports to Agamemnon Achilles' response, Diomedes counsels his fellow Achaeans:

> But now surely, we will let that one alone, he may go, or he may stay:
> he will fight when the heart in his breast calls him and a god arouse him [Homer, *Iliad* 9.701–3].[12]

Clearly Diomedes suggests that it does not matter what Achilles says he will do. He is destined to return to Troy to fight, because that is now his fate. Indeed, while he may have had a choice before—to stay home or to go to war—by setting sail for Troy, Achilles has already made his choice. It is no longer within his power to do otherwise. The gods will ensure that he fulfills his destiny at Troy.

Odysseus, on the other hand, seems to embody free will. He bemoans his fate and his very actions, trying to get home; despite earning the wrath of the gods, Odysseus demonstrates that he places trust more in free will than fate. In the *Odyssey*, after blinding the Cyclops, Odysseus is cursed by Poseidon to wander the sea. One wonders whether it was always Odysseus' fate to wander the sea, or was his act of free will the cause. If it was fated, why did Poseidon need to curse him? At one point Polyphemus declares that an old prophecy had come true.[13] If this is true, then Odysseus, because of his very nature, was always fated to wander. Then again, his choice to reveal his real identity to the Cyclops is what causes his downturn. If he had not shouted out his name, if he had not let *hubris* overtake him, he might have had a chance. His nature then, which the Fates recognized, cinches it. It was only a matter of time.

Let us extend our metaphor of weaving to Penelope. It is interesting to think of her as a weaver, like the Moirai, especially since her and Odysseus's threads are indelibly intertwined. She has decreed that she will not remarry until she has completed weaving a funeral shroud for Laertes. By day she weaves, but by night she slowly unravels, unknots the shroud, elongating her own fate and that of her absent husband, buying them time. Odysseus, too, is able to spin a good yarn. His stories of the Trojan War for example cause the Phaecians to shower him in gifts and speed him on his way home.

Among the ranks of Fate's more famous victims is of course Agamemnon, the king of Mycenae and leader of the Achaeans at Troy. His is a fate, however, generations in the making, one ignited by murder and revenge. His father was Atreus. Atreus and his brother were the sons of Pelops, the hero whose father, Tantalus, had served him up to the gods. After being resurrected by the gods, Pelops goes on to compete in a chariot race for the hand of a princess named Hippodamia. He enlists the aid of a servant named Myrtilus, who helps him sabotage the chariot of his competitor. For this (mis)deed, he promises Myrtilus half of his kingdom and the virginity of Hippodamia, should he win. After winning the race, however, Pelops breaks his word and tosses Mytilus into the sea. With his dying breath, Myrtilus curses Pelops and the entire Atreid line.

Things go from bad to worse. As time goes on, Pelops begets twin sons, Atreus and Thyestes. Eventually they murder their half-brother Chrysippus for the throne of Olympia and are exiled, winding up in the Peloponnese at Mycenae. Later, Atreus discovers that his brother Thyestes is secretly having an affair with his wife and plots to murder his brother's sons in revenge. But he doesn't just kill them. Atreus serves them to Thyestes for dinner and taunts his brother by displaying the hands and heads of his sons, thus giving rise to the term Thyestean feast. Revenge is a dish best served hot. In time, however, Thyestes then sires another two sons, one of which is Aegisthus, who swears revenge on Atreus and his sons. It is the same Aegisthus who will later murder Agamemnon upon his return from Troy.

Before even setting off for Troy, Agamemnon's forces encounter the wrath of the goddess Artemis. Accidentally having slain an animal sacred to the goddess, he faces unfavorable winds and a plague that hinders his expedition. The prophet Calchas claims that to placate the goddess and gain passage to Troy, he must sacrifice his daughter Iphigenia.[14] In some traditions he does, while in others, such as in Euripides' play *Iphigenia at Aulis*, she is substituted for a deer. To say the House of Atreus is cursed would be a supreme understatement. Indeed, but some would argue that Agamemnon's fate was decided by Tantalus's original act of murder, which offended the gods, or when Pelops was cursed by Myrtilus. Others might contend that it was Agamemnon's impious act earning Artemis' wrath and his subsequent decision to blindly follow the prophecy and murder his own daughter that eventually brings about his demise, for it brings his wife Clytemnestra and his enemy Aegisthus closer together as bed fellows, literally and figuratively.

Fate and the gods are at the heart of Aeschylus' play *Agamemnon*. The play centers on the return of Agamemnon to Mycenae. In his absence, his wife and her lover conspire to kill him. At one point, the Chorus decrees that the lives and fates of mortals are determined by the gods. It is an important point and one Clytemnestra has considered. The favor of the gods is indeed powerful, and the gods support Agamemnon, so how does one diffuse it? Upon his return to the palace, Clytemnestra invites him to walk upon a richly dyed purple carpet, which he does, demonstrating to all his hubristic arrogance. He thus loses favor with the gods. Afterwards, he is murdered while bathing. Homer blames Aegisthus,[15] who claims to be acting out of revenge, while many tragedians make it Clytemnestra, who again is acting out of revenge embittered by the death of her daughter.[16] In the end, the two wind up ruling Mycenae, until Agamemnon's son Orestes avenges his father by murdering his own mother. Bad blood, it seems, runs in the family. Orestes, pursued now by the Furies, stands trial in Aeschylus' play appropriately titled *Erinyes*, or *The Furies*. The play makes the poignant point that the cycle of revenge killings can only successfully be concluded by the gods.

Oracles and Prophecy

Many an epic hero's destiny was also guided by prophecy. Prophecies are of course notorious for being vague and tricky.[17] Take for example Vergil's *Aeneid*. In it, Aeneas receives several prophecies, all of which he dutifully tries to interpret. In Book 2, Hector's ghost informs Aeneas he will found a new city across the sea in a western land, where a bride awaits him.[18] Famously in Book 3, the god Apollo tells Aeneas he must seek out his ancient mother, which Aeneas mistakenly interprets as Crete.[19] Apollo then has to send the Penates, the household gods, to help clarify that this is in fact Italy not Crete.[20] Another fine example in Book 7 has one of the harpies, Celaeno, confirm that he and his men will go to Italy but before they lay the foundations of the city, they will be forced to eat their tables, by which she meant stale loaves of bread which they use as plates.[21] As you can see, the more enigmatic, the easier it is for a prophet to make the claim that a message was misunderstood when it goes badly, rather than the prophecy being flat out wrong.

There are innumerable examples of prophecies relating to Troy. Surprisingly, most of these appear prominently outside of Homer's text. We have already mentioned Calchas' prophecy at Aulis, but he was also the one who had foretold that Troy would only fall with the aid of Achilles, which is why Thetis tries hiding him.[22] He also decrees that Troy will fall in its tenth year:

> Not yet, but soon, fate will lay waste the glorious town, if true the tale of Calchas told before the council of Greeks comes to be that the city of Priam be ravaged in the tenth year.[23]

Luckily for Calchas, the prophecies all turned out to be true. Of course, it must have raised many an eyebrow when after the war he was bested by another soothsayer and subsequently died of humiliation and shame. Observe, however, the vagueness of the pronouncements. Achilles simply has to go to Troy and help. Calchas does not say for how long, or if he goes home before the end of the conflict, leaving Achilles' actual fate, and that of Troy's, wide open for interpretation. His prediction that the city should be laid to waste in its tenth year is probably a guess; who could survive a ten-year siege anyway?

Another prophet worth mentioning is Tiresias. In Book 11 of the *Odyssey*, called the *Nekyia*, or summoning of spirits for parlance, the ghostly seer predicts Odysseus' journey will only conclude when he comes to a land where the people know nothing of the sea and mistake a well made oar for a winnowing fan, a threshing tool.[24] There he will make sacrifice to Poseidon and await sleek old age and mysterious death. This prophecy is, like all others, nebulous. Suffice it to say that the event is much further down Odysseus' timeline. Clouding his vision, of course, are Odysseus' actions and those of his men. Will they resist the urge to steal the cattle of the sun? Poseidon has already assured a long and arduous journey, but stealing the cattle will earn them additional wrath and further turmoil.

The Song of Destiny

Perhaps another way of thinking about destiny is as a song. As the scholar Anthony Tuck has suggested, there is a curious link between weaving and singing, particularly in epic poetry.[25] Circe, when Odysseus' men first find her, sings at the loom[26]:

> They heard Circe singing within in a sweet voice the lays of heroes as she went back and forth in front of a great web, befitting the skill of goddesses, finely woven, beautiful and full of glory.

Her actions, back and forth, clearly recall a shuttle on a loom. Also, she is not merely singing, but singing of heroes, like the poet Homer. The metaphor of a tapestry as a web also casts Circe both as a spinner, like the Fates, as well as a spider, laying a clever trap for Odysseus' men who are lured in by her honeyed words. So too might one be lured into the song of the epic poet. Penelope is able achieve the opposite effect—to fend off her wooers rather than lure them—by cleverly weaving a death shroud for Laertes, which earns her glory.[27]

We do not know what exactly is pictured on these tapestries. Like destiny itself, they remain enigmatic, but the very act of singing and weaving with the mention of men's lives is highly suggestive of the spinners of fate, who likewise spin and measure out the lives of mortals. If such is the case, Penelope's act of weaving and unweaving creates a sense that fate may be flexible upon the loom, just as one may sing a song and change the words or tempo. Moreover, she *re*creates the weaving like drafts of an unfinished poem, undoubtedly tweaking it, making the product slightly different each day. If we apply the metaphor of Zeus measuring out the Fates of Achilles and Hector, we may also think of this as the use of weights upon the loom, keeping the life thread taut and inflexible at certain times, perhaps crystalizing at least part of one's final and inevitable fate. There are certain events that must happen, and some that may be altered, and only the weaver knows one from the other.

Fate vs. Free Will

Themes of fate and free will pervade the world of the modern superhero as well. Marvel's Captain America, for example, has faced the hand of destiny on many occasions. Instead of returning home after World War II, he is tossed into the freezing waters of the North Atlantic, his life literally frozen in time. When he is reawakened, it is to a world void of many of his friends. The life he should have had with his love Peggy Carter was not meant to be, or was it? The MCU puts this question to the test in the final installment of the Avengers films, *Endgame*. In the film *Avengers: Infinity War*, audiences witnessed the "Snap," a universal genocide initiated by the mad titan Thanos with the aid of the infinity stones. The event not only wipes out half of the universe, it decimates the ranks of Earth's mightiest superheroes.

In the wake of this annihilation Captain America leads the remaining Avengers on a crusade to recover the stones and reverse the Snap. Encountering Thanos on Planet 0259-S, they learn that he has shrunken them to the atomic level making them virtually impossible to find. After defeating Thanos, Cap believes the stones can be recovered. "The stones are in the past. We can go back and get them." Black Widow declares: "We can snap our own fingers. We can bring everyone back." It is an overt display of free-will over the destiny that has already unfolded, an unwillingness to accept death, and what fate has dealt one, and it is a common trope in modern culture. After recovering the stones and defeating Thanos again, Captain

America travels back in time to return each of the stones to their respective timelines, but instead of returning to the present, he decides to travel back to the 1940s to live out his life with Peggy. His free will determines his fate—not the other way around.

The Infinity Gauntlet

In the film *Avengers: Infinity War*, modern audiences were introduced to the intergalactic warlord Thanos, whose name literally means death. The titan is shown ravaging the universe in a mad quest for the Infinity stones—the Mind Stone, with its power to overcome the minds of others, the Power Stone, Space Stone with the power to bend space and create portals, the Soul Stone with its power to control souls, the Reality Stone, and the Time Stone, also known to Doctor Strange fans as the Eye of Agamotto. When assembled, these six all-powerful gems form a formidable weapon with the power to wipe out half of the universe in a single snap. So powerful are they that they can only be employed using a special gauntlet. He who wields the gauntlet wields power over destiny itself. Marvel began playing with the idea as far back as 1972 with the mention of the Soul Stone in *Marvel Premiere* #1. The story of the stones, however, continued in the 1990 limited series *The Thanos Quest*, where we find the titan Thanos searching for the stones, powerful relics from before the Big Bang used by ancient civilizations. In the miniseries, *Infinity Gauntlet*, he uses the gems to bring the gift of death to the universe, literally controlling the hand of fate.

To many Thanos is Fate incarnate. He even claims, like fate to be "inevitable." His arrival is foreshadowed throughout the MCU. In *Age of Ultron*, the mighty hammer-wielding hero Thor descends into a pool of water and receives a vision of the future. He sees the time stones, and Ragnarok, the fall of his fellow Asgardians. Eventually, he declares that someone is making pawns of Earth's heroes. In *Avengers: Infinity War*, Doctor Strange delivers a prophecy. Using the Time Stone to peer into the future, he tries to find a way of stopping Thanos, or fate. He declares that there are 14,000,605 possible outcomes, but only one in which he foresees them defeating Thanos. The heroes are destined to fail, but there is that one chance. As in the *Iliad*, however, no one knows his or her ultimate fate. The Snap, like Fate of old, is enigmatic. Homer suggests one's destiny is designed by the combination of the Moirai, the gods, and free will; here writers have mixed things up a bit, but it is essentially the same three components, with free-will embodied in the Avengers, the god Thanos an agent of Fate, and fate itself simply randomness and chaos theory guiding the Snap.

In the end, free-will and ingenuity win out over Fate. With knowledge of the future, the Avengers travel back into the past so they can rewrite their own history. This is the major difference between ancient and modern heroes. In a post-enlightenment world of science where man is at the center of universe rather than at its whim, we would like to think we can control nature and by extension our own destiny. It is, however, a bittersweet victory, as some of our heroes inevitably die, but in the modern examples, those that perish have a say in their own deaths. These heroes embrace destiny rather than succumb to it. They are willing to sacrifice themselves for their friends, for their families, and for society as a whole.

Conclusion

If there is one thing we can say about Fate is that it is complicated. Are epic heroes controlled by fate, or do they have the free will to change their life course? What the aforementioned examples demonstrate is that while destiny may appear set in proverbial stone, the ancient Greeks in fact believed that there was a certain degree of flexibility. Achilles claims no matter how a warrior acts in valor, he is incapable of increasing his lot, and yet he himself has the power to choose—either a long and uneventful life or a brief and tumultuous one earning him everlasting glory.

When we say the gods control the fate of mortals, this is not necessarily true. Patroclus' transgressions are based on his overbearing *thymos*. He heeds neither the advice of his friend, nor Apollo, for which he ultimately pays the price. When Zeus holds the lives of Hector and Achilles literally in the balance, what he is really doing is lifting the moratorium on the inevitable, what was always meant to be. So while the gods may have a profound effect on one's life, there is a close interdependence with one's free will. Consider Bellerophon, who, for his act of *hubris,* is forcibly dismounted from Pegasus and suffers a terrible fall. It was still his choice to mount a failed quest for Olympus. Consider also that he may easily have struck his head on a rock, but he didn't. Thus, despite Zeus' efforts, he was not fated to die until his rightful time. Thus the combination of fate, divine intervention, and free-will are all responsible for his destiny. We tend to believe free will is largely a mark of modern culture. Everyone believes that they have the power to change their own fate. Homer and Hesiod, however, interestingly seem to have the same opinion.

What power does the hero have in deciding their own fate, especially in a system where the gods are not just fallible but sometimes downright horrible? They cheat, are unfaithful, and often vengeful. Hesiod, if we recall, characterizes the Muses as liars: ἴδμεν ψεύδεα πολλὰ λέγειν ἐτύμοισιν ὁμοῖα, "We know how to speak many lies the same as true things" (Hesiod,

Theogony 27). Part of the reason Greek philosophy caught on so well and changed the way the Greeks (and others) looked at religion, is because they addressed these inconsistencies. We know that the Greek gods are NOT the best of us and not necessarily inspirational as far as upright behaviors—they aren't people to look up to. Some, such as Ares, one might consider a monster. So why do it? Why believe in or even revere petty gods? As we compose our list of heroes, it is increasingly clear that while the gods have a hand in how things unravel, the hero still has a choice in his or her fate.

Complicating the matter are oracles and prophecies. Prophecies are by nature enigmatic. These are visions given by the gods and thus subject to their influence, and reinterpreted by the human courier. We see what we want to see rather than a range of possibilities. In the end, if the fates are the only ones who know for certain the extent of human life, then prophecies offer a mere snapshot rather than a full picture of what lies ahead and should therefore be viewed with trepidation. Therefore, if we look more broadly, not at single instances but rather a holistic view, we find that it is the joint combination of outside forces and one's own free will that ultimately decides one's fate. Call it Destiny or Thanos, the gods or determinism, there will always be heroes who struggle to fight the forces of nature in order to overcome them. In the end, their struggles earn them glory and everlasting life in story and song.

Epilogue

The Legacy of the Epic Hero

The legacy of the epic hero survives in various forms of modern culture: comics, film, video games, even technology itself. For example, whenever I check my email, I am always cautioned to be wary of Trojan horses and secretly think that a platoon of digital Greek warriors are plotting to crash my computer after I go to sleep. Whenever I hear "an Achilles' heel," whether in sports or in politics, I can't help but think of that fateful arrow that took down the mightiest of the Achaeans, but I also can't help but also think of Kryptonite. Any scene in a film with a funeral pyre, *Return of the Jedi* for example, reminds me of Patroclus. The face that launched a thousand ships always will bring to mind the *femme fatale*, Helen. When we study mythology, we are not simply studying stories but an ongoing continuum and conversation with the past. For many, comics and film provide an alternative way for modern audiences to relate to ancient texts. As scholars and educators, we should celebrate these new forms rather than reject them, for we are, after all, leaving our own human footprint, so to speak, on the sands of time. Our modern mythologies will mix and mingle with those of the past, and two thousand years hence, it will all look exactly the same to a researcher of heroes.

Over the course of the book, we have explored some ancient models of the archer, the berserker, and the semi-divine hero, only to discover that some of these archetypes transcend cultural and temporal boundaries. They are shared by people across the world and across the gulf of time which certainly will not end with us. Comics and film allow oral traditions to be retold in a primarily visual medium. While language is powerful *and* empowering, the language or semiotics of film tends to reach a wider audience. While we may think that we lose the beauty of Homer's song, the characters and the narrative are preserved, in part, and are even reborn. Each telling is slightly different, and while we may mine that ancient vein, each is reformed around modern issues, values, and concerns such as globalism, environmentalism, technophobia, and even xenophobia.

Technology, lest we forget, is also breathing new life into these old heroes. Video games such as *Assassin's Creed Odyssey* provide audiences with newly imagined worlds based on history and myth. Players can assume the role of a Greek mercenary, male (Alexios) or female (Kassandra). Like many epic heroes, you can even receive divine aid using God mode. While the world is set in 431 BCE, which is well into the historic era and no longer the realm of pure myth but rather history, players can engage with monsters such as Medusa, the Cyclops, or the Minotaur, and heroes such as Achilles, Perseus, and Herakles. The game also weaves in its own unique mythology regarding the Assassin Brotherhood. For the purists out there who find these adaptations distasteful, I would remind them of this: Homer's song changed many, many times before stylus was ever set to parchment.

In addition to the traditional storytelling methods, video games, DVDs, and comics also find unique ways of communicating with their audience. One particular method is the Easter egg. An Easter egg is a hidden message or feature, embedded within various media. Gamers, for example, are encouraged to seek out additional features using specialized codes, techniques, or tasks to unlock additional knowledge, characters, or boards. Like the ancient Greek *koine* that enabled people to decipher and draw meaning from figural scenes of Homeric warriors on pottery, modern gamers demonstrate their adeptness as a gamer, knowledge of their virtual world, and the ability to predict the mind of the game developer. In the sci-fi series *Doctor Who*, the Tenth Doctor is able to communicate with a heroine across time by embedding a series of messages across several DVDs, linked by a particular theme. One of the more notorious examples of an Easter egg in comics was Ethan Van Sciver's subtle placement of the word "sex" on every page of the *New X-Men* #118. Another would be the LEGO Batman 3 where players can find a secret level based on using their knowledge of the 1966 Batman television show with Adam West. The Easter egg ultimately rewards the person seeking it with information that enhances the storytelling experience, and the story itself, even if for a select few.

The story of the epic hero is ever-changing, as are the cultures that produce them. Why do we gravitate towards these stories? The hero is the vehicle by which modern audiences search for, and perhaps even find, self-meaning. The hero is *us*, or what we most desire to be. For some the hero is the light, for some the shadow. In the end, he or she is the blazing star streaking through the heavens, on which we hang our hopes and our hearts.

Glossary

Achilles

Son of the sea nymph Thetis and a mortal Peleus, he is the greatest of the Achaeans at Troy. Daring and brave but equally dark and brooding, he is practically invulnerable, save for his heel.

aidos

The fear of disgrace that kept heroes from performing unjust acts.

aisa

One's fate, or destiny, akin to the goddess Atropos.

alter ego

Literally translated, "another self"; originally used in the context of Cicero's letter to his friend Atticus, he is pleased that Pompey the Great views Cicero as "another self" (VII.1.6)

Amazons

A mythical race of warrior woman.

ambrosia/soma

The food or drink of the gods that could grant immortality.

annual

A special, usually oversized, edition released in addition to the regular issues of a comic book.

archetype

Common elements appearing first in the oral traditions and literary traditions of the ancient world that include characters, plots, symbols and themes.

arête

The struggle for greatness, or a noble cause.

Argonaut

One of the men who sailed on the Argo with the hero Jason on his quest for the Golden Fleece.

aristeia
A Greek word meaning "excellence," it is usually shorthand for the particular scene in an epic poem that shows a hero's greatest moment(s).

Atalanta
A fierce virgin huntress, who, abandoned as a child, was raised by bears and accompanied Meleager on the hunt for the Calydonian boar.

bard
A peripatetic storyteller, like Homer, who sang of the great deeds of mortals and gods through epic poetry, usually accompanied by a lyre.

Bellerophon
A Lycian hero who rode Pegasus to victory over the fire-breathing chimaera but whose own hubris caused him to be cast down by the gods.

Boreads
Winged warriors, Calais and Zetes, who aid Jason in defeating the Harpies.

caption
A box used exclusively for narration.

Circe
The beautiful sea witch, daughter of Helios, who transformed Odysseus' men into swine.

closure
The work a viewer has to do in order to find meaning between comic book panels.

colorist
The artist who provides the overall color for the comic.

darshan/darśan
Epiphany experienced when viewing an immortal.

demos
The democratic Greek city; also another way to refer to the people of the Greek city.

deus ex machina
Literally god from the machine, a term used to mean the rescue of a mortal by means of divine favor.

eidolon
An image of a person; specter, phantom, or spirit image of a person; the German term *doppelgänger* is probably the best rendering of this Greek word.

ekphrasis
The (usually poetic) description of an object.

emanata

Symbols used to further describe the actions or feelings of a character. For example, a light bulb drawn above the head to indicate a "bright idea."

encapsulation

Choosing then most pivotal moments in a story to present in a panel.

enthusiasmos

Being filled with the essence, or spirit of a god.

epic

A long narrative poem relating the deeds of great men and women.

epithet

An alternate name used to describe a character in epic, for example, "swift-footed" Achilles. A modern equivalent might be "Man of Steel," for Superman, or the "Dark Knight," for Batman.

erastes

The lover.

eromenos

The beloved, or object of affection in a relationship.

femme fatale

A seductive woman, who uses her charms to lure men into danger.

Golden Age of Comic Books

An era of American comic books from 1938 to 1956.

Gorgon

A hideous snaky-haired woman, whose frightening appearance could turn one into stone. Thought to dwell well beyond the edges of the sea, they lived in seclusion. While Medusa was transformed into one by Athena, Stheno and Euryale were born gorgons. The creature Aege may also have been a gorgon.

habrosyne

Effeminate luxury.

hamartia

A tragic flaw or weakness that ultimately causes the downfall of a hero.

Herakles

All brawn and little in the way of brain, the ancient Greek hero whose incredible strength and Twelve Labors became the stuff of legends. Born of Zeus and Alcmene, he is the frequent target of Hera who eventually drives him to murder his wife and children.

hieratic scale

Artistic method of rendering the more important figures larger than the rest.

Hounds of Hell
Harpies, old beaked women with the ability to fly.

hubris
Pride, especially in terms of stepping beyond one's social class, or station.

Jason
Son of Aeson, king of Iolcos, a Greek hero with one sandal, who led the Argonauts on a quest for the Golden Fleece.

kerostasia
The weighing of an individual's death.

kibisis
Sack used to carry Medusa's head.

kleos
Glory.

koine
A common language/dialect/communication method.

larnax/larnakes
A box or casket, usually terra cotta.

limited series
A comic book with a set number of issues, that usually concludes with the last issue.

male gaze
Term used by Laura Mulvey to indicate a male point of view in film and other media of women usually implying objectification.

Marvel Cinematic Universe (MCU)
The film adaptations of some of classical Marvel characters, themes and storylines.

Medusa
Once a temple priestess, who vainly boasted her hair was more beautiful than that of the goddess Athena's. She was transformed into the dreaded gorgon, a creature with serpentine hair and a face so hideous, a mere glance at it could turn anyone to stone.

Memnon
Ethiopian king and son of the goddess Eos, the dawn; he battles Achilles but ultimately dies at Troy.

menis/menos
Wrath, or rage.

miasma

A pollution of an individual brought on by blood-guilt.

mint condition

Flawlessly preserved (said of comic books). Usually kept in a plastic jacket.

motion lines

Lines drawn in to show the movement of characters and objects.

muthos

Speech, story, myth.

nekuia/nekyia

The summoning of sprits for parlance, i.e., necromancy.

nostos

The return home of the ancient Greek hero; a vital closure of the epic hero's story.

numen

The divine power or spirit that a divinity exudes.

Odysseus

King of Ithaca and the hero of the *Odyssey*, known for his cunning, craftiness, and prolonged return home from Troy. Most beloved of Athena, he defeats the Cyclops, the sirens, and wields a bow like no other.

Other

The opposite of the self, the term is used to refer to a stranger, or outsider to society.

panel

Sometimes referred to as a frame, it is a single box on a comic book page highlighting a scene, or action.

Pegasus

A horse that sprung from the neck of Medusa after Perseus beheaded her.

Penthesilea

Queen of the Amazons, who after accidentally killing her sister seeks redemption before the walls of Troy. Her beauty turns the eye and heart of Achilles, greatest of the Achaeans.

Perseus

One of the most beloved heroes of ancient Greek myth and son of Zeus, who came to the princess Danaë as a shower of gold. With the aid of Pegasus, the cap of Hades, and sandals of Hermes, he fought the gorgon Medusa and used her head to overcome his enemies.

pharmakos

A scapegoat or sacrifice made on behalf of the entire community.

polis
The city state.

poster layout
Panels are discarded in favor of a single full page spread.

Silver Age of Comic Books
American Comic books dating from 1956 to 1970.

simple story layout
A grid shaped layout of panels.

soter
A savior figure.

speech/thought bubble
A drawn bubble containing dialogue, or thoughts of a character.

superhero
A hero with superhuman abilities who defends the weak or innocent.

synesthesia
The simultaneous engagement of the senses, though there is only one sensory input; some who experience this claim to be able to taste colors.

talaria
Winged sandals.

techne
Art or skill, usually used to describe artistry in Homer, but later in Hellenistic times comes to be the polar opposite of *episteme*, or understanding.

therapon
A companion or friend who is a ritual substitute, or stand-in.

thumos/thymos
One's free will, spirit, inner self.

tīmē
Honor.

titanomachy
The war between the Olympian gods and the titans.

two-page spread
When a comic book spread extends across two pages.

Úlfhéðna
The berserker type rage experienced by Viking warriors.

vibranium
A metal mined in Wakanda that originated from the stars.

wanax
A high king during the Bronze Age.

xenia
Guest/host relations.

Chapter Notes

Preface

1. Robin S. Rosenberg and Ellen Winner, "Are Superheroes Just SuperGifted?" in *Our Superheroes, Ourselves*, ed. Robin S. Rosenberg (Oxford: Oxford University Press, 2013), 116.

2. Marco Arnaudo, *The Myth of the Superhero* (Baltimore: Johns Hopkins University Press, 2013), 118.

3. Plutarch, *Life of Alexander* 8.26. Although the story is probably an exaggeration, Alexander probably kept a copy with him on his campaigns.

4. Contrastingly, the term *mythologia*, mythology, was used to mean the fashioning of tales. Plato equates this with storytelling or even lying.

5. C.G. Jung, *Two Essays on Analytical Psychology* (London: Routledge, 1953), 108.

6. Edmund Leach, *Claude Lévi-Strauss: Modern Masters* (Ann Arbor: Viking Press, 1974), 9.

7. Carl G. Jung, et al., *Man and His Symbols* (London: Arkana, 1990), 67.

8. Fitz Roy Richard Somerset Raglan, *The Hero: A Study in Tradition, Myth, and Drama* (Mineola, NY: Dover Publications, 2016), 1741–75.

9. See Andrew Bahlmann, *The Mythology of the Superhero* (Jefferson, NC: McFarland, 2016), 10, where the author astutely observes that such qualities are embedded in the modern superhero.

10. Adam Bradley, *Book of Rhymes: The Poetics of Hip Hop* (New York: Basic Civitas, 2017).

11. Vergil, *Aeneid* 2.5265–30.

12. Scott McCloud, *Understanding Comics: The Invisible Art* (New York: Harper Perennial, 1994), 63 defines closure as "the phenomenon of observing the parts but perceiving the whole."

13. Apollodorus, *Library* 2.5.9.

14. For more discussion of these panels in particular, see Jaś Elsner and Michael Meyer, eds., *Art and Rhetoric in Roman Culture* (Cambridge: University Printing House, 2014), 375, and Michael Squire, *The Iliad in a Nutshell: Visualizing Epic on the Tabulae Iliacae* (Oxford: Oxford University Press, 2012), 139.

15. Roland Barthes, *A Barthes Reader*, trans. and ed. Susan Sontag (New York: Hill and Wang, 1982), 94.

16. Umberto Eco, *A Theory of Semiotics* (Bloomington: Indiana University Press, 1976), 7.

17. Umberto Eco, *The Island of the Day Before* (New York: Harcourt, 2006), 207.

18. Daniel Chandler, *Semiotics: The Basics* (New York: Routledge, 2007), 2.

19. *Ibid.*

20. As an example, see Jonathan Ostenson, "Exploring the Boundaries of Narrative: Video Games in the English Classroom," *English Journal* 102, no. 6 (2013): 717–8.

Introduction

1. Hesiod, *Works and Days* 1561–69b refers to the Age of Heroes as one nobler and more righteous, a god-like race of heromen who called themselves demigods.

2. Laura Mulvey, *Visual and Other Pleasures* (New York: Palgrave Macmillan, 2009).

3. Homer, *Iliad* 4.370.

4. Pseudo-Apollodorus, *Bibliotheca* E5.6; see Quintus Smyrnaeus' *Fall of Troy*, where he slays sheep instead of cows.

5. Quintus Smyrnaeus, *Fall of Troy* 2.4174–26.

6. *Wonder Woman, Swan Song!* #288 (February 1982).

Chapter 1

1. Tony Stark in *Captain America: Civil War* notes he wishes he could kick Rogers in his perfect teeth.

2. Homer, *Iliad* 19.345–348, 351–354.

3. οἶσθ᾽ οἷαι νέου ἀνδρὸς ὑπερβασίαι τελέθουσι
κραιπνότερος μὲν γάρ τε νόος, λεπτὴ δέ τε μῆτις (Homer, *Iliad* 23.589–590).

4. Hephaestus exclaims: "…many a one among the multitude of men shall marvel, whosoever shall behold it" (…οἱ τεύχεα καλὰ παρέσσεται, οἷά τις αὖτε/ἀνθρώπων πολέων θαυμάσσεται, ὅς κεν ἴδηται, Homer, *Iliad* 18.462).

All translations, whether from Greek or Latin, in this book are my own unless otherwise noted.

5. χαλκὸν δ᾽ ἐν πυρὶ βάλλεν ἀτειρέα κασσίτερόν τε
καὶ χρυσὸν τιμῆντα καὶ ἄργυρον: αὐτὰρ ἔπειτα
θῆκεν ἐν ἀκμοθέτῳ μέγαν ἄκμονα, γέντο δὲ χειρὶ
ῥαιστῆρα κρατερήν, ἑτέρηφι δὲ γέντο πυράγρην.
ποίει δὲ πρώτιστα σάκος μέγα τε στιβαρόν τε
πάντοσε δαιδάλλων, περὶ δ᾽ ἄντυγα βάλλε φαεινὴν
τρίπλακα μαρμαρέην, ἐκ δ᾽ ἀργύρεον τελαμῶνα.
πέντε δ᾽ ἄρ᾽ αὐτοῦ ἔσαν σάκεος πτύχες: αὐτὰρ ἐν αὐτῷ
ποίει δαίδαλα πολλὰ ἰδυίῃσι πραπίδεσσιν (Homer, *Iliad* 18.474–482).

6. ὣς ἄρα φωνήσασα θεὰ κατὰ τεύχε᾽ ἔθηκε
πρόσθεν Ἀχιλλῆος: τὰ δ᾽ ἀνέβραχε δαίδαλα πάντα.
Μυρμιδόνας δ᾽ ἄρα πάντας ἕλε τρόμος, οὐδέ δε ἔτλη
ἄντην εἰσιδέειν, ἀλλ᾽ ἔτρεσαν. αὐτὰρ Ἀχιλλεὺς
ὡς εἶδ᾽, ὥς μιν μᾶλλον ἔδυ χόλος, δε δέ οἱ ὄσσε
δεινὸν ὑπὸ βλεφάρων ὡς εἰ σέλας ἐξεφάανθεν:
τέρπετο δ᾽ ἐν χείρεσσιν ἔχων θεοῦ ἀγλαὰ δῶρα (Homer, *Iliad* 19.12–19).

7. I discuss this more at length in my forthcoming book *Stolen Fire: Technology and Artifice in Ancient Greek Myth*, which views the fate of technology in the ancient world and how we might see it as a mirror to our own modern technology-obsessed society.

8. Elizabeth McGowan, "Tumulus and Memory: The Tumulus as a Locus for Ritual Action in Greek Imagination," in *Tumulus as Sema: Space, Politics, Culture and Religion in the First Millennium BC 174*, ed. Olivier Henry and Ute Kelp (Berlin: Walter de Gruyter, 2016), 163–180.

9. Jim Shooter, Paul Neary, and Michael Carlin, *Captain America* 1, #303 (March 1985).

10. Plutarch, *Parallel Lives: Numa Pompilius* §XIII.1–3.

11. In *Civil War*, when Tony notes his father's role in creating the shield, Cap tosses it aside, preferring humanity to technology.

12. Although Hoplite warfare is deemed later, possible signs of it may appear in the Peisistratid canonization of the epic.

13. Homer, *Iliad* 17.411; Gregory Nagy, *The Best of the Achaeans* (Baltimore: Johns Hopkins University Press, 1999), 105, notes that the specific nature of this relationship is what ultimately lures Achilles back into the fray.

14. See Robin Fox, *The Tribal Imagination: Civilization and the Savage Mind* (Cambridge: Harvard University Press, 2011); W.M. Clarke, "Achilles and Patroclus in Love," *Hermes* 106 (1978): 381–96; Bernard Sergeant *Homosexuality in Greek Myth* (Boston: Beacon Press 1986), 250–258; and David Halperin, *One Hundred Years of Homosexuality: and Other Essays on Greek Love* (New York: Routledge, 2012), 75–87.

15. Pseudo-Apollodorus, *Bibliotheca* 3.13.8.

16. Thank you, Chris Aguirre, for your insight as a veteran; thank you also for your service to our country.

17. One of the more famous suicides of the Homeric cycle is Ajax's, but his actions have a different motivation entirely, namely divinely inspired madness and then Homeric shame.

18. Stan Lee, Jack Kirby, and Artie Simek, *The Avengers: Captain America Lives Again!* 1, #4 (March 1964).

19. *Captain America* Vol. 5 #26 (May 2007).

20. *Captain America* Vol. 5 #30 (November 2007).

21. *Captain America* Vol. 5 #33 (February 2008).

22. Gregory Nagy, *The Ancient Greek Hero in 24 Hours* (Cambridge: Harvard University Press, 2013), 166, refers to *Iliad* 16.244 and the Greek term, *therapon*, i.e., ritual substitute used to refer to Patroclus.

23. Pierre Bourdieu, *Distinction* (London: Routledge, 1986), 471.

Chapter 2

1. Apollonius Rhodius, *Argonautica* 2. 985–988.

2. The Greek conception of the half-breasted Amazon appears in both vase painting and sculpture, e.g., the Mattei Amazon, a Roman copy of a Greek original by Phidias, perpetuated in later works such as the Byzantine mosaic of Melanippe at Urfa.

3. Homer, *Iliad* 3.189.

4. At the time of writing this book, the Russian government recently uncovered a tomb of three female warriors while excavating for airport construction. Here is a link to the most recent information: https://www.smithsonianmag.com/smart-news/tomb-containing-three-generations-amazon-warrior-women-unearthed-russia-180973877/.

5. Perhaps the best treatment—academic or mainstream—*Across the Ancient World* (Princeton: Princeton University Press, 2016).

6. Bettany Hughes, *Helen of Troy: Goddess, Princess, Whore* (London: Pimlico, 2005), 585–9.

7. See Sue Blundell, *Women in Ancient Greece* (Cambridge: Harvard University Press, 1995), 157, where she discusses Plutarch's *Moralia* 240e 6.

8. Aristotle, *Politics* 2.1269b.30.

9. Herodotus, *Histories* 4; Diodorus Siculus, *Bibliotheca Historica*, 3.52

10. Apollonius Rhodius, *Argonautica* 2; Hyginus, *Fab.* 225; Schol. *ad Apollon. Rhod.* i. 1033.

11. Hyginus, *Fabulae* 30; Apollodorus E.5.1; Hyginus, *Fab.* 112.

12. Euripides, *Hercules Furens* 408–415; Apollonius Rhodius, *Argonautica* 2. 777–779 and 964 sqq.; Diodorus Siculus, *Bibliotheca Historica* IV.16; Ps.-Apollodorus *Bibliotheke* II. 5. 9; Pausanias, *Hellados Periegesis* V. 10. 9.

13. Pseudo-Apollodorus, *Bibliotheke* II. 5. 9

14. Plutarch, *Life of Theseus* 27.

15. Arctinus, *Aethiopis* fr.1.

16. Pseudo-Apollodorus, *Epitome of the Bibliotheke* 5.1.

17. No. 1836,0224.127.

18. Pausanias, *Description of Greece* 5.11.6.

19. The semantics of left and right in the Greek mind-set are easily seen in all kinds of examples from epic to the stage, science to philosophy. For a (still) excellent study of how the Greek mind processed such polarities, see G.E.R. Lloyd, "Right and Left in Greek Philosophy," *Journal of Hellenic Studies* 82 (1962): 56–66.

20. Readers of Greek tragedy will recall Aeschylus' bloody wife, Clytemnestra, who murdered her recently-returned husband, Agamemnon, in his bath and calls for her axe in the subsequent play, *Libation Bearers* (889). Otherwise neither the axe nor the sword are terribly feminine weapons. There has, of course, been some scholarly debate on the matter: Malcolm Davies, "Aeschylus' Clytemnestra: Sword or Axe?" *Classical Quarterly* 37, no. 1 (1987): 65–75; A.H. Sommerstein, "Again Klytaimestra's Weapon," *Classical Quarterly* 39, no. 2 (1989): 296–301; A.J.N.W. Prag, "Clytemnestra's Weapon Yet Once More," *Classical Quarterly* 41, no. 1 (1991): 242–246.

21. Pausanias, *Description of Greece* 7.10.6 mentions the King Abrupolis, while Strabo, *Geography* 12.3.20.1–2, recalls that the Saii, were the Sapaei, a tribe of Thracians.

22. According to Aelian (Hist. Misc. 13.1) the bear was bereft of her cubs, killed by hunters, suggesting a symbiotic relationship. The bear also has links to Artemis, whose companion Calisto was transformed into a bear after losing her virginity to Zeus, and at the site of Brauron where young women dressed like bears.

23. Apollodorus, *Bibliotheca* 1.1291–33.

24. Jacques Grasset de Saint-Sauveur, *Encyclopédie des voyages: América*, 1796. Bibliothèque Nationale de France.

25. Helen May, Baljit Kaur, and Larry

Prochner, *Empire, Education, and Indigenous Childhoods: Nineteenth-Century Missionary Infant Schools in Three British Colonies. Studies in Childhood, 1700 to the Present* (London: Routledge, 2016), 13.

26. Columbia first appears in the revolutionary poetry of Phillis Wheatley.

27. "Be Patriotic" poster by Paul Stahr, ca. 1917–1918, at the Herbert Hoover Library, National Archives and Records Administration.

28. *All Star Comics* Vol. 1 # 8 (December–January 1941–42).

29. In the later tradition, she discovers she is a child of Zeus and Hippolyta.

30. *All Star Comics* Vol. 1 # 8 (December–January 1941–42).

31. *Wonder Woman* (Volume 4) #7.

32. *Wonder Woman* (Volume 1) #95.

33. Laura Mulvey, *Visual and Other Pleasures* (New York: Palgrave Macmillan, 2009).

34. Women were typically excluded from competing in and even watching some games. Only *hetaerai*, paid companions, were supposedly allowed at the symposium.

Chapter 3

1. Homer, *Odyssey* 8.51–2: δουράτεον μέγαν ἵππον. Though Quintus Smyrnaeus attributes the building to Odysseus, various traditions, however, attribute the idea of the horse to Athena, and the actual construction of it to Epeius, including Homer (*Odyssey* 8.4929–3).

2. See Apollodorus, *Bibliotheca* 1.9.16, who discloses that Hermes, often the trickster figure, has a son named Autolycus, who is the grandfather of Odysseus.

3. Homer, *Odyssey* 12.280 where Eurylochos exclaims that Odysseus is σιδήρεα πάντα τέτυκται, "wholly made of iron." Telemachus calls him iron-hearted, "κραδίη γε σιδηρέη" (*Od.* 4.293). See Ruth Russo, "The Heart of Steel: A Metallurgical Interpretation of Iron in Homer," *Bulletin for the History of Chemistry* 30, no.1 (2005): 232–4.

4. Homer, *Odyssey* 12.48.

5. Homer, *Odyssey* 5.243–260.

6. Κύκλωψ, αἴ κέν τίς σε καταθνητῶν ἀνθρώπων

ὀφθαλμοῦ εἴρηται ἀεικελίην ἀλαωτύν,

φάσθαι Ὀδυσσῆα πτολιπόρθιον ἐξαλαῶσαι,

υἱὸν Λαέρτεω, Ἰθάκῃ ἔνι οἰκί' ἔχοντα (Homer, *Odyssey* 9.502–505).

7. Robert Downey Jr.'s "ghosting" of his own performance or even character appears also in *Sherlock Holmes*. A confirmed bachelor and "playboy," Holmes is always intrigued by and drawn to the strong, intellectual character of Irene Adler. Whether or not this ghosting is intentional on the actor's part or simply a story-telling trope (and a quite ancient one, as we have seen) is not certain.

8. In the comics they come to realize that their romance is ill-suited, and Pepper marries Happy Hogan.

9. …ἱμειρόμενός περ ἰδέσθαι

σὴν ἄλοχον, τῆς τ' αἰὲν ἐέλδεαι ἤματα πάντα.

οὐ μέν θην κείνης γε χερείων εὔχομαι εἶναι,

οὐ δέμας οὐδὲ φυήν, ἐπεὶ οὔ πως οὐδὲ ἔοικεν

θνητὰς ἀθανάτῃσι δέμας καὶ εἶδος ἐρίζειν. Homer, *Odyssey* 5.209–213.

10. For the use of περίφρων and Penelope see Patricia Marquardt, "Penelope 'Polutropos,'" *The American Journal of Philology* 106, no. 1 (1985): 32–48.

11. In *Spiderman: Far from Home*, the trope is reversed, after Peter is shown a picture of his former mentor, Stark.

12. Homer, *Odyssey* 24.

13. In *Marvel Team-Up* #9, "The Tomorrow War," Iron Man refuses to work with the young protégé, going so far as to call him "web-head."

Chapter 4

1. Homer, *Iliad* 1.75; *Odyssey* 3.135.

2. Herodotus, *Histories* 7.134.1, when referring to Talthybius, Agamemnon's herald.

3. Aeschylus, *Agamemnon* 155.

4. Hesiod, *Shield of Herakles* 21; Herodotus, *Histories* 7.229.

5. We will return to this concept later in the last chapter of the book on Fate and Free Will.

6. See Homer, *Iliad* 21.116–221, where Achilles kills Lycaon and Asteropaeus and gloats over their dead bodies remanding them to the River Scamander, who takes exception. After killing Thersilochus, Mydon, Astypylus, Mnesus, Thrasius,

Œneus, and Ophelestes, Scamander finally rises up against him.

7. Ἕκτορ μή μοι ἄλαστε συνημοσύνας ἀγόρευε:
ὡς οὐκ ἔστι λέουσι καὶ ἀνδράσιν ὅρκια πιστά,
οὐδὲ λύκοι τε καὶ ἄρνες ὁμόφρονα θυμὸν ἔχουσιν,
ἀλλὰ κακὰ φρονέουσι διαμπερὲς ἀλλήλοισιν,
265ὣς οὐκ ἔστ᾽ ἐμὲ καὶ σὲ φιλήμεναι, οὐδέ τι νῶϊν
ὅρκια ἔσσονται, πρίν γ᾽ ἢ ἕτερόν γε πεσόντα
αἵματος ἆσαι Ἄρηα ταλαύρινον πολεμιστήν (Homer, *Iliad* 22.261–267).

8. Georg Autenrieth, collator of the benchmark lexicon for students of Homer suggests that, based on the reading of many texts with these terms, *thuon* refers to rage in the human realm. Georg Autenrieth, *A Homeric Dictionary* (Norman: University of Oklahoma Press, 1976), *loc sit.*

9. ὁρμήθη δ᾽ Ἀχιλεύς, μένεος δ᾽ ἐμπλήσατο θυμὸν/ἀγρίου (Homer, *Iliad* 22.312–313).

10. In the Greco-Roman world, as opposed to the Judeo-Christian one, the gods are not necessarily the best versions of ourselves, but rather usually the worst. God-driven rage is more base than the rage of mere mortals. For example, Athena blinds Tiresias for spying on her in the nude but later regrets it. She reacts without thinking, lacking the human filter. Since the word of the gods is binding, she cannot take it back, but instead she bestows him with miraculous powers of second sight. In contrast, Christians want to live in the way of Christ, and the Jews in the way of the prophets. For modern audiences, some of us want to be most like the superhero.

11. αἲ γάρ πως αὐτόν με μένος καὶ θυμὸς ἀνήη/ὤμ᾽ ἀποταμνόμενον κρέα ἔδμεναι… (Homer, *Iliad* 22.346–347).

12. Statius, *Thebaid* 8.751–766.

13. Attic black-figure amphora signed by Exekias, c. 530–525 BCE in the British Museum Collection, #1836,0224.127. This vase has already been discussed and is pictured in Chapter 2 on the Amazons and Wonder Woman.

14. See Pindar *Nemean* 10.

15. Homer, *Iliad* 5.115–120.

16. ʽθαρσῶν νῦν Διόμηδες ἐπὶ Τρώεσσι μάχεσθαι:
ἐν γάρ τοι στήθεσσι μένος πατρώϊον ἧκα
ἄτρομον, οἷον ἔχεσκε σακέσπαλος ἱππότα Τυδεύς:
ἀχλὺν δ᾽ αὖ τοι ἀπ᾽ ὀφθαλμῶν ἕλον ἣ πρὶν ἐπῆεν,
ὄφρ᾽ εὖ γιγνώσκῃς ἠμὲν θεὸν ἠδὲ καὶ ἄνδρα (Homer, *Iliad* 5.124–128).

17. Homer, *Iliad* 5.909.

18. ὥς κεν Τυδέος υἱὸν ἀπόσχῃ Ἰλίου ἱρῆς
ἄγριον αἰχμητὴν κρατερὸν μήστωρα φόβοιο,
ὃν δὴ ἐγὼ κάρτιστον Ἀχαιῶν φημι γενέσθαι.
οὐδ᾽ Ἀχιλῆά ποθ᾽ ὧδέ γ᾽ ἐδείδιμεν ὄρχαμον ἀνδρῶν,
100ὅν πέρ φασι θεᾶς ἐξέμμεναι: ἀλλ᾽ ὅδε λίην
μαίνεται, οὐδέ τίς οἱ δύναται μένος ἰσοφαρίζειν (Homer, *Iliad* 6.96–101).

19. Homer, *Iliad* 6.132; see *Odyssey* 9.350, where Odysseus accuses Polyphemus of raging beyond all measure as well.

20. τοῖος ἔην Τυδεὺς Αἰτώλιος: ἀλλὰ τὸν υἱὸν
γείνατο εἷο χέρεια μάχῃ, ἀγορῇ δέ τ᾽ ἀμείνω.
ὣς φάτο, τὸν δ᾽ οὔ τι προσέφη κρατερὸς Διομήδης
αἰδεσθεὶς βασιλῆος ἐνιπὴν αἰδοίοιο (Homer, *Iliad* 4.399–402).

21. Pseudo-Apollodorus, *Bibliotheca* E5.6.

22. ὣς ἄρ᾽ ἔφη δολόεντα μετὰ κταμένοις Ὀδυσῆα
κεῖσθαι ἰϊόμενος μεμορυγμένον αἵματι πολλῷ:
καὶ τότε οἱ Τριτωνὶς ἀπὸ φρενὸς ἠδὲ καὶ ὄσσων
ἐσκέδασεν Μανίην βλοσυρὴν πνείουσαν ὄλεθρον (Quintus Smyrnaeus, *Fall of Troy* 5.449–452).

23. λυγρὸν ἀνεστονάχησεν, ἔπος δ᾽ ὀλοφύρετο τοῖον:
ʽὤ μοι ἐγώ, τί νυ τόσσον ἀπέχθομαι ἀθανάτοισιν;
οἵ με φρένας βλάψαντο, κακὴν δ᾽ ἐπὶ λύσσαν ἔθεντο,
μῆλα κατακτεῖναι, τά μοι οὐκ ἔσαν αἴτια θυμοῦ (Quintus Smyrnaeus, *Fall of Troy* 5.464–467).

24. Pseudo-Hyginus, *Fabulae* 107.

25. οἷον δή νυ θεοὺς βροτοὶ αἰτιόωνται:
ἐξ ἡμέων γάρ φασι κάκ᾽ ἔμμεναι, οἱ δὲ καὶ αὐτοὶ

σφῇσιν ἀτασθαλίῃσιν ὑπὲρ μόρον ἄλγε᾽ ἔχουσιν (Homer, *Odyssey* 1.32–34).

26. Homer, *Odyssey* 22.471–473.

27. Homer, *Odyssey* 22.203.

28. Euripides, *Hēraklēs Mainomenos* 1002–1006.

29. Euripides, *Hēraklēs Mainomenos* 1313–1333.

30. See Mary Lefkowitz, *Euripides and the Gods* (Oxford: Oxford University Press, 2015), xiix–iii, who argues that Euripides is not attempting to subvert traditional Greek religion, but that the gods did not necessarily work to the benefit of mortals.

31. Aelian, *Varia Historia* 3.32.

32. Initially, the Hulk appeared gray.

33. Simcha Weinstein, *Up, Up, and Oy Vey!* (Baltimore: Leviathan Press, 2006), 82–97.

34. *Tales to Astonish* # 59 (1964).

35. Kristin W. Samuelson, "Post-traumatic Stress Disorder and Declarative Memory Functioning: A Review," *Dialogues in Clinical Neuroscience* 13, no. 3 (2011): 346–351.

36. *The Incredible Hulk* #180 (November 1974).

37. Homer, *Iliad* 18.353–8.

38. Homer, *Iliad* 5.114.

39. Homer, *Iliad* 5.302 uses the verb ἰάχων, meaning to shriek, or give a battle cry.

40. Homer, *Iliad* 9.702–703.

41. Rudolf Simek, *Lexikon der germanischen Mythologie* (Stuttgart: Alfred Kröner, 1995); Hilda R.E. Davidson, *Shape Changing in Old Norse Sagas.* (Cambridge: Cambridge University Press, 1978).

42. Howard Fabing, "On Going Berserk: A Neurochemical Inquiry," *Scientific Monthly* 83, no. 5 (1956): 232–37.

43. Jonathan Shay, *Achilles in Vietnam* (New York: Scribner, 1994), 98.

44. Vergil, *Aeneid* 7.462–463.

45. Vergil, *Aeneid* 12.680. Vergil states: *Hunc, ōrō, sine mē furere ante furōrem.* I interpret this to mean "let me give vent to this fury before I go mad."

Chapter 5

1. *Avengers* Vol. 1 #55 (1968). T'Challa to Chen Lu.

2. He appeared in a two-part story in the *Fantastic Four* #525–3 (July-August 1966).

3. Hesiod, *Theogony* 984–985.

4. Homer, *Odyssey* 11.522 has Odysseus call him the handsomest man he ever saw, placing him again on par with Achilles.

5. Look to the Byzantine encyclopedic work, *Suda,* for the information about Arctinus (*s.lem.*).

6. Homer, *Odyssey* 4.188, which simply calls him the son of radiant dawn.

7. Dictys Cretensis, *Chronicle of the Trojan War* 4.4. See also Pseudo-Apollodorus, *Bibliotheca* E5.3.

8. 'οὐ μὲν χρὴ παρὰ δαιτὶ πελώριον εὐχετάασθαι
οὐδ᾽ ἄρ᾽ ὑποσχεσίην κατανευέμεν, 1 ἀλλὰ ἕκηλον
δαίνυσθ᾽ ἐν μεγάροισι καὶ ἄρτια μηχανάασθαι: (Quintus Smyrnaeus, *Fall of Troy* 2.148–150).

9. Ἠοῦς ὄβριμος υἱός, ὃν ἔκποθι λειριόεσσαι
Ἑσπερίδες θρέψαντο παρὰ ῥόον ὠκεανοῖο.
τοὔνεκά σευ καὶ δῆριν ἀμείλιχον οὐκ ἀλεείνω
εἰδὼς μητέρα δῖαν, ὅσον προφερεστέρη ἐστὶ
Νηρεΐδος, τῆς αὐτὸς ἐρεύχεαι ἔκγονος εἶναι:
ἡ μὲν γὰρ μακάρεσσι καὶ ἀνθρώποισι φαείνει,
τῇ ἐπὶ πάντα τελεῖται ἀτείρεος ἔνδον Ὀλύμπου
ἐσθλά τε καὶ κλυτὰ ἔργα, τά τ᾽ ἀνδράσι γίνετ᾽ ὄνειαρ: (Quintus Smyrnaeus, *Fall of Troy* 2.418–425). Adapted from the translation by A.S. Loeb Classical Library Volume 19 (London: William Heinemann, 1913).

10. Manetho, who was Egyptian, claims Memnon was also Egyptian (*Aegyptica* 2).

11. Philostratus, *Imagines* 1.7.

12. Herodotus, *Histories* 7.69.

13. Object number 26.7.1415.

14. Kv 62.

15. Quintus Smyrnaeus, *Fall of Troy* 2.248–249, uses λέων ὥς ὀβριμόθυμος καπρίῳ, "as though a lion leaping onto a boar."

16. *Black Panther* Vol. 1 #7 (January 1978).

17. *Black Panther* Vol. 3 #5 highlights Bashenga's role in establishing Wakanda and his connection with Bast.

18. *Fantastic Four* #52 (1966).

19. Homer, *Odyssey* 10.305.

20. ἀλλ' οὐδ' ὧς θέλξαι σε δυνήσεται: οὐ γὰρ ἐάσει
φάρμακον ἐσθλόν, ὅ τοι δώσω, ἐρέω δὲ ἕκαστα (Homer, *Odyssey* 10.291–292).

21. Athenaeus, *Deipnosophistae* 7.48.

22. Quintus Smyrnaeus, *Fall of Troy* 2.109.

23. Quintus Smyrnaeus, *Fall of Troy* 2.101.

24. Philostratus, *Imagines* 1.7. It is important to note that slavery and all the baggage that comes along with it here in America would be completely unfounded in ancient Greece. There identity would be *ethnic* rather than *racial*, and purely dependent on whether or not you or your ancestors won a particular war, not based on the color of your skin.

25. Metropolitan Museum of Art, New York 56.171.25.

26. Compare with the relief of Perehu, consort of Queen Ati from Hateshepsut's temple at Deir el-Bahri.

Chapter 6

1. Homer, *Odyssey* 4.455–459. He also turns himself into a boar and a tree.

2. Ovid, *Metamorphoses* 11.250–254; Sophocles: *Troilus* quoted by scholiast on Pindar's *Nemean Odes* 3.35; Apollodorus: iii.13.5; Pindar, *Nemean Odes* 4.62; Pausanias v.18.5.

3. Ovid, *Metamorphoses* 11.241–246.

4. Apollodoros, *Bibliotheca* 2.5.11.

5. *Gilgamesh* I.9; XI 305.

6. Isaac Preston Cory, *Ancient Fragments of the Phoenician, Chaldaean, Egyptian, Tyrian, Carthaginian, Indian, Persian and Other Writers: With an Introductory Dissertation, and an Inquiry into the Philosophy and Trinity of the Ancients* (London: Pickering, 1832).

7. Carolyn Nakamura, "Dedicating Magic: Neo-Assyrian Apotropaic Figurines and the Protection of Assur," *World Archaeology* 36, no. 1 (2004): 112–5.

8. For Proteus, see Apollodorus, *Bibliotheca* 2.5; for Nereus, see Hesiod, *Theogony* 233.

9. See Nobou Komita, "The Indo-European Attribute of Poseidon Was a Water-god," *Research Reports of the Kanagawa Institute of Technology* 14 (1990).

10. Homer, *Iliad* 1.358; 538.

11. Hesiod, *Theogony* 234–236.

12. Hesiod, *Theogony* 237–239.

13. nunc adeste, saeva ponti monstra, nunc vastum maris, ultimo quodcumque Proteus aequorum abscondit sinu (Seneca, *Phaedra* 1204–1205).

14. Compare with Glaucus, whose name means bluish green, or glimmering, a sea god, who began life as a mortal, but who was turned immortal by ingesting a magic herb. The myth seems to echo other stories of transformative herbs such as the underwater blossom meant to grant Gilgamesh immortality. For more information on Phorcys and his offspring, see Hesiod's *Theogony* 270–297. For Glaucus, see Philostratus the Elder, *Imagines* 2.15, and Ovid's *Metamorphoses* 13.898–968 & 14.1–74.

15. Homi Bhabha in *The Locations of Culture* (New York: Routledge, 1994), 2, 5, 37, 223 argues that hybridity is more than even a mixing of two cultures, but also a channel for negotiation between culture and the outside world. He uses the analogy of the stairwell, as an excellent example.

16. ὃ δ' ἄρ' ἐκ δίνης ἀνορούσας
ἤϊξεν πεδίοιο ποσὶ κραιπνοῖσι πέτεσθαι
δείσας: οὐδέ τ' ἔληγε θεὸς μέγας, ὦρτο δ' ἐπ' αὐτῷ
ἀκροκελαινιόων, ἵνα μιν παύσειε πόνοιο
δῖον Ἀχιλλῆα, Τρώεσσι δὲ λοιγὸν ἀλάλκοι (Homer, *Iliad* 21.246–250).

17. The term means "blonde" or "golden," which for a river could mean silty sand or even that the river itself carried gold ore from the mountains of its origin. Both definitions are certainly possible.

18. Diodorus Siculus, *Library of History* 4.75.1 claims the first to rule as king over the land of Troy was Teucer, the son of the River-god Scamander and a Nymph of Mt. Ida.

19. Homer, *Iliad* 21.218–220.

20. Quintus Smyrnaeus, *Fall of Troy* 11.245–246.

21. Since Scamander was believed to be the father of Teucer, the original founder of Troy, the war would be seen as a personal attack on his own family.

22. Nonnus, *Dionysiaca* 24.93–94.

23. Nonnus, *Dionysiaca* 14.36–37; 21.195–196 (Scelmis is the name Nonnos gives this particular Telchine); 27.105.

24. Callimachus, *Hymn to Delos* (4).313–3.

25. Diodorus Siculus, *Library of History* 5.55.3.

26. Ovid, *Metamorphoses* 7.365–366; Eustathius of Thessalonica was a scholar of Greek and archbishop of the church in the Byzantine period. His work isn't necessarily original, but he gathers the work of many Homeric scholiasts, both from the *Iliad* and the *Odyssey*, some of which we no longer possess. The most complete editions we have of these texts now are translated into Latin by M. Van Der Valk: *Eustathii Archiepiscopi Thessalonicensis* Commentarii ad Homeri Iliadem Pertinentes (Leiden: Brill, 1971).

27. Nonnus, *Dionysiaca* 14.46–49.

28. Not to be confused with the comic version of Proteus created by DeMatteis, Buidansky and Bulandi, who can also change his form like the Proteus of Greek myth. See *Prince Namor the Sub-Mariner* #2 (October 1984).

29. *Human Torch* #4 (Spring 1941, "The Serum Must Get Through!"). Bill Everett (w.), Bill Everett (p.), Bill Everett (i.).

30. *The Fantastic Four. Volume 1 #4* (2010). New York, NY: Marvel Worldwide. Stan Lee (w.), Jack Kirby, Artie Simek, Chic Stone, Frank Giacoia, Vince Colletta, and Sam Rosen.

31. *Sub-Mariner* #37, "The Way to Dusty Death" (May 1971). Roy Thomas (w.), Ross Androu (p.), Mike Esposito (i.).

32. *Adventure Comics* #260 (May 1959).

33. Plato, *Critias.*

Chapter 7

1. Douglas Frame, "Achilles and Patroclus as Indo-European Twins: Homer's Take," http://nrs.harvard.edu/urn-3:hlnc.essay:Frame.Achilles_and_Patroclus_as_Indo-European_Twins.2013.

2. See Gregory Nagy, *The Best of the Achaeans: Concepts of the Hero in Archaic Greek Poetry* (Baltimore: John Hopkins University Press, 1999), 292–295 where he discusses twinning and the concept of the *therapon*; and Olga Davidson, *Poet and Hero in the Persian Book of Kings* (Ithaca, NY: Cornell University Press, 1994), 144 where she discusses the terms *dioscurism* and *therapon* with Achilles as the aggressive twin and Patroclus as the passive, when they are together, but different when they are apart.

3. Λητὼ δ' Ἀπόλλωνα καὶ Ἄρτεμιν ἰοχέαιραν,
ἱμερόεντα γόνον περὶ πάντων Οὐρανιώνων,
γείνατ' ἄρ' αἰγιόχοιο Διὸς φιλότητι μιγεῖσα (Hesiod, *Theogony* 918–920).

4. Pseudo-Apollodorus, *Bibliotheca* 1.4.1.

5. Nonnus, *Dionysiaca* 27. 271 writes that they are twins, δίζυγα, i.e., double-yolked.

6. See Antoninus Liberalis, *Metamorphoses* 35, who discusses the tale of Leto and the Lycian shepherds.

7. Pseudo-Apollodorus, *Bibliotheca* 1.4.1.

8. Homer, *Iliad* 24.602–604. Pseudo-Apollodorus, *Bibliotheca* 3.5.6.

9. Homer, *Iliad* 5.445–448.

10. Pseudo-Hyginus, *Astronomica* 2.26 (on Scorpio).

11. See Martin L. West, *The East Face of Helicon: West Asiatic Elements in Greek Poetry and Myth* (Oxford: Clarendon Press, 2003), 440, where the author discusses twins Crissus and Ponopeus fighting in the womb. Sibling rivalry and constant fighting is apparently something even the gods do.

12. Fritz Blakolmer, "A Pantheon Without Attributes?" in *Divine Images and Human Imaginations in Ancient Greece and Rome*, ed. Joannis Mylonopoulos (Leiden: Brill, 2009), 25.

13. Hesiod, *Catalogues of Women* Frag. 66; Homer, *Homeric Hymn* 21; Hyginus, *Fabulae* 77.

14. Pindar, *Nemean Ode* 10.55–60.

15. Stasinus, *Cypria* Frag.1; Pseudo-Apollodorus, *Bibliotheca* 3.11.2; Pseudo-Hyginus, *Fabulae* 80.

16. Pseudo-Hyginus, *Astronomica* 2.22.

17. Diodorus Siculus, *Library of History* 4.43.1–2.

18. *Homeric Hymn* (33) *to the Dioscuri*, lines 6–8: σωτῆρας τέκε παῖδας ἐπιχθονίων ἀνθρώπων/ὠκυπόρων τε νεῶν, ὅτε τε σπέρχωσιν ἄελλαι/χειμέριαι κατὰ πόντον ἀμείλιχον....

19. Callimachus, *Lyric* Frag. 227 (trans. Trypanis)

20. Ovid, *Fasti* 5.699–700.

21. Hyginus, *Astronomica* 2.22; Apollonius, *Argonautika* 2.40–43 states: "the son of Tyndareus was like a star of heaven whose rays are the brightest as they shine through the night sky at eventide," (ὁ δ'

οὐρανίῳ ἀτάλαντος/ ἀστέρι Τυνδαρίδης, οὗπερ κάλλισται ἔασιν/ ἑσπερίην διὰ νύκτα φαεινομένου ἀμαρυγαί).

22. Giulia Sfameni Gasparro, *Soteriology and Mystic Aspects in the Cult of Cybele and Attis* (Leiden: Brill, 1985).

23. Ferrara T18CVP, Beazley No. 211599.

24. Callimachus, *Aetia* Frag.115 (trans. Trypanis). *Orphic Hymn* 30 to the Curetes, refers to the heavenly twins (*The Hymns of Orpheus*, trans. by Thomas Taylor, Philadelphia: University of Pennsylvania Press, 1792, 1999). For a more modern translation, please see Apostolos Athanassakis' and Ben Wolkow's version from Johns Hopkins University Press, 2013.

25. Diodorus Siculus, *Bibliotheca Historica* 5.70.1–2; See also Strabo, *Geography* 10. 3.7–8.

26. Herodotus, *Histories* 3.37.2–3.

27. Diodorus Siculus, *Library of History* 4.43.1–2.

28. Nonnus, *Dionsyiaca* 29.213–214.

29. Hesiod, *Shield* 15–50.

30. Homer, *Iliad* 19.100–105; Diodorus Siculus, *Library of History* 4.9.4.

31. Ovid, *Metamorphoses* 9.281–315.

32. Pindar, *Nemean Odes* 1.33–59; Diodorus Siculus, *Library of History* 4.10.1; Apollodorus 2.4.8

33. Pseudo-Apollodorus, *Bibliotheca* 2.4.8.

34. Pseudo-Apollodorus, *Bibliotheca* 2.7.3.

35. Schol. Homer, *Iliad* 13.638, 639; cp. *Iliad*. 11.709–710.

36. Ibycus fragment 16, preserved in Athenaeus, *Deipnosophistae* 2.50; "with equal heads in one body," ἰσοκεφάλους ἐνιγυίους.

37. P 4885; for an argument against see M.K. Dahm, "Not Twins at All: The Agora Oinochoe Reinterpreted," *Hesperia* 76 (2007): 717–730.

38. Lekythos, Delos, B 6137.546; Stahler 13.

39. Paris Medailles 202.

40. Pseudo-Apollodorus, *Bibliotheca* 2.7.2.

41. Alexander Krappe, "Herakles and Greek Dioskouroi Legends," *The Classical Journal* 18, no. 8 (May 1923): 502–504.

42. See *Rig Veda* 1.22.1–2, where it is mentioned they yoke the horses to their cart in the morning; see also *Rig Veda* 1.34, 1.46, 1.47, 1.112, 1.116, 1.117, 1.118, 1.119, and 1.120, which are all hymns to the divine Aśhvin twins.

43. M.L. West, *Indo-European Poetry and Myth* (Oxford: Oxford University Press, 2009), 187.

44. *Ibid*., 188; *didiyagni* (*Rig Veda* 1.15.11; 8.57.2); *puruścandra*, "a bright light to men," (*Rig Veda* 1.92.17, 182.3).

and "much gleaming, resplendent" (*Rig Veda* 8.5.32).

45. *Rig Veda* 1.34.6, for providing knowledge of medicine and 1.116, *passim* for poet referring to the twins as Nāsatyas.

46. *Rig Veda* 10.39.9.

47. *Rig Veda* 1.119.4.

48. Compare with the Syrian St. Cosmas and Damien, twin brothers and physicians.

49. *Rig Veda* 1.22.1, for example.

50. KBo 1 1. Gary M. Beckman, *Hittite Diplomatic Texts* (Riga, Latvia: Scholars Press, 1999), 53.

51. Michael Coe, "Hero Twins: Myth and Image," in *The Maya Vase Book*, Vol.1 (New York: Kerr Associates, 1989), 165.

52. Allen J. Christenson, *Popol Vuh: The Sacred Book of the Maya: The Great Classic of Central American Spirituality, Translated from the Original Maya Text* (Norman: University of Oklahoma Press, 2007).

53. Apollodoros, *Bibliotheca* 2.5.11

54. Stan Lee, Jack Kirby, and Dick Ayers, "The Old Order Changeth," *The Avengers* 16 (May 1965).

Chapter 8

1. Homer, *Iliad* 21.453–455. Priam's father, Laomedon once threatened to bind the feet and hands of Poseidon and Apollo, in human guise, in order to sell them on the islands. The king also exhibits bad *xenia* by refusing Herakles the horses given to him by Zeus, in exchange for rescuing his daughter Hesione from a terrible fate at the hands of a sea-monster. Likewise, Paris abuses *xenia* when, as a guest in Sparta, he absconds with Queen Helen, stealing her from the home of King Menelaus. It seems that the Trojan royal line lacks manners.

2. It is generally believed that Homer is probably living in the 9th c. The text we have now is most certainly redacted by the Peisistratid tyrants of Athens in the late 6th/ early 5th c. BCE.

3. Homer, *Iliad* 2.12 (εὐρυάγυιαν). Streets are the bloodlines of the city. In Book II, Zeus sends a dream to Agamemnon to rally the Greeks against the Trojans. Here, he refers to Troy as "wide-streeted," εὐρυάγυια, an epithet typically used for great cities.

4. For the Tomb of Ilus see Homer, *Iliad* 11.166–167, for the oak (φηγὸν), *Iliad* 11.170–171.

5. Homer, *Iliad* 4.378 mentions the walls of Thebes (τείχεα Θήβης).

6. Homer, *Iliad* 4.34: τείχεα μακρὰ, "great walls"; εὐτείχεον, "well-walled," *Iliad* 1.129; ξεστοῖο λίθοιο, "polished stone," twice within the lines *Iliad* 6.243–249.

7. An excellent example of a daughter supportive of her father in his old age is Antigone. She goes with her father, Oedipus, into exile from Thebes to Athens, as he seeks absolution and purification for his blind misdeeds.

8. Homer, *Iliad* 21.295: Ἰλιόφι κλυτὰ τείχεα; cp τείχους (n) wall πύλας καὶ τείχεα μακρὰ *Iliad* 4.34.

9. Scott Montgomery, *Push Me, Pull You: Imaginative, Emotional, Physical, and Spatial Interaction in Late Medieval and Renaissance Art.* (Brill: Leiden, 2011) 578–579.

10. Homer, *Iliad* 4.34 uses πύλας καὶ τείχεα μακρὰ; πύλας comes from the feminine πύλη, meaning "gate."

11. Homer, *Iliad* 3.145, 149, 263; 6.237, 307, 393; 9.354; 11.170; 16.712.

12. Homer, *Iliad* 22.5–6.

13. Homer, *Iliad* 22.344–349.

14. Homer, *Iliad* 6.237–240; 9.352–354.

15. Zeus' Sanctuary at Dodona is where prophecies were revealed by the oak leaves. *Iliad* 5.692–695; *Odyssey* 14.327–230.

16. Homer, *Odyssey* 11.260–265 claims Thebes could not have survived without its towers.

17. Homer, *Iliad* 22.466–472; cp. *Odyssey* 1.332–334. For the concept of the headdress and a city's crenellations, see Michael Nagler, *Spontaneity and Tradition: A Study in the Oral Art of Homer* (Berkeley: University of California Press, 1967), 279–280; and Steve Reece, "Headdresses and Citadels in Early Greek Epic," in *Homer's Winged Words. The Evolution of Early Greek Epic Diction in the Light of Oral Theory*, ed. Steve Reese (Leiden: Brill, 2009), 249–260.

18. Homer, *Iliad* 6.242–250 (ἀλλ' ὅτε δὴ Πριάμοιο δόμον περικαλλέ' ἵκανε/ ξεστῇς αἰθούσῃσι τετυγμένον: αὐτὰρ ἐν αὐτῷ/ πεντήκοντ' ἔνεσαν θάλαμοι ξεστοῖο λίθοιο/ πλησίον ἀλλήλων δεδμημένοι, ἔνθα δὲ παῖδες/ κοιμῶντο Πριάμοιο παρὰ μνηστῇς ἀλόχοισι,/ κουράων δ' ἑτέρωθεν ἐναντίοι ἔνδοθεν αὐλῆς/ δώδεκ' ἔσαν τέγεοι θάλαμοι/ ξεστοῖο λίθοιο/ πλησίον ἀλλήλων δεδμημένοι, ἔνθα δὲ γαμβροὶ/ κοιμῶντο Πριάμοιο παρ' αἰδοίῃς ἀλόχοισιν:).

19. Eric Cline, *The Oxford Handbook of the Bronze Age Aegean* (Oxford: Oxford University Press, 2012), 201–202.

20. Robert Fagles and Berard Knox, *The Iliad* (London: Penguin Books, 1998), 31.

21. Leslie Kurke, "The Politics of ἁβροσύνη in Archaic Greece," *Classical* Antiquity 11, no. 1 (1992): 91–120. See also Edith Hall, *Inventing the Barbarian: Greek Self-Definition through Tragedy* (Oxford: Oxford University Press, 1989), 128.

22. Homer, *Iliad* 6.45–56.

23. Homer, *Iliad* 2.311–320.

24. In Homer, *Iliad* 12.243: Hector exclaims, "Fight for your country! That is the best and only omen," (εἷς οἰωνὸς ἄριστος ἀμύνεσθαι περὶ πάτρης).

25. Homer, *Iliad* 22.454–460.

26. Eugene N. Lane, *Cybele, Attis and Related Cults: Essays in Memory of M.J. Vermaseren* (Brill: Leiden, 1996), 157.

27. Homer, *Iliad* 24.729.

28. Homer, *Iliad* 7.92–93: "A hushed silence rang through the Achaean ranks, ashamed to refuse, but afraid to accept the challenge," (ὣς ἔφαθ', οἱ δ' ἄρα πάντες ἀκὴν ἐγένοντο σιωπῇ:/ αἴδεσθεν μὲν ἀνήνασθαι, δεῖσαν δ' ὑποδέχθαι:).

29. *Batman*, Vol.3 #36 (February 2018).

30. *Batman: The Cult*, Vol. 1# 1(August 1988).

31. *Batman: Legends of the Dark Knight*, Vol.1 #27 (February 1992); *Gates of Gotham*, Vol.1 #2 (August 2011).

32. In the most recent incarnation of the Batman series of stories, Fox's *Gotham* indicates in the latest season that the "walls" of the city were really the bridges, and when the criminal mastermind known as The Joker blows them up, evil really was locked inside.

33. *Gotham* (2014) Season 4 Episode 1, "Pax Penguina."

Chapter 9

1. See Dictys Cretensis, *Chronicle of the Trojan War* 3.1 where he mentions all of these as examples of prime archers.

2. For a well-researched and well-written account of things like plague-carrying arrows in Greek lore, see Adrienne Mayor's *Greek Fire, Poison Arrows, and Scorpion Bombs: Biological and Chemical Warfare in the Ancient World* (New York: Harry N. Abrams, 2004).

3. For Hector's rebuke see Homer, *Iliad* 3.38–57; for Helen's see 6.349–351, and briefly at 3.410–412 where afterwards Aphrodite demands she attend Paris after his duel with Menelaus. Helen initially refuses Aphrodite's request, calling it a shameful act. The goddess, however, has her way with both Helen and Paris in the end.

4. Clearly, Hector likens him to Apollo, master of the bow and the lyre; Apollo is not necessarily known for any martial prowess, and ironically, his romantic prowess is often unsuccessful as well.

5. τοξότα λωβητὴρ κέρᾳ ἀγλαὲ παρθενοπῖπα
εἰ μὲν δὴ ἀντίβιον σὺν τεύχεσι πειρηθείης,
οὐκ ἄν τοι χραίσμῃσι βιὸς καὶ ταρφέες ἰοί:
νῦν δέ μ᾽ ἐπιγράψας ταρσὸν ποδὸς εὔχεαι αὔτως (Homer, *Iliad* 11.385–388).

6. In Hyginus, *Fabulae* 107, the author can't even bring himself to admit that Paris killed Achilles, the best of the Achaeans. In fact, in his version, Apollo disguises himself as Paris.

7. Homer, *Iliad* 4.85–185.

8. ‘ἦ ῥά νύ μοί τι πίθοιο Λυκάονος υἱὲ δαΐφρον.
τλαίης κεν Μενελάῳ ἐπιπροέμεν ταχὺν ἰόν,
πᾶσι δέ κε Τρώεσσι χάριν καὶ κῦδος ἄροιο,
ἐκ πάντων δὲ μάλιστα Ἀλεξάνδρῳ βασιλῆϊ.
τοῦ κεν δὴ πάμπρωτα παρ᾽ ἀγλαὰ δῶρα φέροιο,
αἴ κεν ἴδῃ Μενέλαον ἀρήϊον Ἀτρέος υἱὸν
σῷ βέλεϊ δμηθέντα πυρῆς ἐπιβάντ᾽ ἀλεγεινῆς (Homer, *Iliad* 4.93–99).

9. Hoplite warfare is not common until long after Homeric times, and even longer after the Bronze Age. If there is a nod to Hoplite warfare in the text, this would further speak to the Peisistratid recension.

10. She is the daughter of the former King Laomedon of Troy and sister of Priam.

11. Homer, *Iliad* 15.458–466.

12. Servius on *Aeneid* 1.619–621. Some traditions hold that Teucer returned home where he was disowned by his father for not ensuring his brother's return and joining Bellus II in the war on Cyprus; he eventually founded the city of Salamis.

13. Dictys Cretensis, *Chronicle of the Trojan War* 3 claims Philoctetes was the best, and he also mentions the contest between Odysseus and Meriones.

14. Ovid, *Metamorphoses* 9.229–232. See also Quintus Smyrnaeus, *Fall of Troy* 9.393–397, who says he has a quiver full of arrows with the deadly venom of a water snake and the bow of Herakles himself.

15. Homer, *Iliad* 2.716–725; *Cypria* frag.1.

16. Quintus Smyrnaeus, *Fall of Troy* 10.237–245.

17. *Aesop's Fables*, trans. Laura Gibbs (Oxford: Oxford University Press, 2008), 123, mentions Orion watches during the night with a golden bow. Hesiod, *Astronomy* Fr. 4 mentions he is the son of Poseidon and Euryale, daughter of Minos.

18. Herodotus, *Histories* 7.61.1 refers to these as τόξα…μεγάλα.

19. See A. Rumpf, *Chalkidische Vasen* (Berlin/Leipzig: Walter de Gruyter, 1927), 12, which shows the drawing of a Chalchidian amphora in the Pembroke Hope collection in Deepdene England, now lost; this vase illustrates the Trojan prince Paris slaughtering the enemy with his bow and quiver.

20. *Tales of Suspense* #57 (September 1964).

21. Mark Gruenwald; Bob Layton (1983). "Till Death Do Us Part." *Hawkeye* 1 (4).

Chapter 10

1. Clark's biological mother, whom he leaves behind on the planet Krypton, sews his red and blue costume and cape, whereas Thetis has her son's armor made by the divine blacksmith, Hephaestus.

2. This vulnerability is foreshadowed with Paris' devastating blow to Diomedes.

3. *Superman* #61 (November 1949).

4. Sophocles, *Antigone* 944–953.

5. Compare with Dionysus whose mother Semele was incinerated with a lightning bolt while he was still *in utero*. Zeus saves him, ripping the child from the mother and sewing him into his leg, making him twice born.

6. Pseudo-Apollodorus, *Bibliotheca* 2.4.1.

7. *Homeric Hymn to Demeter* 275–281.

8. Callimachus, *Hymn* 5.

9. Other examples include Aphrodite's self-revelation to Anchises, *Homeric Hymn to Aphrodite*, and Zeus to Semele in Ovid, *Metamorphoses* 3.306–307; see also Hygnius, *Fabulae* 179; Nonnus, *Dionysiaca* 8.316–334.

10. See *DC One Million*, 1998.

11. By Hellenistic times Apollo had been conflated with Helios, the Sun, and Phoebus meaning bright. Alexander the Great, after arriving in Egypt had also earned the title the son of Ra, or the son of the sun.

12. See Friedrich Wilhelm Nietzsche, *Also Sprach Zarathustra*, trans. Thomas Common (New York: Courier Corporation, 2004), 8, who asserts that "Der Übermensch ist der Sinn der Erde." When first introduced, by Jerry Siegel in 1933, Superman was portrayed as a bald-headed villain. Recognizing the difficulty in promoting a villain, he recreated Superman into the titular character we see today.

13. Homer, *Iliad* 1.352–354; Ovid, *Metamorphoses* 13.162–163; Pseudo-Hyginus, *Fabulae* 96.

14. Matthew 4:4.

15. Matthew 4:7.

16. Matthew 4:8.

17. Ian Dawe, "'The Last Temptation of Supe' Christian Overtones in 'For the Man Who Has Everything,'" *Sequart* (2014): http://sequart.org/magazine/50445/the-last-temptation-of-supe-christian-overtones-in-for-the-man-who-has-everything/.

18. *Superman Annual* #11 (1985).

19. Snorri Sturluson, *Prose Edda, Gylfaginning* 51 "Þórr berr banaorð af Miðgarðsormi ok stígr þaðan braut níu fet"; For an excellent translation see Jesse L. Byock, *The Prose Edda: Norse Mythology (Penguin Classics) by Snorri Sturluson* (London: Penguin Classics, 2006).

20. *Thor* Vol.1 #379 (May 1987), #380 (June 1987).

Chapter 11

1. Apollonius Rhodius, *Argonautica* 1.211–224.

2. Gilgamesh's mother is the goddess Ninsun. The 21st c. BCE king Utu-hengal takes Gilgamesh as his patron deity; see Jeremy Black and Anthony Green, *Gods, Demons and Symbols of Ancient Mesopotamia: An Illustrated Dictionary* (Austin: University of Texas Press, 1992), 166–168.

3. ἀλλ᾽ ὥς τ᾽ ὀρνίθων πετεηνῶν αἰετὸς αἴθων
ἔθνος ἐφορμᾶται ποταμὸν πάρα βοσκομενάων
χηνῶν ἢ γεράνων ἢ κύκνων δουλιχοδείρων,
ὣς Ἕκτωρ ἴθυσε νεὸς κυανοπρῴροιο
ἀντίος ἀΐξας (Homer, *Iliad* 15.690–694).

4. οἱ δ᾽ ὥς τ᾽ αἰγυπιοὶ γαμψώνυχες ἀγκυλοχεῖλαι,
ἐξ ὀρέων ἐλθόντες ἐπ᾽ ὀρνίθεσσι θόρωσι (Homer, *Odyssey* 22.302–303).

5. Homer, *Odyssey* 19.518–523. χλωρηῒς ἀηδών, a nightingale perched in the fresh (or green) foliage.

6. ἡ μὲν ἄρ᾽ ὣς εἰποῦσ᾽ ἀπέβη γλαυκῶπις Ἀθήνη,/ὄρνις δ᾽ ὣς ἀνόπαια διέπτατο (Homer, *Odyssey* 1.319–320); for a more detailed look at the unique relationship the goddess shares with the son of her favorite hero, see Michael Murrin, "Athena and Telemachus," *International Journal of the Classical Tradition* 13, no. 4 (2007): 495–514.

7. Apollonius Rhodius, *Argonautica* 2.273–277.

8. Apollodorus, *Bibliotheca* 3.15.2. υἱοὺς δὲ Ζήτην καὶ Κάλαϊν πτερωτούς, οἳ πλέοντες σὺν Ἰάσονι καὶ τὰς ἁρπυίας διώκοντες ἀπέθανον, ὡς δὲ Ἀκουσίλαος λέγει, περὶ Τῆνον ὑφ᾽ Ἡρακλέους ἀπώλοντο.

9. Apollonius Rhodius, *Argonautica* 1.130 ff–1304 ff.

10. Pindar, *Pythian Ode* 4.179–183. …πτεροῖσιν νῶτα πεφρίκοντας ἄμφω πορφυρέοι "…bristling purple wings on their backs."

11. Apollonius Rhodius, *Argonautica* 1.210–223. Mentions they are on the feet ποδῶν, and that they are χρυσείαις φολίδεσσι διαυγέας, "golden, scaly, and translucent."

12. Pseudo-Hyginus, *Fabulae* 14.18.2–3 "hi capita pedesque pennatos habuisse

feruntur crinesque caeruleos, qui pervio aere usi sunt." These are said to have had feathers on their heads and feet and dark blue locks" they flew through the air.

13. Ovid, *Metamorphoses* 6.714–718.

14. Pseudo-Apollodorus, *Bibliotheca* 2.4.3; Pindar, *Pythian Ode* 12.16.

15. Hyginus, *Fabulae* 64.2.1 says that Perseus received the sandals from Mercury (Hermes); Compare with Pseudo-Apollodorus, *Bibliotheca* 2.4.5, who says the sandals were given to Perseus by the Nymphs.

16. This is a common trope, for Phaedra does the same thing to her stepson Hippolytus. This same theme occurs in the tale of Potiphar's wife in the Hebrew Bible, where she tries to seduce Joseph. When he does not succumb, she accuses him of rape.

17. Pindar, *Olympian Ode* 13.65–66 claims that Athena supplies him with a golden bridle and headband to charm the horse.

18. Pindar, *Isthmian Ode* 7.44–47.

19. Hortaturque sequi damnosasque erudit artes
et movet ipse suas et nati respicit alas.
Hos aliquis tremula dum captat harundine pisces,
aut pastor baculo stivave innixus arator
vidit et obstipuit, quique aethera carpere possent
credidit esse deos (Ovid, *Metamorphoses* 8.215–220).

20. Genesis 6:4.

21. See W.B. Henning, *The Book of Giants* (London: Forgotten Books 2017), 12: Manuscript B, Uygur "the sun's light and heat will descend and set your wings alight. You will burn and die."

22. *Book of Giants*, Fragment 4Q530 Col. 3 in Florentino Garcia Martinez, *The Dead Sea Scrolls Translated: The Qumran Texts in English*. (Leiden: Eerdmans, 1996), 261.

23. A nod perhaps to the real-life Egyptian archaeologist Howard Carter.

24. *Captain America* #170.

Chapter 12

1. Homer, *Iliad* 3. Translated by Robert Fagles. Penguin, 1991. The Greek reads αἰνῶς ἀθανάτῃσι θεῇς εἰς ὦπα ἔοικεν, which literally translated "terrible like the deathless goddess she beseems."

2. Fragment 67, Scholiast on Euripides, *Orestes* 249 says: "Steischorus says that while sacrificing to the gods Tyndareus forgot Aphrodite and that the goddess was angry and made his daughters twice and thrice wed and deserters of their husbands." See *Hesiod, Homeric Hymns, Epic Cycle, Homerica*, trans. Evelyn-White, H G. Loeb Classical Library Volume 57. (London: William Heinemann, 1914).

3. Others have thought Helen heroic as well, for example, the Roman writer Ovid includes her in his *Heroides* (17). In it, she writes a letter to Paris giving him a well-deserved verbal lashing for breaking *xenia*. She accuses him of stalking her, another man's wife, and being a poor hero, more interested in affairs of love. She eschews his advances, the promise of riches, and sees Paris' persistence as a source of constant fear—fear of shame and the mark of adultery. Now, Helen does not completely rule their affair out. Her letter, like so much of Roman (especially Ovidian) elegy, may simply stand as an example of the beloved, Helen, playing hard to get—verbal foreplay if you will.

4. See Aristophanes, *Lysistrata* 1551–56 and Scholiast *loc sit.*

5. Pseudo-Apollodorus, *Bibliotheca* E6.29.

6. Homer, *Iliad* 3.410–412.

7. τὼς δέ σ' ἀπεχθήρω ὡς νῦν ἔκπαγλ' ἐφίλησα,
μέσσῳ δ' ἀμφοτέρων μητίσομαι ἔχθεα λυγρὰ
Τρώων καὶ Δαναῶν, σὺ δέ κεν κακὸν οἶτον ὄληαι (Homer, *Iliad* 3.415–417).

8. Phiroze Vasuni, *The Gift of the Nile: Hellenizing Egypt from Aeschylus to Alexander* (Berkeley: University of California Press), 61.

9. ἄκουσον, ἤν τι καὶ γυνὴ λέξῃ σοφόν.
βούλῃ λέγεσθαι, μὴ θανών, λόγῳ θανεῖν;
(Euripides, *Helen* 1049–1050)

10. 0αἰνῶ σε, Μενέλα', εἰ κτενεῖς δάμαρτα σήν.
ὁρᾶν δὲ τήνδε φεῦγε, μή σ' ἕλῃ πόθῳ.
αἱρεῖ γὰρ ἀνδρῶν ὄμματ', ἐξαιρεῖ πόλεις,
πίμπρησιν οἴκους: ὧδ' ἔχει κηλήματα.
ἐγώ νιν οἶδα, καὶ σύ, χοἱ πεπονθότες.
(Euripides, *Troades* 890–894)

11. Aegisthus was the son Thyestes, brother of King Atreus who fathered Agamemnon and Menelaus. When he learned that his real father was Thyestes, who had been banished years before by Atreus after

having an affair with the queen, he plotted to kill the king and seize the throne for himself and his blood father. Try wrapping your head around that one. Years later, Agamemnon reclaims the throne and drives out Aegisthus.

12. Joseph Campbell, *The Hero with a Thousand Faces* (Novato: New World Library, 2008), 102.

13. *Wonder Woman, Swan Song!* #288 (February 1982).

14. *Tales of Suspense: Featuring the Power of Iron Man* Vol. 1 #57. Stan Lee (w), Don Heck (p), Sam Rosen (i).

15. *Batman* #181 (June 1966).

Chapter 13

1. Quintus Smyrnaeus, *Fall of Troy* 13.545

2. Tyrtaeus, Solon, Theognis, Mimnermus, *Greek Elegiac Poetry: From the Seventh to the Fifth Centuries BC*, ed. and trans. Douglas E. Gerber, Loeb Classical Library 258 (Cambridge, MA: Harvard University Press, 1999), 128–130.

3. Homer, *Odyssey* 3.208–210.

4. μήτηρ γάρ τέ μέ φησι θεὰ Θέτις ἀργυρόπεζα
διχθαδίας κῆρας φερέμεν θανάτοιο τέλος δέ.
εἰ μέν κ' αὖθι μένων Τρώων πόλιν ἀμφιμάχωμαι,
ὤλετο μέν μοι νόστος, ἀτὰρ κλέος ἄφθιτον ἔσται:
εἰ δέ κεν οἴκαδ' ἵκωμι φίλην ἐς πατρίδα γαῖαν,
ὤλετό μοι κλέος ἐσθλόν, ἐπὶ δηρὸν δέ μοι αἰὼν
ἔσσεται, οὐδέ κέ μ' ὦκα τέλος θανάτοιο κιχείη (Homer, *Iliad* 9.410–416).

5. Homer, *Iliad* 9.319–322. See also *Iliad* 6.487–489 in which the poet presents us with a fascinating doublet; this time it is Hector's sentiments, where he tells Andromache no man will deliver him to Hades beyond what fate has allotted and that fate is inescapable both for the brave man and the coward: οὐ γάρ τίς μ' ὑπὲρ αἶσαν ἀνὴρ Ἄϊδι προϊάψει:/μοῖραν δ' οὔ τινά φημι πεφυγμένον ἔμμεναι ἀνδρῶν,/οὐ κακὸν οὐδὲ μὲν ἐσθλόν, ἐπὴν τὰ πρῶτα γένηται.

6. For an interesting discussion on the *thymos* (or *thumos*) and other more anthropological views on the concept of free will and fate, see Esther Eidinow, "Oracular Consultation, Fate, and the Concept of the Individual," in *Divination in the Ancient World: Religious Options and the Individual*, ed. V. Rosenberger (*Potsdamer Altertumswissenschaftliche Beiträge*, vol. 46, Stuttgart: Franz Steiner Verlag) 21–39.

7. Homer, *Iliad* 22.209–213.

8. Compare this with the Egyptian weighing of the heart ceremony, when after death, an individual's soul is weighed against the feather of Maat. If the soul proves heavier, it descends to the underworld, to be consumed by demons.

9. J.V. Morrison, "*Kerostasia*, the Dictates of Fate, and the Will of Zeus in the *Iliad*." *Arethusa* 30, no. 2 (1997): 291–292.

10. ἔνθά κεν ὑψίπυλον Τροίην ἕλον υἷες Ἀχαιῶν
Πατρόκλου ὑπὸ χερσί, περὶ πρὸ γὰρ ἔγχεϊ θῦεν,
εἰ μὴ Ἀπόλλων Φοῖβος ἐϋδμήτου ἐπὶ πύργου (700)
ἔστη τῷ ὀλοὰ φρονέων, Τρώεσσι δ' ἀρήγων.
τρὶς μὲν ἐπ' ἀγκῶνος βῆ τείχεος ὑψηλοῖο
Πάτροκλος, τρὶς δ' αὐτὸν ἀπεστυφέλιξεν Ἀπόλλων
χείρεσσ' ἀθανάτῃσι φαεινὴν ἀσπίδα νύσσων.
ἀλλ' ὅτε δὴ τὸ τέταρτον ἐπέσσυτο δαίμονι ἶσος (705)
δεινὰ δ' ὁμοκλήσας ἔπεα πτερόεντα προσηύδα:
'χάζεο διογενὲς Πατρόκλεες: οὔ νύ τοι αἶσα
σῷ ὑπὸ δουρὶ πόλιν πέρθαι Τρώων ἀγερώχων,
οὐδ' ὑπ' Ἀχιλλῆος, ὅς περ σέο πολλὸν ἀμείνων.'
ὣς φάτο, Πάτροκλος δ' ἀνεχάζετο πολλὸν ὀπίσσω (710)
μῆνιν ἀλευάμενος ἑκατηβόλου Ἀπόλλωνος.
Then would the sons of the Achaeans would have taken high-walled Troy
By Patroclus' hands, for all around him he raged with his spear,
If Phoebus Apollo had not stood on the well-wrought wall (700)
Considering terrible thoughts toward him and helping the Trojans.
Three times Patroclus approached the corner of the lofty wall,
And three times did Apollo throw him back with his deathless hands,

Pushing back against [his] glimmering shield.
But when indeed the fourth time he pushed forward in equal force to a god (705)
Having shouted terrifyingly, responded with winged words:
"Step back, Zeus-born Patroclus: It is not your fate
To topple the city of the venerable Trojans by your spear,
nor by that of Achilles, who is better than you by far."
Thus he spoke, and Patroclus stepped far back (710)
Avoiding the wrath of far-shooting Apollo.

11. 'ἤδη νῦν Ἕκτορ μεγάλ' εὔχεο: σοὶ γὰρ ἔδωκε
845νίκην Ζεὺς Κρονίδης καὶ Ἀπόλλων, οἵ με δάμασσαν
ῥηιδίως: αὐτοὶ γὰρ ἀπ' ὤμων τεύχε' ἕλοντο. *Iliad* 16.844–846.
And:
ἀλλά με μοῖρ' ὀλοὴ καὶ Λητοῦς ἔκτανεν υἱός,
ἀνδρῶν δ' Εὔφορβος: σὺ δέ με τρίτος ἐξεναρίζεις, *Iliad* 16.849–850.

12. ἀλλ' ἤτοι κεῖνον μὲν ἐάσομεν ἤ κεν ἴῃσιν
ἤ κε μένῃ: τότε δ' αὖτε μαχήσεται ὁππότε κέν μιν
θυμὸς ἐνὶ στήθεσσιν ἀνώγῃ καὶ θεὸς ὄρσῃ (*Iliad* 9.701–703).

13. Homer, *Odyssey* 9.584–595.

14. Homer, *Iliad* 2.

15. Homer, *Odyssey* 3:266.

16. Aeschylus, *Agamemnon* 1389.

17. Historically, consider Herodotus' account of the famous pronouncement to the Athenians by the oracle at Delphi. When asked how to go about the Persian War, she replied Athens must build a wall of wood. Being impractical and combustible, few saw the value in building a wooden wall, but one young soldier by the name of Themistocles, interpreted this to mean a wall of wooden ships. Athens builds a navy, rather than a wall and that is that.

18. Vergil, *Aeneid* 2.268–297; 730–795.

19. Vergil, *Aeneid* 3.84–120

20. Vergil, *Aeneid* 3.135–191.

21. Vergil, *Aeneid* 7.107–147.

22. Apollodorus, *Library* 3.13.8.

23. καὶ δ' οὔπω δὴ μοῖρα διαπραθέειν κλυτὸν ἄστυ,
εἰ ἐτεὸν Κάλχαντος ἐτήτυμος ἔπλετο μῦθος
τόν ῥα πάρος κατέλεξεν ὁμηγερέεσσιν Ἀχαιοῖς
δηῶσαι Πριάμοιο πόλιν δεκάτῳ ἐνιαυτῷ.' Quintus Smyrnaeus, *Fall of Troy* 8.474–478; see also Apollodorus, *Epitome* 3.15.

24. Homer, *Odyssey* 11.121–131. See also Douglas S. Olson's article on the winnowing fan: "Odysseus' "Winnowing-Shovel" (Hom. *Od.* 11.119–137) and the Island of the Cattle of the Sun," *Illinois Classical Studies* 22 (1997): 7–9.

25. For the concept of singing and weaving as a trope in pan-Mediterranean culture, see Anthony Tuck, "Singing the Rug: Patterned Textiles and the Origins of Indo-European Metrical Poetry," *American Journal of Archaeology* 110 no. 4 (2006): 539–550. For some excellent work on women, weaving, and song, see all of Ann Bergren, *Weaving Truth: Essays on Language and the Female in Greek Thought* (Cambridge, MA: Harvard University Press, 2008).

26. ἔσταν δ' ἐν προθύροισι θεᾶς καλλιπλοκάμοιο,
Κίρκης δ' ἔνδον ἄκουον ἀειδούσης ὀπὶ καλῇ,
ἱστὸν ἐποιχομένης μέγαν ἄμβροτον, οἷα θεάων
λεπτά τε καὶ χαρίεντα καὶ ἀγλαὰ ἔργα πέλονται (Homer, *Odyssey* 10.221–224).

27. Homer, *Odyssey* 2.94–106.

Bibliography

Arnaudo, Marco. *The Myth of the Superhero.* Baltimore: Johns Hopkins University Press, 2013.
Athanassakis, Apostolos, and Ben Wolkow. *The Orphic Hymns.* Baltimore: Johns Hopkins University Press, 2013.
Autenrieth, Georg. *A Homeric Dictionary.* Norman: University of Oklahoma Press, 1976.
Bahlmann, Andrew. *The Mythology of the Superhero.* Jefferson, NC: McFarland, 2016.
Barthes, Roland. *A Barthes Reader.* Edited by Susan Sontag. New York: Hill and Wang, 1982.
Bergren, Ann. *Weaving Truth: Essays on Language and the Female in Greek Thought.* Cambridge, MA: Harvard University Press, 2008.
Bhabha, Homi. *The Locations of Culture.* New York: Routledge, 1994.
Blakolmer, Fritz. "A Pantheon without Attributes?" In *Divine Images and Human Imaginations in Ancient Greece and Rome.* Leiden: Brill, 2009.
Bourdieu, P. *Distinction.* New York: Routledge, 1986.
Byock, Jesse L. *The Prose Edda: Norse Mythology (Penguin Classics) by Snorri Sturluson.* London: Penguin Classics, 2006.
Campbell, Joseph. *The Hero with a Thousand Faces.* Novato, CA: New World Library, 2008.
Carlson, Marvin. *The Haunted Stage: The Theatre as Memory Machine.* Ann Arbor: University of Michigan Press, 2003.
Chandler, Daniel. *Semiotics: The Basics.* New York: Routledge, 2007.
Christenson, Allen J. *Popol Vuh: The Sacred Book of the Maya: The Great Classic of Central American Spirituality, Translated from the Original Maya Text.* Norman: University of Oklahoma Press, 2007.
Clarke, W.M. "Achilles and Patroclus in Love." *Hermes* 106 (1978): 381–396.
Cline, Eric. *The Oxford Handbook of the Bronze Age Aegean.* Oxford: Oxford University Press, 2012.
Cocca, Carolyn. *Superwomen: Gender, Power, and Representation.* London: Bloomsbury Academic, 2016.
Coe, Michael. "Hero Twins: Myth and Image." In *The Maya Vase Book,* Vol.1 New York: Kerr Associates, 1989.
Cory, Isaac Preston. *Ancient Fragments of the Phoenician, Chaldaean, Egyptian, Tyrian, Carthaginian, Indian, Persian and Other Writers: With an Introductory Dissertation, and an Inquiry into the Philosophy and Trinity of the Ancients.* London: Pickering, 1832.
Dahm, M.K. "Not Twins at All: The Agora Oinochoe Reinterpreted." *Hesperia* 76 (2007): 717–730.
Davidson, Hilda R.E. *Shape Changing in Old Norse Sagas.* Cambridge: Cambridge University Press, 1978.
Davidson, Olga. *Poet and Hero in the Persian Book of Kings.* Ithaca, NY: Cornell University Press, 1994.
Davies, Malcom. "Aeschylus' Clytemnestra: Sword or Axe?" *Classica Quarterly* 37, no. 1 (1987): 65–75.
Dawe, Ian. "'The Last Temptation of Supe' Christian Overtones in 'For the Man Who Has Everything,'" *Sequart,* 2014.

de Saint-Sauveur, Jacques Grasset. *Encyclopédie des voyages: América, 1796.* Bibliothèque Nationale de France.

Diak, Nicholas. *The New Peplum. Essays on Sword and Sandal Films and Television Programs Since the 1990s.* Jefferson, NC: McFarland, 2017.

Dover, Kenneth J. *Greek Homosexuality.* New York: Vintage Books, 1978.

Eco, Umberto. *A Theory of Semiotics.* Bloomington: Indiana University Press, 1976.

Eidinow, Esther. "Oracular Consultation, Fate, and the Concept of the Individual." In *Divination in the Ancient World: Religious Options and the Individual,* edited by Veit Rosenberger, 21–39. (Potsdamer Altertumswissenschaftliche Beiträge; Vol. 46). Stuttgart: Franz Steiner Verlag, 2013.

Fabing, Howard. "On Going Berserk: A Neurochemical Inquiry." *Scientific Monthly* 83, no. 5 (1956): 232–237.

Fagles, Robert, and Berard Knox. *The Iliad.* London: Penguin Books, 1998.

Fox, Robin. *The Tribal Imagination: Civilization and the Savage Mind.* Cambridge, MA: Harvard University Press, 2011.

Frankel, Valerie Estelle. *Superheroines and the Epic Journey: Mythic Themes in Comics, Film and Television.* Jefferson, NC: McFarland, 2017.

Gasparro, Giulia Sfameni. *Soteriology and Mystic Aspects in the Cult of Cybele and Attis.* Leiden: Brill, 1985.

Gruenwald, Mark and Bob Layton. "Till Death Do Us Part," *Hawkeye.* 1(4), 1983.

Hall, Edith. *Inventing the Barbarian: Greek Self-Definition through Tragedy.* Oxford: Oxford University Press, 1989.

Halperin, David. *One Hundred Years of Homosexuality: and Other Essays on Greek Love.* New York: Routledge, 2012.

Hughes, Bettany. *Helen of Troy: Goddess, Princess, Whore.* London: Pimlico, 2005.

Jung, C.G. *Man and His Symbols.* New York: Dell Publishing, 1968.

_____. *Two Essays on Analytical Psychology.* New York, Pantheon Books, 1953.

Komita, Nobou. "The Indo-European Attribute of Poseidon Was a Water-god." *Research Reports of the Kanagawa Institute of Technology,* 1990.

_____. "Poseidon the Horse-god and the Early Indo-Europeans." *Research Reports of Ikutoku Tech. University,* 1995.

Krappe, Alexander. "Herakles and Greek Dioskouroi Legends." *The Classical Journal* 18, no. 8 (May 1923): 502–504.

Kurke, Leslie. "The Politics of ἁβροσύνη in Archaic Greece." *Classical* Antiquity 11, no. 1 (1992): 91–120.

Lane, Eugene. *Cybele, Attis and Related Cults: Essays in Memory of M.J. Vermaseren.* Leiden: Brill, 1996.

Leach, Edmund. *Claude Lévi-Strauss: Modern Masters.* Ann Arbor: Viking Press, 1974.

Lefkowitz, Mary. *Euripides and the Gods.* Oxford: Oxford University Press, 2015.

Lewis, A. David. *Graven Images: Religion in Comic Books & Graphic Novels.* New York: Continuum, 2010.

Lloyd, G.E.R. "Right and Left in Greek Philosophy." *Journal of Hellenic Studies* 82 (1962): 56–66.

Madrid, Mike. *The Supergirls: Feminism, Fantasy, and the History of Comic Book Heroines.* Minneapolis: Exterminating Angel Press, 2016.

Mallowan, M.E.L. "The Excavations at Nimrud (Kalhu), 1953." *Iraq* 16, no. 1 (1954): 86–93.

Marquardt, Patricia. "Penelope 'Polutropos.'" *The American Journal of Philology* 106, no.1 (1985): 32–48.

Maslov, Boris. "The Semantics of Aoidos and Related Compounds: Towards a Historical Poetics of Solo Performance in Archaic Greece." *Classical Antiquity* 28 (2009): 1–38.

May, Helen, Baljit Kaur, and Larry Prochner. *Empire, Education, and Indigenous Childhoods: Nineteenth-Century Missionary Infant Schools in Three British Colonies.* London: Routledge, 2014.

Mayor, Adrienne. *The Amazons. Lives and Legends of Warrior Women Across the Ancient World.* Princeton: Princeton University Press, 2016.

McCloud, Scott. *Understanding Comics: The Invisible Art.* New York: William Morrow Paperbacks, 1994.

McGowan, Elizabeth. "Tumulus and Memory. The Tumulus as a Locus for Ritual Action in Greek Imagination." In *Tumulus as Sema: Space, Politics, Culture and Religion in the First Millennium BC 174*. Edited by Olivier Henry and Ute Kelp. Leiden: Walter de Gruyter, 2016.

Montgomery, Scott. *Push Me, Pull You: Imaginative, Emotional, Physical, and Spatial Interaction in Late Medieval and Renaissance Art*. Leiden: Brill, 2011.

Morrison, Grant. *Supergods: What Masked Vigilantes, Miraculous Mutant, and a Sun God from Smallville Can Teach Us About Being Human*. London: Spiegel & Grau, 2012.

Morrison, J.V. "*Kerostasia*, the Dictates of Fate, and the Will of Zeus in the *Iliad*." *Arethusa* 30, no. 2 (1997): 273–296.

Mulvey, Laura. *Visual and Other Pleasures*. New York: Palgrave Macmillan, 2009.

Nagler, Michael. *Spontaneity and Tradition: A Study in the Oral Art of Homer*. Berkeley: University of California Press, 1967.

Nagy, Gregory. *The Ancient Greek Hero in 24 Hours*. Cambridge, MA: Harvard University Press, 2013.

_____*The Best of the Achaeans: Concepts of the Hero in Archaic Greek Poetry*. Baltimore: John Hopkins University Press, 1999.

Nakamura, Carolyn. "Dedicating Magic: Neo-Assyrian Apotropaic Figurines and the Protection of Assur." *World Archaeology* 36, no. 1 (2004): 11–25.

Ostenson, Jonathan. "Exploring the Boundaries of Narrative: Video Games in the English Classroom." *The English Journal* 102, no. 6 (2013): 71–78.

Prag, A.J.N.W. "Clytemnestra's Weapon Yet Once More," *Classical Quarterly* 41, no. 1 (1991): 242–246.

Raglan, Fitz Roy Richard Somerset. *The Hero: A Study in Tradition, Myth, and Drama*. Mineola, N.Y.: Dover Publications, 2016.

Reece, Steve. "Headdresses and Citadels in Early Greek Epic." In *Homer's Winged Words. The Evolution of Early Greek Epic Diction in the Light of Oral Theory*. Leiden: Brill, 2009.

Reynolds, Richard. *Super Heroes: A Modern Mythology (Studies in Popular Culture)*. Jackson: University Press of Mississippi, 1994.

Rosenberg, Robin S. *Our Superheroes, Ourselves*. Oxford: Oxford University Press, 2013.

_____. *The Psychology of Superheroes an Unauthorized Exploration*. Prince Frederick, MD: Recorded Books & Jennifer Canzoneri, 2008.

Rosenberg, Robin S. and Tom DeFalco. *Superhero Origins: What Makes Superheroes Tick and Why We Care*. CreateSpace Independent Publishing Platform, 2013.

Rouse, W.H.D., H.J. Rose, and Lind L.R. Nonnus, *Dionysiaca*. Cambridge, MA: Harvard University Press, 1940.

Rumpf, A. *Chalkidische Vasen*. Berlin/Leipzig: de Gruyter, 1927.

Russo, Ruth. "The Heart of Steel: A Metallurgical Interpretation of Iron in Homer." *Bulletin in the History of Chemistry* 30, no. 1 (2005): 23–24.

Saunders, Ben. *Do the Gods Wear Capes? Spirituality, Fantasy, and Superheroes (New Directions in Religion and Literature)*. New York: Continuum, 2011.

Sergeant, Bernard. *Homosexuality in Greek Myth*. Boston: Beacon Press, 1986.

Shay, Jonathan. *Achilles in Vietnam: Combat Trauma and the Undoing of Character*. New York: Scribner's, 1994.

Simek, Rudolf. Lexikon der germanischen Mythologie, Stuttgart: Alfred Kröner, 1995.

Sommerstein, A.H. "Again Klytaimestra's Weapon." *Classical Quarterly* 39, no. 2 (1989): 296–301.

Stuller, Jennifer. *Ink-Stained Amazons and Cinematic Warriors: Superwomen in Modern Mythology*. London: I.B. Tauris, 2010.

Taylor, Thomas, trans. *The Hymns of Orpheus*. Philadelphia: University of Pennsylvania Press, 1792, 1999.

Tuck, Anthony. "Singing the Rug: Patterned Textiles and the Origins of Indo-European Metrical Poetry." *American Journal of Archaeology* 110 no. 4 (2006): 539–50.

Van Der Valk, M. *Eustathii Archiepiscopi Thessalonicensis* Commentarii ad Homeri Iliadem Pertinentes. Leiden: Brill, 1971.

Vasuni, Phiroze. *The Gift of the Nile: Hellenizing Egypt from Aeschylus to Alexander*. Berkeley: University of California Press, 2001.

Wandtke, Terrence. *The Meaning of Superhero Comic Books.* Jefferson, NC.: McFarland, 2012.
Weinstein, Simcha. *Up, Up, and Oy Vey!* Baltimore: Leviathan Press, 2006.
West, Martin, L. *The East Face of Helicon: West Asiatic Elements in Greek Poetry and Myth.* Oxford: Clarendon Press, 2009.
_____. *Indo-European Poetry and Myth.* Oxford: Oxford University Press, 2009.

Comics and Graphic Novels

Adventure Comics #260 (May 1959). "How Aquaman Got His Powers!" Script: Robert Bernstein. Art: Ramona Fradon.
All Star Comics #8 (October 1941). "Introducing Wonder Woman." Script: William Moulton Marston. Art: Harry G. Peter.
Avengers Vol. 1 # 4 (March 1964). " Captain America Lives Again!" Script: Stan Lee. Art: Jack Kirby, George Roussos, Stan Goldberg, and Artie Simek.
Avengers Vol. 1 # 16 (May 1965). "The Old Order Changeth." Script: Stan Lee. Art: Jack Kirby, Dick Ayers, Stan Goldberg, and Artie Simek.
Avengers Vol. 1 #55 (August 1968). "Mayhem Over Manhattan." Script: Roy Thomas. Art: John Buscema, George Klein, and Sam Rosen.
Batman: Gates of Gotham Vol.1 #2 (August 2011). "The Four Families of Gotham." Script: Scott Snyder and Kyle Higgins. Art: Trevor McCarthy, Guy Major, and Jared K. Fletcher.
Batman: Legends of the Dark Knight Vol.1 #27 (February 1992). "The Destroyer, Part Two: Solomon." Script: Dennis O'Neill. Art: Chris Sprouse, Bruce D. Patterson, Steve Oliff, and John Costanza.
Batman: The Cult Vol 1# 1 (August 1988). "Book One: Ordeal." Script: Jim Starlin. Art: Bernie Wrightson, Bill Wray, and John Costanza.
Batman Vol.3 #36 (February 2018). "Superfriends, Part 1." Script: Tom King. Art: Clay Mann, Seth Mann, Jordie Bellaire, and Clayton Cowles.
Captain America Vol.1 # 303 (March 1985). "Double Dare." Script: Michael Carlin. Art: Paul Neary, Dennis Janke, Ken Feduniewicz, and Diana Albers.
D.C. One Million (1998). Script: Grant Morrison and Val Semeiks.
Fantastic Four #53 (August 1966). "The Way It Began...!" Script: Stan Lee. Art: Jack Kirby, Joe Sinnott, and Artie Simek.
Fantastic Four #52 (July 1966). "The Black Panther." Script: Stan Lee. Art: Jack Kirby, Joe Sinnot, Stan Goldberg, and Sam Rosen.
Fantastic Four Vol 1 #4 (May 1962). "The Coming of...Sub-Mariner!" Script: Stan Lee. Art: Jack Kirby, Artie Simek, Sol Brodsky, and Stan Goldberg.
Human Torch Comics Vol. 1 #4 (March-April 1941). "The Serum Must Get Through!" Script: Bill Everett. Art: Bill Everett.
The Incredible Hulk Vol. 1 #180 (October 1974). "And the Wind Howls...Wendigo!" Script: Len Wein. Art: Herb Trimpe, Jack Abel, Christie Scheele, and Artie Simek.
Sub-Mariner Vol 1 #37 (May 1971). "The Way to Dusty Death." Script: Roy Thomas. Art: Ross Androu, Mike Esposito, and Artie Simek.
Superman Annual Vol 1 #11 (1985). "For the Man Who Has Everything..." Script: Alan Moore. Art: Dave Gibbons and Tom Ziuko.
Superman Vol 1 #61 (November 1949). "Superman Returns to Krypton!" Script: Bill Finger. Art: Al Plastino.
Tales of Suspense Vol 1 #57 (September 1964). "Hawkeye, the Marksman!" Script: Stan Lee. Art: Don Heck and Sam Rosen.
Wonder Woman Vol. 1 #95 (January 1958). "Wonder Woman—The World's Most Dangerous Human!" Script: Robert Kanigher. Art: Harry G. Peter.
Wonder Woman Vol. 4 #7 (May 2012). "Il Gangster Dell'Amore." Script: Brian Azzarello. Art: Cliff Chiang, Matthew Wilson, Jared K. Fletcher.

Primary Sources

Although all translations in the previous text are my own, I have provided below the references for text and translation from a well-known and well-loved series from the Loeb Classical Library, where available. Otherwise I have cited the most easily available translation.

Aeschylus II, *Oresteia: Agamemnon. Libation-Bearers. Eumenides*, trans. Alan H. Sommerstein Loeb Classical Library. Cambridge, MA: Harvard University Press, 2009.

Antoninus Liberalis, *Metamorphoses*, ed. & trans. Francis Celoria. New York: Routledge, 1992.

Apollodorus, *Bibliotheca.* Volumes I & II, trans. James G. Frazer. Loeb Classical Library. New York: Macmillan, 1921.

Apollonius Rhodius, *Argonautica*, trans. William H. Race. Loeb Classical Library. Cambridge, MA: Harvard University Press, 2009.

Athenaeus, *The Learned Banqueters*, Volume III: Books 6–7, trans. S. Douglas Olson. Loeb Classical Library. Cambridge, MA: Harvard University Press, 2008.

Callimachus, *Aetia, Iambi, Hecale and Other Fragments.* Hero and Leander. trans. C.A. Trypanis, T. Gelzer, and Cedric H. Whitman. Loeb Classical Library. Cambridge, MA: Harvard University Press, 1973.

Callimachus, *Hymns and Epigrams.* Lycophron: *Alexandra.* Aratus: *Phaenomena*, trans. A.W. Mair. Loeb Classical Library. New York: Macmillan, 1921.

Dictys Cretensis. *Chronicle of the Trojan War.* transl. R.M. Frazer. Bloomington: Indiana University Press, 1966.

Diodorus Siculus, *Library of History Volume IV*, trans. C.H. Oldfather. Loeb Classical Library. Cambridge, MA: Harvard University Press, 1946.

Euripides III, *Suppliant Women. Electra. Heracles*, trans. David Kovacs. Loeb Classical Library. Cambridge, MA: Harvard University Press, 1998.

Greek Epic Fragments: From the Seventh to the Fifth Centuries BC, trans. Martin L. West. Loeb Classical Library. Cambridge, MA: Harvard University Press, 2003.

Greek Lyric. Sappho. Alcaeus, trans. David A. Campbell. Loeb Classical Library. Cambridge, MA: Harvard University Press, 1982.

Herodotus. *The Persian Wars.* Vols. I-IV, trans. A.D. Godley. Loeb Classical Library. New York: Macmillan, 1920–1925.

Hesiod. *Homeric Hymns, Epic Cycle, Homerica*, trans. Evelyn-White, H G. Loeb Classical Library Volume 57. London: William Heinemann, 1914.

Hesiod. *The Shield. Catalogue of Women. Other Fragments*, trans. Glenn W. Most. Loeb Classical Library. Cambridge, MA: Harvard University Press, 2018.

Hesiod. *Theogony. Works and Days. Testimonia*, trans. Glenn W. Most. Loeb Classical Library. Cambridge, MA: Harvard University Press, 2018.

Homer. *Iliad. Volumes I & II*, trans. A.T. Murray. Loeb Classical Library. New York: Macmillan, 1924.

Homer. *Odyssey. Volumes I & II*, trans. A.T. Murray. Loeb Classical Library. New York: Macmillan, 1919.

Homeric Hymns. Homeric Apocrypha. Lives of Homer, trans. Martin L. West. Loeb Classical Library. Cambridge, MA: Harvard University Press, 2003.

Hyginus. *Fabulae*, trans. Mary Grant [The Myths of Hyginus]. 1960. reproduced without notes and introduction at https://www.theoi.com/Text/HyginusFabulae1.html.

Nonnus. *Dionsyiaca. Volumes I-III*, trans. W.H.D. Rouse. Loeb Classical Library. Cambridge, MA: Harvard University Press, 1940.

Orphic Hymn 30 to the Curetes see: https://www.theoi.com/Text/OrphicHymns1.html.

The Orphic Hymns, trans. Apostolos Athanassakis and Benjamin Wolkow. Baltimore: Johns Hopkins University Press, 2013.

Ovid. *Fasti*, trans. James G. Frazer. Loeb Classical Library. New York: Macmillan, 1931.

Ovid. *Metamorphoses. Volumes I & II*, trans. Frank Justus Miller. Loeb Classical Library. New York: Macmillan, 1916.

Pausanias. *Description of Greece. Volumes I-V*, trans. W.H.S. Jones, H.A. Omerod, and R.E. Wycherley. Loeb Classical Library. New York: Macmillan, 1918–1935.

Philostratus the Elder. *Imagines*, trans. Arthur Fairbanks. Loeb Classical Library. New York, Macmillan: Harvard University Press, 1931.

Pindar. *Nemean Odes. Isthmian Odes. Fragments*, trans. William H. Race. Loeb Classical Library. Cambridge, MA: Harvard University Press, 1997.

Plutarch. *Lives, Volume I: Theseus and Romulus. Lycurgus and Numa. Solon and Publicola*, trans. Bernadotte Perrin. Loeb Classical Library. New York: Macmillan, 1914.

Quintus Smyrnaeus. *Posthomerica*, trans. Neil Hopkinson. Loeb Classical Library. Cambridge, MA: Harvard University Press, 2018.

Rig Veda 1, trans. T.H. Griffith. Available online: https://www.sacred-texts.com/hin/rigveda/rvi01.htm.

Sophocles. *Antigone. The Women of Trachis. Philoctetes. Oedipus at Colonus*, trans. Hugh Lloyd-Jones. Loeb Classical Library. Cambridge, MA: Harvard University Press, 1994.

Sophocles *Fragments,* trans. Hugh Lloyd-Jones. Loeb Classical Library. Cambridge, MA: Harvard University Press, 1996.

Statius. *Thebaid. Volumes I & II*, trans. D.R. Shackleton Bailey. Loeb Classical Library. Cambridge, MA: Harvard University Press, 2004.

Strabo. *Geography*. Vol. V, trans. Horace Leonard Jones. Loeb Classical Library. New York: Macmillan, 1928.

Vergil. *Aeneid*. Volumes I & II, trans. Rushton H. Fairclough. Loeb Classical Library. Cambridge, MA: Harvard University Press, 2001.

Index

Numbers in ***bold italics*** indicate pages with illustrations